Picture Credits:
All pictures by Bruce Bennett Studios, except
C. Andersen: 27, 66, 67, 96, 97; Paul Angers: 43;
Brian Bennett: 15, 22, 71, 84, 120; Rick Berk: 85, 91;
Gary Bettman: 17; D. Carroll: 70; M. Desjardins: 88;
M. Di Giacomo: 122; J. Di Maggio: 121; A. Foxall:
20, 95; D. Giacopelli: 31; J. Giamundo: 18, 35, 42,
48, 63, 65, 76, 82, 106, 107, 108; Hockey Hall Of
Fame: 8, 118; G. James: 57; P Laberge: 21, 32, 37,
46, 52, 68; J. Leary: 92; Scott Levy: 26, 29, 48, 54,
56, 78, 81, 83, 87, 103, 104, 112; R. Lewis: 30, 40, 60;
R. McCormick: 39; Jim McIsaac: 7, 23, 25, 36, 49,
51, 55, 64, 79, 80, 98; Layne Murdoch: 44, 89;
W. Robers: 45; J. Tremmel 4; Nick Welsh: 94;
B. Winkler: 3, 19, 41, 69, 74, 99, 105; B. Wippert: 24.

Published in Canada in 1997 by
Raincoast Books
8680 Cambie Street
Vancouver, B.C. V6P 6M9
(604) 323-7100

**Canadian Cataloguing in Publication Data**
MacKinnon, John, 1953-
  NHL hockey

Includes index.
ISBN 1-55192-120-0

  1. National Hockey League -- Miscellanea. I. Title.
GV847.8.N3M37 1997   796.962'64   C97-910452-1

Printed and bound in Italy

# NHL HOCKEY

## AN OFFICIAL FANS' GUIDE

# John MacKinnon

RAINCOAST BOOKS

*Vancouver*

# CONTENTS

**Top Notch:** Avalanche goaltender Patrick Roy (left) solidified his position as one of, if not the, best netminders in hockey with another stellar season for Colorado.

# INTRODUCTION

The transformation of the National Hockey League from a parochial league into an organization with a global vision began with the 1972 Summit Series between Canadian stars and the great national team of the Soviet Union—the Big, Red Machine.

After years of seeing their understaffed team whipped by the Soviets at the Olympics and World Championships, Canadians were finally given the chance to see their best players, their professionals, the stars of the NHL, supposedly deliver an overdue lesson to the big, bad Russians. It didn't work out quite that way.

The Canadians won, but it took some desperate, last-minute play and a goal by Paul Henderson with 34 seconds remaining in the final game to give Canada a 6-5 victory in the game and a slender series triumph—four games won, three lost, one game tied. The Canadian-invented sport—and the NHL—would never be the same.

NHL teams soon began to copy the superior Russian training methods, to blend their intricate, purposeful drills into often unimaginative North American practices, to pay more attention to the game's technical aspects.

The Russians, and other European teams, grafted the North Americans' never-say-die competitiveness and physical courage onto their highly skilled brand of hockey.

As the NHL expanded, first from six to 12 teams, then to 14, then 18, then 26 and now, with the granting of franchises to Nashville, Atlanta, Columbus and St. Paul, Minnesota, to 30 teams by the turn of the century, teams have to cast their nets wider and wider in search of major-league talent. The talent search has hauled in US high-schoolers and collegians, Russians, Finns, Swedes, Germans, Czechs, Slovaks and Polish-born players.

The NHL, dominated for its first half-century by Canadian stars like Frank McGee, Howie Morenz, Aurel Joliat, George Hainsworth, Maurice (Rocket) Richard, Gordie Howe, Glenn Hall, Bobby Hull, Bobby Orr and Frank Mahovlich, was adjusting to an influx of European talent.

NHL fans grew to admire players like Borje Salming, Anders Hedberg, Ulf Nilsson, Peter, Anton and Marian Stastny and, in the 1990s, Sergei Fedorov, Pavel Bure, Jaromir Jagr and Teemu Selanne.

As the NHL moves toward the 21st Century, it has blossomed from a six- to a 30-team league. By 2000 there will be teams in 16 US states, as well as the District of Columbia and four Canadian provinces. Along with its traditional strength along the Eastern Seaboard and in the Northeast and Midwest, the NHL has planted its pennant in such previously unlikely spots as North Carolina, Tennessee, Georgia, Texas, Florida and Arizona.

The cliché that the NHL appeals merely to regional interests in the US simply does not apply any longer.

In the fall of 1996, the inaugural World Cup of Hockey was held, a joint venture involving the NHL and the NHL Players' Association. Team USA beat Canada in a best-of-three final series, stunning the favored Canadians and setting the stage rather dramatically for the Winter Olympics in Nagano, Japan in February 1998.

Those Olympics will put the Dream Teams on display in the men's Olympic hockey tournament for the first time in history.

In other words, the best from the NHL from each country will compete for Olympic gold as the NHL shuts down for three weeks to enable its stars to shine in the Olympic Arena.

A worldwide audience will be able to revel in the exploits of Paul Kariya, Joe Sakic and Patrick Roy of Canada; Finland's Teemu Selanne and Saku Koivu; Pavel Bure and Alexander Mogilny of Russia; Brian Leetch, Keith Tkachuk and Mike Richter of Team USA; and Jaromir Jagr and Dominik Hasek of the Czech Republic. Among many others.

The NHL has come a long way indeed since Henderson's legendary goal on a cold September night in Moscow in 1972. The ongoing progress—including Hockey Night in Nagano in 1998—should be great fun to witness.

**Growing Center: With Wayne Gretzky and Mark Messier at the end of brilliant careers, and Mario Lemieux in retirement, Eric Lindros' time to emerge as the dominant player in the NHL is at hand.**

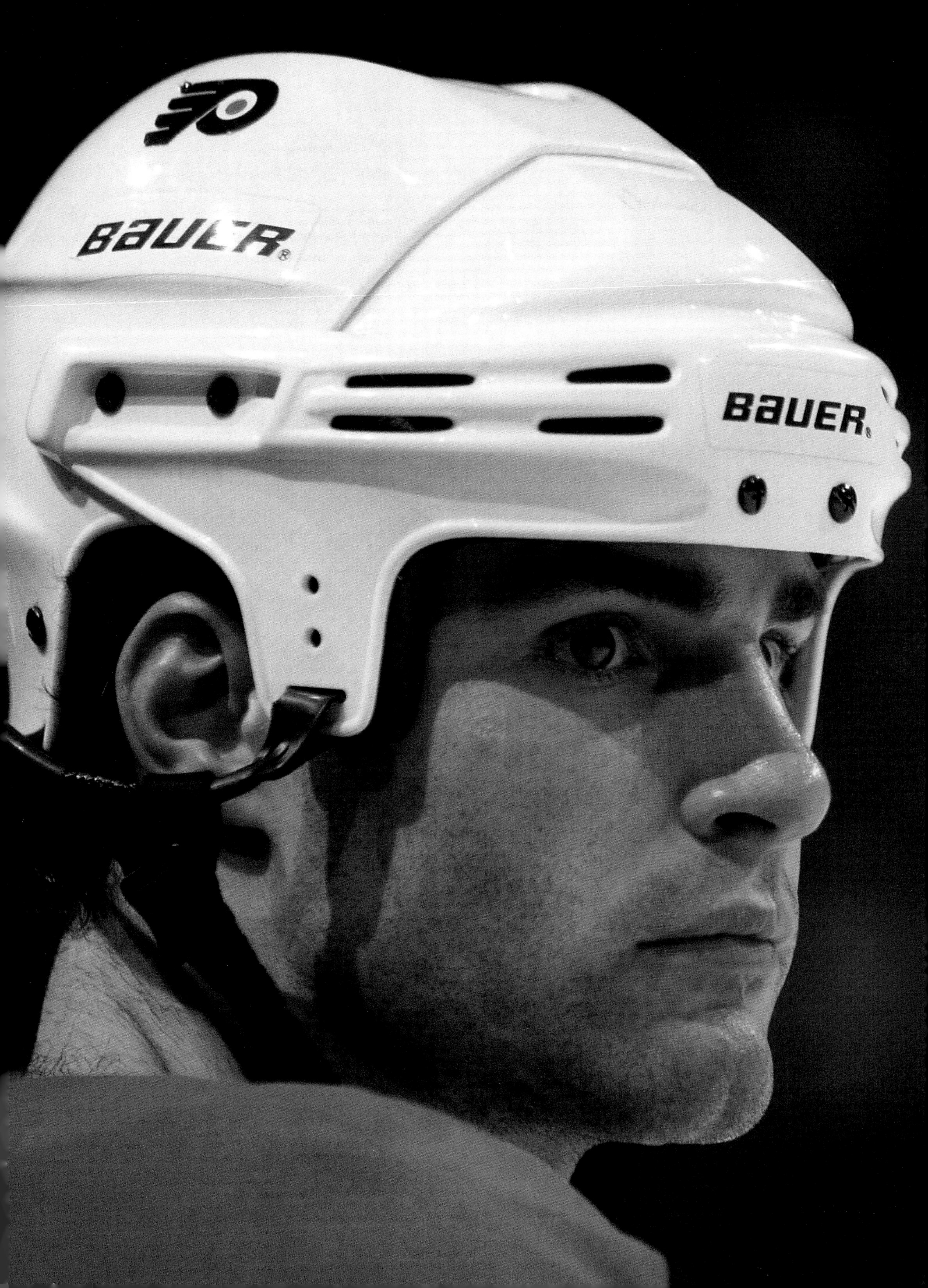
BAUER
BAUER

# BIRTH OF A HOCKEY LEAGUE

**T**he whole world was not watching when a small cluster of men met in a downtown Montreal hotel on November 22, 1917 and formed the National Hockey League. The National Hockey Association, a forerunner of the NHL, had suspended operations, so the heads of the Montreal Canadiens, Montreal Wanderers, Ottawa Senators and Quebec Bulldogs attended a founding meeting and formed a new league.

A single reporter—Elmer Ferguson, of the *Montreal Herald*—reported on the somewhat shaky launch. For starters, the Bulldogs, a poor draw in Quebec City, decided not to operate in the NHL's first season, so the Toronto Arenas were admitted to the league as a replacement.

The league was down to three teams early into the first season, though, after the Westmount Arena, home to the Montreal Wanderers, burned down. With nowhere to play, the Wanderers, too, dropped out. The NHL, then, featured the Original Three for most of its initial season, not the Original Six, a term that would gain common usage years later.

The first president of the NHL was Frank Calder, a soccer-playing British émigrée to Canada who had grown to love the Canadian game of hockey. His name would eventually be etched onto a trophy given annually to the best first-year, or rookie, player in the NHL.

In that first season, the league held the first of many dispersal drafts to distribute the players from the Bulldogs, including their scoring star, Joe Malone, who was chosen by the Canadiens.

In one of two opening-night games for the new league on December 19, 1917, Malone scored five goals as the Canadiens defeated Ottawa 7-4. Malone went on to score 44 goals during the 22-game regular season, easily winning the scoring title and setting a scoring pace never equalled in NHL history. The new league had its first superstar.

The league suffered its first major setback the following season, 1918-19. An influenza epidemic enfeebled many of the players on both finalists in the Stanley Cup playoffs—the Montreal Canadiens and Seattle Metropolitans of the Pacific Coast Hockey Association. Joe Hall, one of Montreal's star players died of the disease and so many players were stricken that the series was cancelled with no winner declared.

## Building a Following

Interest in NHL hockey grew appreciably through the 1920s and 1930s, but the popularity curve was far from smooth.

In 1919, the Mount Royal Arena was built as the home of the Montreal Canadiens and five years later, the Montreal Forum was constructed to house the Maroons, the other NHL team in that hockey-mad city. In Ottawa, Frank Ahearn built a 10,000-seat arena called the Auditorium in 1923. And in Toronto, Maple Leaf Gardens was completed in 1931.

When Ottawa met the Canadiens in the 1923-24 playoffs,

11,000 jammed into the Auditorium to see the Canadiens, with Howie Morenz, defeat the Senators 4-2. The Canadiens went on to defeat Vancouver to win the Stanley Cup, the first of 24 they would win in the NHL's 80 years.

The Forum, the Canadiens' home for most of the century, was actually built as the home of the Maroons. But a warm spell spoiled the natural ice at the Mount Royal Arena in the fall of 1924, so the Canadiens asked to play at the Forum, which had artificial ice. So it was that the Canadiens opened the Forum on November 29, 1924, whipping the Toronto Maple Leafs 7-1.

The 1924-25 season witnessed the first labor-management dispute when the players of the Hamilton Tigers, where the Quebec Bulldogs had shifted in 1920, went on strike before the playoffs. They wanted to be paid an extra $200 Cdn. per player for work during the playoffs, a seemingly reasonable request since Hamilton had made a record profit.

**Fans' Target: NHL president Clarence Campbell enraged Montreal fans in March 1955 when he suspended their hero, Maurice (Rocket) Richard.**

League president Calder, though, acted in support of the owners, in the belief that giving in to the players would put at risk the owners' "…large capital investment in rinks and arenas, and this capital must be protected."

Accordingly, Hamilton was disqualified from the playoffs, and the players were suspended and fined $200 Cdn. each. The Hamilton players' stand on playoff pay would be echoed in a similar stand later in the century by all NHL players, but at the time it seemed a minor obstacle on the league's pathway to success.

By the 1927-28 season, the NHL had grown from three teams to ten, split into two divisions: the Canadian and American. The Canadian division included the Toronto St. Patricks, the Ottawa Senators, the New York Americans, the Montreal Maroons and Montreal Canadiens. The American division consisted of the Boston Bruins, the New York Rangers, the Pittsburgh Pirates, the Chicago Blackhawks and the Detroit Cougars. This two-division alignment remained intact for 12 seasons, although this era was hardly immune from franchise shifts.

After winning the Stanley Cup in 1927, the Ottawa Senators, increasingly cashstrapped as the Great Depression approached, slid downhill. In 1930, the Senators sold star defenseman Frank (King) Clancy to the Toronto Maple Leafs for $35,000 Cdn., the largest sum ever paid for a hockey player. But even that cash infusion couldn't staunch the financial hemorrhage and, after suspending operations for the 1931-32 season, the Senators moved to St. Louis. The Eagles, as they were called, staggered through one season, before folding. Franchises also sprung up, struggled and folded or moved, in Pittsburgh and Philadelphia.

There was no shortage of star players in this era, which featured the scoring exploits of Nels Stewart, Cy Denneny, Aurel Joliat, Babe Dye, Montreal's incomparable Morenz, Harvey (Busher) Jackson, Charlie Conacher, Bill Cook and Cooney Weiland.

The game was evolving, finding itself, through the NHL's early days. Forward passing of the puck was not permitted at all until the 1927-28 season, when a rule change legalized this radical change in the defensive and neutral zones. When another rule change in 1929-30 gave players the green light to pass the puck ahead to a teammate in all three zones, goalscoring doubled. Ace Bailey led the league with 22 goals in 1927-28, compared to 43 goals for the league-leading Weiland the following season.

Play in the NHL was often vicious in the early days, but no incident horrified fans quite like Eddie Shore's attack on Ace Bailey on December 12, 1933 at the Boston Garden. Shore had been bodychecked into the boards by Red Horner and got up seeking revenge. He skated up to Bailey, who had his back to him, and knocked his feet out from under him. Bailey's head smacked against the ice and he went into convulsions. Horner responded by knocking Shore out with one punch, opening up a seven-stitch cut. Surgeons had to drill a hole in Bailey's skull to remove a blood clot that had formed near his brain. He remained unconscious, near death for 15 days and never played again.

The NHL of the 1930s produced many sublime evenings, also, but none like the Longest Game, a playoff encounter that began March 24 and ended March 25 in 1936.

That night, the Montreal Maroons and the Detroit Red Wings faced off in a Stanley Cup semifinal series opener that lasted 176 minutes 30 seconds. The only goal was scored by Detroit's Modere (Mud) Bruneteau at 16:30 of the sixth overtime period, provoking momentary stunned silence among the 9,000 fans at the Montreal Forum, followed by a huge ovation of relief. The game that began at 8:34 pm had ended at 2:25 am the following morning and all in attendance were utterly exhausted. None deserved a rest

more than Detroit goaltender Norm Smith, a Maroons castoff, who stopped 90 shots in his first NHL playoff game.

The Forum was also the scene for one of the saddest days in NHL history—the funeral of Canadiens great Howie Morenz on March 10, 1937. Morenz had died from complications arising from a broken leg. More than 25,000 fans filed past the coffin at center ice in the Forum.

As the 1930s progressed, teams began to die as well, as the NHL shrank from a ten-team, two-division league to a one-division league with seven teams by 1940.

## The War Years

In the early 1940s, a rule change introduced a center red line to the NHL ice surface. The idea was to speed up play and reduce offside calls. The change marked the onset of the league's so-called Modern Era.

As the NHL moved into this new phase, one player dominated the transition—Maurice (Rocket) Richard. Playing

Mr. Hockey: Gordie Howe's marvellous career stretched over five decades. His legendary longevity permitted him to play in the NHL with his sons, Mark and Marty.

Russian Bear: Anatoli Tarasov has been called the father of Soviet hockey. In fact, he studied the hockey writings of Toronto's Lloyd Percival.

Rubbing salt in the fans' wounds, he replaced Drillon with Don Metz, a raw rookie, putting him on a line with Nick Metz, his brother, and Dave (Sweeney) Shriner. The trio dominated the rest of the series as the Leafs, who got spectacular goaltending from Turk Broda, did the seemingly impossible and won the Stanley Cup. Drillon never played for the Leafs again.

Many NHL stars of this era enlisted in the Canadian armed forces and served in the war, including Broda, Syl Apps, Bob Goldham, the Metz brothers, Jimmy Orlando, Sid Abel, Mud Bruneteau and Bucko McDonald. The league operated throughout the wartime era, but the quality of competition was thinned by military service.

It was in the 1940s, too, that the NHL stabilized as a six-team league, its constituent members coming to be known as the 'Original Six.' The general managers, the sporting architects of those teams, became as legendary as the players: Frank J. Selke in Montreal; Toronto's Smythe; Jack Adams, who built the great Detroit Red Wings teams of the 1950s; Tommy Ivan with the Chicago Blackhawks.

## The Richard Riot

Sports journalist Rejean Tremblay once said: "The Rocket once told me that when he played he felt he was out there for all French Canadians."

Accordingly, all of French Canada was outraged in March 1955 when NHL president Clarence Campbell suspended Richard from the final three regular-season games and the entire playoffs for slugging a linesman in a fracas during a game in Boston.

Campbell, who embodied Anglophone dominance for many French-Canadians, attended the Canadiens' next game, against Detroit, at the Montreal Forum and quickly became a target for the irate Montreal fans seeking revenge for what they perceived as unjustly severe treatment of their hero.

At the end of the first period, a young man approached the NHL executive, extending his hand. But when Campbell held out his for an expected handshake, the man slapped his face. Moments later, a tear-gas bomb was set off behind one of the goals and soon after, the city's fire chief stopped the game, which was forfeited to Detroit.

The 15,000 fans filed out onto Ste-Catherine Street and a procession of pillaging unfolded along the street for several blocks.

The next day, Richard went on radio and television to appeal for calm in Montreal. The incident resonates to this day in Quebec. Many cite it as the spark that touched off the so-called Quiet Revolution, a period of profound and peaceful social change in the early 1960s.

right wing with center (Elegant) Elmer Lach and left winger Hector (Toe) Blake, Richard was the scoring star for the Montreal Canadiens, a symbol of competitive excellence for all French-Canadians and one of the most fiery, combative athletes ever to play any professional sport.

In the 1944-45 season, Richard scored 50 goals in 50 games, setting the standard for scoring brilliance for years to come. Lach (80 points), Richard (73) and Blake (67) finished 1-2-3 in the scoring race, earning the nickname, the 'Punch Line'.

Richard set a single-game scoring record that season, too, by scoring five goals and adding three assists as the Canadiens whipped the Red Wings 9-1 in Montreal on December 28.

The Stanley Cup highlight of the World War II period had to be the Toronto Maple Leafs' dramatic comeback victory in 1942, the only time in NHL history that a team overcame a 3-0 deficit in games to win a seven-game final series.

The Maple Leafs, second-place finishers during the 48-game regular season, found themselves in that predicament against the Detroit Red Wings, who had finished fifth in regular-season play.

At that point in the series, Maple Leafs' manager Conn Smythe, the man who built Maple Leaf Gardens and whose hockey credo was: "If you can't beat 'em in the alley, you can't beat 'em on the ice," took extreme measures.

Smythe benched right winger Gordie Drillon, the Leafs' top scorer, provoking outrage among Maple Leafs' supporters.

The league entered the 1950s with its depth of talent restored, its membership rock solid and the quality of play impressive.

### The Rocket and Mr. Hockey

If the overall quality of play was high, two teams stood out head and shoulders above the pack—the Detroit Red Wings and the Montreal Canadiens. Between them the Red Wings and Canadiens won ten of 11 Stanley Cups from 1950-1960. From 1951 through to 1960, the Canadiens made the Stanley Cup finals ten straight times, winning the Cup six times, including five in a row from 1956-60.

Beginning with the 1948-49 season and ending with the 1954-55 campaign, the Red Wings finished first in the regular season seven straight times, topping things off with a Stanley Cup victory four times during that run of excellence.

The Red Wings were constructed around Gordie Howe—Mr. Hockey, a prolific scorer and physically powerful player with a legendary mean streak he often expressed by delivering a pile-driver elbow to an opponent.

The Canadiens' leader was Maurice (Rocket) Richard, a passionate star with a burning desire to win at all costs. Richard's eyes, it was said, lit up like a pinball machine as he crossed the opposition blue line and homed in on the net to score.

In the Stanley Cup semifinals against Boston in 1952, Richard scored one of his most memorable goals. After a thunderous check by Boston's Leo LaBine, Richard left, semi-conscious, for the Forum clinic to have a nasty gash to the head stitched. He returned to the game late in the third period, with the score tied 1-1. His head bandaged, still groggy, Richard fashioned an end-to-end rush that he completed by fending off defenseman Bill

Quackenbush with one hand and shovelling a one-handed shot past goaltender Sugar Jim Henry.

With two spectacular stars like Howe and Richard, the NHL's popularity soared, and television broadcasts of NHL games only added to its appeal.

It was a period of consistently fat profits for the club owners: Conn Smythe in Toronto; the Norris family, which owned or controlled the Detroit Red Wings, Chicago Blackhawks and New York Rangers; Weston Adams in Boston; and the Molson family in Montreal.

Some of the players, notably Ted Lindsay of Detroit and Doug Harvey of Montreal, did some figuring and estimating and concluded that they were reaping a small slice of a revenue pie that was much larger than the owners let on.

In 1957, Lindsay was the driving force behind the formation of the National Hockey League Players' Association. The group wanted to take control of the players' pension fund, and channel broadcast revenues from the All-Star game directly into the fund.

The owners were, to say the least, hostile to the players' efforts. Jack Adams, the Red Wings' GM, traded Lindsay and goaltender Glenn Hall, both first-team All-Stars, to the Chicago Blackhawks. The Canadiens, unwilling to lose their best defenseman, waited three years before trading Harvey to the New York Rangers. Ownership battled the players every step of the way and in 1958 the players dropped their attempt to form a legally recognized association.

The exciting on-ice wars between the Red Wings, Canadiens, Bruins and Maple Leafs obscured the decade-ending labor-management skirmish. Far more prominent in the public imagination was the dominance of the Canadiens, who won a record five straight Stanley Cups to close the decade.

The Canadiens of that era were so proficient on the power play they forced a rule change. In 1956-57, the NHL ruled that a penalized player could return to the ice if the opposing team scored a goal in his absence. Previously, a player had to sit out the full two minutes, during which time the potent Canadiens power-play unit sometimes scored two or even three times.

As the league moved into a new decade, Richard retired, but another brilliant player emerged with the Chicago Blackhawks—Bobby Hull. Actually, it was Bernie Geoffrion, one of Richard's ex-teammates, who became the second player to score 50

**The Fog: Fred Shero coached the Philadelphia Flyers to two straight Stanley Cups in the 1970s but couldn't rekindle that magic as coach of the New York Rangers.**

Skill Set: Along with Hedberg, Hull and Lars-Erik Sjoberg, the flashy Winnipeg Jets had plenty of skill and helped change the way hockey is played in North America.

## ICE TALK

### "THERE IS NO WAY (THE CANADIENS) CAN BEAT US WITH A JUNIOR B GOALTENDER,"

*GEORGE (PUNCH) IMLACH, TORONTO MAPLE LEAFS' GENERAL MANAGER AND HEAD COACH ON ROOKIE MONTREAL GOALIE ROGATIEN VACHON ON THE EVE OF THE 1967 STANLEY CUP FINAL SERIES*

goals in a season. Of course, Geoffrion recorded the feat in the 1960-61 season, a 70- not a 50-game season. Hull recorded the first of his five 50-plus goal seasons the following year.

Hull and teammate Stan Mikita were at the top of an impressive list of 1960s scoring stars that included Frank Mahovlich, the still-impressive Howe, Jean Beliveau, Andy Bathgate, Red Kelly, Alex Delvecchio, Rod Gilbert, Ken Wharram, John Bucyk and Norm Ullman.

The Toronto Maple Leafs supplanted the Canadiens as the dominant team in the early 1960s, winning three straight Stanley Cups from 1962-64, but the Canadiens won four in five years from 1964-69. They might have won five straight, except for Toronto's stunning upset victory over Montreal with an aging team in 1967.

That Stanley Cup final was truly the last of an era, because the NHL was preparing for unprecedented growth as the decade wound down.

## A Victory for the Aged—Toronto's 1967 Stanley Cup Win

The Montreal Canadiens had won two straight Stanley Cups and seemed a solid bet to win a third as they prepared to meet the Maple Leafs in the final pre-expansion final series.

The Maple Leafs, third-place finishers during the season, had surprised lots of people by knocking off the first-place Chicago Blackhawks in the semifinals, but the younger, speedier Canadiens had swept the New York Rangers in four games, going with rookie goalie Rogatien Vachon.

The Maple Leafs' lineup had an average age of more than 31 years that included 42-year-old goalie Johnny Bower, and 41-year-old defenseman Allan Stanley. Twelve members of the roster were over 30—seven of them over 35.

When the Canadiens won Game 1, 6-2, with Henri Richard recording the hat-trick and Yvan Cournoyer scoring twice, it seemed to confirm the experts' analysis—the younger, quicker Canadiens were simply too good for the aging Leafs.

Then the ageless Bower went out and shut out the Canadiens as Toronto won Game 2, 3-0. The Leafs won Game 3 in overtime 3-2, with Bower brilliant again, making 60 saves. But when he strained his groin in the Game 4 pre-game warm-up, Maple Leafs' coach Punch Imlach had to insert Terry Sawchuk in goal.

The Canadiens seemed to solve Sawchuk, winning 6-3 to even the series 2-2. But Sawchuk only gave up two goals in the final two games—as Toronto stunned the hockey world by winning the series 4-2. The ageless wonders had turned back the clock and rediscovered their prime.

"I felt sick for a month afterwards," said Montreal defenseman Terry Harper. "To lose the Stanley Cup, that was horrible, but to lose to Toronto and have to live in Canada afterwards, oh man—everywhere you'd go you'd run into Leafs' fans, well, that was like losing twice."

# ICE TALK

## "A MISTAKE HAS BEEN MADE."

*NHL PRESIDENT CLARENCE CAMPBELL, AFTER MISTAKENLY ANNOUNCING THAT THE EXPANSION VANCOUVER CANUCKS WOULD SELECT FIRST OVER THE BUFFALO SABRES IN THE 1971 ENTRY DRAFT*

## So Long, Original Six, Hello Expansion

The success—artistic and financial—of the Original Six had attracted interested investors as early as the mid-1940s. In 1945-46, representatives from Philadelphia, Los Angeles and San Francisco had applied for franchises. The Original Six owners, jealously guarding their rich profit margins, were hostile to the notion for years.

But envious of the lucrative TV contracts U.S. networks were signing with the National Football League, American Football League and Major-League baseball, and recognizing that such riches were definitely beyond the grasp of a six-team, Canadian-

## Broad Street Bounty

"We take the shortest distance to the puck and arrive in ill humor." That was the Philadelphia Flyers credo, as enunciated by head coach Fred Shero. He wasn't kidding.

The Flyers were constructed around a core of stellar players: goaltender Bernie Parent; defensemen Jim Watson and Bob Dailey; centers Bobby Clarke and Rick MacLeish; and wingers Bill Barber and Reggie Leach.

The supporting cast included some honest checkers like Bill Clement, Terry Crisp and Ross Lonsberry and a platoon of enforcers like Dave (The Hammer) Schultz, Bob (Houndog) Kelly, Don (Big Bird) Saleski, Jack McIlhargey and Andre (Moose) Dupont.

The blend of goaltending brilliance, team defense, toughness and scoring punch helped make the Flyers the first expansion club to win one Stanley Cup, let alone two.

Shero was nicknamed 'The Fog' by his players because he was given to cryptic sayings.

On the day of Game 6 in Philadelphia's Stanley Cup victory over the Boston Bruins in 1974, Shero wrote this message on the chalkboard in the dressing room: "Win together today and we'll walk together forever."

The Flyers won, and carved their names into the Stanley Cup.

based league, the league governors decided to proceed with expansion. The decision was spurred, in part, by aggressive efforts by the Western Hockey League, a development league, to push for major-league status.

The NHL governors received 15 applications for new franchises and in February, 1966, granted teams to Los Angeles, San Francisco, St. Louis, Pittsburgh, Philadelphia and Minnesota. The new franchises cost $2 million U.S. each.

The new teams were grouped together in the West Division, which enabled them to be competitive amongst themselves, even if they weren't really competitive with the six established teams in the East Division. The first three years of expansion, the St. Louis Blues, coached by Scotty Bowman, and staffed with aging stars like Glenn Hall, Jacques Plante, Doug Harvey, Dickie Moore and others, advanced to the Stanley Cup final. Each year, the Blues lost in four straight games.

The third of those three four-game sweeps of the Blues was administered by Bobby Orr and the Boston Bruins. Orr had become the first defenseman in NHL history to record 100 points in 1969-70, when he scored 33 goals and added 87 assists for 120 points to win the scoring championship. Many thought it was the first Stanley Cup of a Boston dynasty, but Orr's career was foreshortened by a series of knee injuries. He left the NHL before he was 30, with just two Stanley Cup rings—1970 and 1972.

Expansion coincided with the establishment of the NHL Players' Association—ten years after Ted Lindsay's effort had failed. A Toronto lawyer named Alan Eagleson had helped striking players on the minor-league Springfield Indians win their dispute with Eddie Shore, the club's miserly, ogre-like president and manager.

That victory helped him win the players' support when, led by a core group of Toronto Maple Leafs players, the association was established in 1967, with Eagleson as its executive director.

**King of Kings: After Wayne Gretzky was traded to Los Angeles in 1988, it suddenly became chic to be seen at an NHL game in La-La Land.**

13

Players' salaries, kept artificially low for decades, were about to increase dramatically, but it was a rival league—the World Hockey Association—far more than the Eagleson-led NHLPA that would be responsible.

The Winnipeg WHA franchise provided instant credibility for the rival league by signing Bobby Hull for $1 million Cdn. Then they borrowed Hull's nickname—The Golden Jet—to name their own club. Other high-profile players who followed included J.C. Tremblay, Marc Tardif, Gerry Cheevers and Derek Sanderson.

Many clubs signed players to lucrative contracts rather than lose them to WHA teams.

To combat the upstart league, the NHL kept on expanding, adding Vancouver and Buffalo in 1970. That year, the great Gilbert Perreault was the prize available for the expansion club fortunate enough to choose first in the entry draft. To decide between the Sabres and Canucks, the league brought in a wheel of fortune apparatus, the kind popular at country fairs. The Sabres were assigned numbers one through ten, with the Canucks getting 11-20. The wheel was given a spin and came to rest at the number 1—or so it seemed. Clarence Campbell, the league president announced that the Sabres had won, prompting elation among the Buffalo supporters. But the wheel had stopped at 11. Campbell stepped back to the microphone and uttered this phrase: "A mistake has been made."

Perreault played 17 seasons for the Sabres and scored 512 goals, while Dale Tallon, selected by the Canucks, had a solid, but unspectacular career with Vancouver, Chicago and the Pittsburgh Penguins. Expansion continued in 1972, when Atlanta and the New York Islanders were added, and in 1974 the Kansas City Scouts and the Washington Capitals joined the league. The NHL had tripled in size in just seven years, severly depleting the talent base.

The dilution was made more apparent by the 1972 Summit Series between Canada and the Soviet Union. Canadians expected their pros, who had been banned for years from competing in World Championships or Olympic competitions, to drub the Soviets, but were stunned when the Soviets beat Canada 7-3 in the opening game at the Forum. The Soviet game, with legendary coach Anatoli Tarasov directing its development, had caught up to and, in many areas, passed the Canadian style. That realization stunned a country which prided itself on producing the best hockey players in the world.

Canada, playing on pride, guts and determination, won a narrow series victory with four victories, three losses and one game tied. But the game had changed forever.

On the expansion front, meanwhile, not all the franchises took root where they were first planted. The California Golden Seals moved to Cleveland in 1976, then merged with the struggling Minnesota North Stars in 1979. The Kansas City Scouts moved to Denver, Colorado in 1976 and then in 1982 to East Rutherford, New Jersey, where they remain as the Devils.

In the early expansion days, Montreal general manager Sam Pollock took advantage of expansion to build a 1970s dynasty in Montreal. The Canadiens, rich in solid talent throughout their farm system, swapped good young players, and sometimes established but aging players, to talent-starved expansion clubs for high draft picks.

Swedish Import: Anders Hedberg was Bobby Hull's linemate in his WHA days with the Winnipeg Jets, but he became a Ranger when the Jets entered the NHL in 1979.

In this fashion, the Canadiens obtained Guy Lafleur, Steve Shutt, Bob Gainey, Doug Risebrough, Michel Larocque, Mario Tremblay—the building blocks of the six Stanley Cup champions during the 1970s.

Many complained that the rapid expansion drastically diluted the talent in the NHL. The Philadelphia Flyers, the first post-expansion club to win the Stanley Cup, certainly weren't overloaded with talent. Their canny coach, Fred Shero, made the most of a small nucleus of excellent talent, led by goalie Bernie Parent, center Bobby Clarke, and wingers Bill Barber and Reggie Leach, and a belligerent style of play that intimidated the opposition.

That formula led the Flyers to back-to-back Stanley Cup championships in 1974 and 1975. By 1976, the Canadiens load of drafted talent—particularly Guy Lafleur—had matured, and Montreal rolled to four straight Stanley Cup championships to close out the 1970s.

The turn of the decade also saw the ten-year war with the WHA resolved, when the only four surviving teams from the rival league—the Quebec Nordiques; Hartford Whalers; Edmonton Oilers; and Winnipeg Jets joined the NHL. The teams were stripped of the talent they had recruited, often in bidding wars with NHL clubs, and denied access to TV revenue for five years after joining the NHL.

As a result, the Jets lost stars Anders Hedberg and Ulf Nilsson, both of whom played for the New York Rangers thereafter. The Oilers were permitted to keep Wayne Gretzky, who had signed a personal services contract with Oilers owner Peter Pocklington. And the Whalers iced a lineup that included 50-year-old Gordie Howe, playing with his sons, Mark and Marty.

The Nordiques' response was be to creative in its recruiting efforts. Club president Marcel Aubut arranged for Slovak stars Peter and Anton Stastny to defect from Czechoslovakia, and the pair were joined one year later by older brother Marian. The Stastnys, especially Peter and Anton, became the scoring stars on the rebuilt Nordiques.

The success of the Stastnys helped convince NHL managers that there were rich veins of talent in Europe that had to be tapped. Communism was one major obstacle to doing so immediately, however.

There were few large impediments to importing Scandinavian talent, though, as the New York Islanders found out. They won four straight Stanley Cups, beginning in 1980, with some talented Scandinavians, like Tomas Jonsson, Stefan Persson, Anders Kallur and Mats Hallin, playing important roles.

The European influence really took hold in the NHL, though, with the Edmonton Oilers, who supplanted the Islanders as the NHL's pre-eminent team in 1984, when they won the first of five Stanley Cups in seven years.

Glen Sather, the Oilers' general manager and coach, sprinkled some talented Europeans like Jari Kurri, Esa Tikkanen, Reijo Ruotsalainen, Kent Nilsson and Willy Lindstrom around the Edmonton lineup, with good results.

But Sather went one step further, borrowing much from the flowing, speed-based European style and adapting it to the NHL.

Sather once described the Oilers' style as the Montreal Canadiens (of the 1970s) updated for the 1980s.

The style of play—executed by great players like Gretzky, Mark Messier, Glenn Anderson, Paul Coffey and Kurri—helped Sather construct a Canadiens-like 1980s dynasty.

## Thinking Globally

As the NHL moved toward the 1990s the governors began to develop a larger vision. This was not an easy process. The traditions and mind-set of the Original Six had continued to dominate the league well after expansion had transformed a small, regional league into a continental one, albeit a weak sister compared to major-league baseball, football and basketball.

The NHL had evolved into a 21-team league but was controlled by the triumvirate of league president John Ziegler, Chicago Blackhawks owner Bill Wirtz and NHLPA executive-director Alan Eagleson.

The league had traditionally been gate-driven, dominated by shrewd entrepreneurs like Smythe, the Norrises, the Wirtz family and the Molsons, who owned their own arenas and knew how to fill them but had little feel for or interest in marketing the league as a whole.

A series of linked events began to change this. By the summer of 1988, Wayne Gretzky had led the Edmonton Oilers to four Stanley Cups and established himself as the best player in hockey. But to Oilers owner Peter Pocklington he was a depreciating asset whose value had peaked.

Pocklington traded Gretzky to the Los Angeles Kings—sending Edmontonians, and Canadians in general, into mourning, and stunning NHL ownership.

Bruce McNall, then the Kings' owner, promptly raised Gretzky's salary. He reasoned that Gretzky would generate far greater revenues for the Kings, both at the gate and through advertising and he was proved right.

Two years later, the St. Louis Blues used similar logic when they signed Brett Hull, their franchise player, to a three-year contract. Then they signed restricted free agent defenseman Scott Stevens to a four-year deal.

While salaries were rising, there were other parts of the hockey business taking off as well. In the United States more people watched NHL hockey on Fox and ESPN than ever before. In Canada, Saturday became a double dream as *Hockey Night in Canada* began running doubleheaders. And in the U.S. and Canada the NHL found success in five new markets. Anaheim, Ottawa, San Jose, Miami Florida and Tampa Bay all greeted the game with excitement and big crowds. The value of an NHL franchise rose and the level of people wanting to own a team grew.

As the economics of major professional hockey changed, the NHL realized that the old, gate-driven model would not work anymore. Hockey entrepreneurs began to build new, larger arenas, which featured scores of so-called luxury suites, hotel-plush boxes designed to enable corporate executives and guests to enjoy a game in high style.

**In With the New:** By importing European talents like Esa Tikkanen, Jari Kurri, **Risto Siltanen** and others to the Edmonton Oilers' talent-rich lineup in the 1980s, general manager Glen Sather helped change the face of the game in the NHL.

Labor Man: Under executive-director Bob Goodenow, the NHL Players' Association has become more proactive about getting its share of the NHL revenue pie.

New forms of advertising opportunities—on scoreboards, rink boards, even on the ice itself—were deployed to generate more money. And the NHL, long a marketing luddite among major professional leagues, got into the merchandising business in a concerted way.

As the hockey business grew more sophisticated, the players became more assertive about their interests, also. Dissatisfaction with NHLPA executive-director Alan Eagleson's autocratic, company-union style had been growing and, in 1990, the players selected former agent Bob Goodenow, the man who had negotiated Brett Hull's blockbuster contract, as their new director.

At the end of the 1992 season, the players staged an 11-day strike, demanding, among other things, the marketing rights to their own likenesses. They wanted a chunk of the revenue pie, in other words, and were prepared to fight to get it. The players also sought more relaxed free agency guidelines enabling them to sell themselves on the market.

As the league adjusted to a new economic and labor reality, it sought new leadership capable of achieving peace with the players and the league's on-ice officials, and proactively directing its newly ambitious business aspirations.

In 1992, a search committee selected Gary Bettman, a lawyer and former executive with the marketing-slick National Basketball Association to become the league's first commissioner.

Early in his tenure, Bettman made a business statement by recruiting two powerful new partners to set up NHL franchises—the Disney Corporation and Blockbuster Entertainment.

Michael Eisner, the Disney CEO, named his company's team the Mighty Ducks of Anaheim, after a commercially successful movie of the same name. Wayne Huizenga, head of Blockbuster,

established a second team in Florida, the Panthers, based in Miami.

It had long been a cliché that pro sports was an entertainment business, but recruiting the likes of Eisner and Huizenga suggested that NHL head office had actually begun to believe this maxim.

One team—the Ottawa Senators—misread the market and grossly overestimated the promotional opportunities available to young stars when they signed untried No. 1 draft pick Alexandre Daigle to a five-year contract in June 1993. The deal included a marketing component that was unrealistically generous for an unproven rookie.

If the Gretzky, Hull and Stevens contracts had lifted the salary ceiling, the Daigle deal significantly raised the entry level and helped cause an ownership backlash. The notion of a rookie salary cap took hold and a second owner-player showdown in three years loomed.

The result was a lockout that cancelled 468 games from October 1, 1994 to January 19, 1995, shrinking the regular season to 48 games with no inter-conference play. The deal finally struck included a rookie salary cap and provided somewhat greater freedom of movement for older players.

The new, five-year deal couldn't help franchises stuck with outmoded arenas, however, and two Canadian teams, the Quebec Nordiques and Winnipeg Jets, moved south to Denver and Phoenix, respectively—Quebec for 1995-96, Winnipeg for the 1996-97 season. The move proved successful for Colorado when they won the Stanley Cup in their first year.

## The Next One

Eric Lindros was so dominant as a junior hockey player that he was dubbed 'The Next One'—Wayne Gretzky being 'The Great One'—well before he was drafted No. 1 overall by the Quebec Nordiques in 1991.

He was also supremely confident in his ability and secure in the knowledge that his extraordinary skill and potential as a marketing vehicle gave him unprecedented leverage to negotiate.

He warned Nordiques president Marcel Aubut, with whom he did not get along, not to draft him, saying he would refuse to report if he were selected. Sure enough, Quebec drafted him and Lindros, true to his word, did not report. He played another year of junior and for Canada's Olympic team at the 1992 Olympics in Albertville, France.

In June 1992, Aubut invited a bidding contest for Lindros and thought he had made a blockbuster deal with the New York Rangers. But the Philadelphia Flyers also had an offer on the table that included $15 million U.S., six players and two first-round draft picks.

An arbitrator was called in and he awarded Lindros to the Flyers in one of the most bizarre transactions in NHL history.

## Going For Gold

The 1997-98 season is an historic one for the NHL, which will, for the first time ever, suspend operations to enable the stars from all participating countries to join their respective national teams to compete at the 1998 Winter Olympics in Nagano, Japan.

The so-called Dream Teams concept is the result of years of negotiating among the NHL, NHLPA, the International Ice Hockey Federation and its member federations, and the International Olympic Committee. The result is the first-ever best-against-best men's hockey tournament at the Winter Olympics.

The Olympic Games is an extraordinary opportunity for the National Hockey League to further establish itself as a major force on the international sporting market.

As the league's vision continues to expand globally, it has granted expansion franchises to four more cities: Atlanta, Nashville, Columbus, Ohio and St. Paul, Minnesota, which has been without a franchise since the Stars moved to Dallas.

Unlike previous expansion efforts, the NHL, under Bettman, is deploying its considerable marketing forces not merely to ensure that the individual franchises succeed, but to implant a hockey culture across the United States.

Through its state-of-the-art website, grassroots programs such as the NHL's involvement with In-Line and Street hockey, as well as its growing involvement with women's hockey, the league is, in fact, raising the profile of the NHL as well as the sport of hockey itself.

As the NHL heads into the next century, the marketing momentum is building; the league and the sport are growing. Its future has never been more exciting.

Mightiest Duck: Disney Company CEO Michael Eisner transposed cinematic marketing techniques to help sell the sport of hockey in Southern California.

# TEAMS IN THE NHL

**W**ith the growth of the National Hockey League in North America and the influx of bright international stars like Jaromir Jagr, Sergei Fedorov and Peter Forsberg, the NHL is showcasing more individual talent in the 1990s than it ever has. Yet the team concept continues to endure as the bedrock principle of the sport. It's a cliché in hockey that no player—no matter how spectacular his contribution—is bigger than his team.

Consider Eric Lindros, whom many regard the heir apparent to the mantle of the greatest player in the NHL, now that Mario Lemieux has retired and Wayne Gretzky's brilliant career is drawing to a close.

Lindros entered the NHL with Philadelphia in the 1992-93 season, loaded down with achievements. He had helped the Oshawa Generals win the Memorial Cup as Canada's best junior team, helped Canada's National Junior Team win the World Junior Hockey Championship, helped Team Canada win the 1991 Canada Cup (now the World Cup of Hockey) tournament, and helped Canada's Olympic team win a silver medal at the 1992 Winter Olympics in Albertville, France.

He has continued to pile up awards in the NHL, winning the Hart Trophy as the league's most valuable player in 1995. But Lindros and his growing number of followers had to wait while the Flyers surrounded their awesomely talented star with the right supporting cast before seeing their hero lead Philadelphia into the Stanley Cup Finals for the first time in his era in 1997.

## The ultimate standard

Successful hockey teams are an amalgam of coaching acumen, solid team defense, great goaltending, timely scoring, leadership, fan support and the most elusive factor of all—team chemistry.

Coaches set the tone for success and none was more successful than Hector (Toe) Blake, the legendary coach of the Montreal Canadiens in the 1950s and 1960s.

In his first meeting with his team, in October 1955, Blake told his players: "There are some guys in this room who play better than I ever did. I have nothing to teach them. But what I can show you all is how to play better as a team."

Blake obviously succeeded. In 13 years as coach of the Canadiens, the team finished first in the regular season nine times and won eight Stanley Cups, including five straight from 1956-60.

Scoring titles and individual awards may be the measure of a

**Doom Trooper:** Big, strong-skating, offensively skilled John Leclair is a key component in Philadelphia's Legion of Doom line, along with Eric Lindros and Michael Renberg.

player's excellence, but NHL teams are measured by one standard only—their ability to win the Stanley Cup.

An entire generation of Toronto Maple Leafs fans has grown to adulthood without seeing their club win the Cup, yet the legend of an aging Leafs club that did win it in 1967 lives on.

In the early 1970s, the New York Islanders entered the NHL as an expansion club and were carefully crafted into a formidable group by general manager Bill Torrey. The validation of Torrey's genius in drafting Denis Potvin, Mike Bossy, Bryan Trottier, Clark Gillies and others was the four straight Stanley Cups the Islanders won, beginning in 1980.

As great as those stars were, though, the Islanders championship chemistry didn't click until Torrey traded for Butch Goring, a speedy, gritty, centerman. Goring checked the opposing team's top center and, a keen student of the game, designed the Islanders' penalty killing system.

The Edmonton Oilers of the 1980s were loaded with offensive firepower, boasting the likes of Wayne Gretzky, Jari Kurri, Glenn Anderson, Paul Coffey and Mark Messier. But they didn't become champions until coach Glen Sather had taught them to play solid, if not necessarily brilliant, team defense.

Mario Lemieux, arguably the game's best player, led Pittsburgh to two straight Stanley Cup triumphs in the early 1990s, but a key member of both teams was Trottier, who brought invaluable playoff experience to those Pittsburgh teams.

New York fans of a certain age have fond memories of stars like Jean Ratelle, Rod Gilbert and Vic Hadfield, the famous GAG (Goal-a-game) line of the 1970s. But none of those players ever won a Stanley Cup.

The Rangers faithful had to wait until 1994, after Messier, who learned how to be a champion with the Oilers, had moved to New York and instilled team values in his new teammates.

**Fair Trade:** When Colorado Avalanche traded Owen Nolan to the San Jose Sharks for defenseman Sandis Ozolinsh they acquired one of the most offensively talented defensemen in all of the National Hockey League.

## Saving goals

And no team can succeed without great goaltending: the Islanders' Billy Smith; Grant Fuhr of the Oilers; the Rangers' Mike Richter; Tom Barrasso of the Penguins.

No goalie can boast a Stanley Cup performance chart quite like Patrick Roy of the Colorado Avalanche. He led the Canadiens to a Stanley Cup as a rookie in 1986 and backstopped them to another in 1993, when he cooly closed the door on the opposition as Montreal won 10 games in overtime.

In 1996, Roy's stingy netminding was central to Colorado winning the Stanley Cup. In that four-game sweep of the Florida Panthers, Roy gave up just four goals total—one per game.

In 1995-96, the talent-rich Red Wings won a record 62 regular-season games, breaking the old record for most victories in a season (60) set in 1976-77 by the Canadiens. But that Montreal team was in the process of winning four straight Stanley Cups.

The Red Wings berth in the 1997 Stanley Cup final was, for them, another chance to measure themselves against the other great teams in NHL history by the only yardstick that matters— a Stanley Cup championship.

# MIGHTY DUCKS OF ANAHEIM

## After a weak start to the season, the Mighty Ducks rallied to reach the playoffs, and second place in the Pacific Division.

Eleven games into the 1996-97 NHL season, the Mighty Ducks of Anaheim were more like sitting ducks for their opponents. A seven-game losing skid dropped their record to 1-8-2 and drove them deeper into the league basement. Then, in Hollywood fashion, a white knight arrived to the rescue in the person of immensely talented forward Paul Kariya, who missed the first 11 games with an abdominal injury sustained near the end of the previous season.

His return meant that the equally-gifted Teemu Selanne had his linemate back. And, playing alongside center Steve Rucchin, things quickly started to click for the trio. In the following months they combined for 114 goals, the most by any line in the league. The Mighty Ducks shrugged off their miserable start and piled up victories, including a 13-3-7 run in the season's final 23 games.

### Late success

The late charge not only got the Mighty Ducks into the playoffs for the first time in their history, but pushed them into second place in the Pacific Division and fourth overall in the Western Conference with a 36-33-13 record.

Not surprisingly, Selanne, Kariya and Rucchin were the team's top three goal-scorers with 51, 44 and 19 respectively. Selanne set a team record with 109 points, while Kariya produced 99 and Rucchin, who forsook a medical career after Anaheim picked him in the 1994 supplemental draft, collected 67 points.

The emergence of goaltender Guy Hebert, who compiled a 2.67 goals-against average while handling the bulk of the netminding chores—including 23 straight games at one point— was an integral part of the Mighty Ducks' success.

The success continued in the opening round of the playoffs, as the Mighty Ducks rallied from a 3-2 deficit in games to knock off Phoenix in a seven-game series. The Ducks were swept by Detroit in the second round, but not before sending three of the games into overtime, including a double-overtime session in the fourth game.

A few weeks after the playoff elimination, Mighty Ducks general manager Jack Ferreira announced that the team was parting company with Ron Wilson, their only coach so far, and the man behind the bench for the World Cup victory by the United States squad last fall. Ferreira said the reason for the change were "philosophical differences" between Wilson and club management.

### Celluloid birth

The NHL's Mighty Ducks probably wouldn't exist if it hadn't been for Emilio Estevez and a rag-tag bunch of skaters who turned a low-budget Disney production into a celluloid success.

"The movie was our market research," recalls Disney chairman Michael Eisner, who approached the NHL about an

**Finnish Duck: Teemu Selanne continued his scoring groove with linemate Kariya, to propel the Ducks, after a weak early season, to fourth overall in the Western Conference.**

## ★ ROLL OF HONOR ★

| | |
|---|---|
| Conference/Division | **Western/Pacific** |
| First Season | **1993-94** |
| Honor roll | **Share record for most wins (33) by first-year team** |
| Home rink/Capacity | **Arrowhead Pond/17,174** |
| Stanley Cups | **0** |

### Playing Record

| | W | L | T | Pts |
|---|---|---|---|---|
| Regular Season | 120 | 145 | 31 | 271 |
| Playoffs | 4 | 7 | | |

expansion franchise after the screen version of the Mighty Ducks grossed almost $60 million.

In the fall of 1993, the real-life Mighty Ducks became the NHL's third California-based member, joining the Los Angeles Kings and San Jose Sharks, and were the league's big surprise that first year, tying an NHL first-year team record with 33 victories, including 19 road wins, the most ever by a first-year club.

In the shortened 1994-95 season, they developed their first star players, such as Kariya and defenseman Oleg Tverdovsky, who was then traded, along with center Chad Kilger, to obtain the high-scoring Selanne from the Winnipeg Jets on February 7, 1996. Selanne and Kariya provide the Mighty Ducks with a formidable 1-2 offensive punch.

The Mighty Ducks are equally powerful at the marketing and merchandising level. Their logo—a goalie mask resembling an angry duck—and team colors of purple, jade, silver, and white are big sellers well beyond the Magic Kingdom.

**Gretzky's Heir: Many hockey observers believe that the speedy Paul Kariya is the 1990s version of Wayne Gretzky, combining speed, skill and an uncanny ability to anticipate how plays will develop.**

# BOSTON BRUINS

## Bad omens before the season's start came all too true, as the Bruins blundered through chaos to miss the Cup playoffs.

Spring-time just wasn't the same around Boston in 1997. For the first time in 30 years, the beloved Bruins failed to qualify for the Stanley Cup playoffs, ending the longest such streak in major professional sports.

There were bad omens even before the season started, as Cam Neely, the club's major scoring threat, was forced to retire because of chronic pain in his hip. Besides being the team's inspirational leader, Neely had led the Bruins in scoring in seven of his ten seasons with the club.

In December, forward Steve Heinze, the Bruins top scorer at the time, was lost for the remainder of the season because of damaged knee ligaments. Center Adam Oates openly commented about what he perceived was management's lack of commitment to winning. And veteran right-winger Rick Tocchet grumbled about his reduced playing time.

It wasn't a surprise when Bruins general manager Harry Sinden packaged goaltender Bill Ranford, Oates and Tocchet in a trade with the Washington Capitals for goaltender Jim Carey and young prospects Anson Carter and Jason Allison, a center and right-winger, respectively.

### Build again

Amid the Bruins' chaotic season was the courage and inspiration of forward Sheldon Kennedy, who went public with the shocking details of his sexual abuse by a coach while he was playing junior hockey. Kennedy was hailed by both friends and on-ice foes for his revelations, which raised awareness about a disturbing societal issue.

Grit and determination were also part of Kennedy's on-ice characteristics. But even those qualities weren't enough to save Kennedy's job. He was released in the off-season. Sadly for the Bruins, too many of Kennedy's teammates failed to exemplify the Bruins' trademark lunch-bucket style. The result was an NHL-worst 26-47-9 record, the team's poorest performance since it was 17-43-10 in 1966-67, the last time it missed the playoffs.

"It's everyone's fault," said Mike O'Connell, the Bruins assistant general manager, said of the team's demise, which included allowing a league-high 300 goals. But second-year coach Steve Kasper paid the steepest price—he was relieved of his duties and replaced by Pat Burns, the former head coach with Montreal and Toronto, who was given a four-year contract to put the Bruins back on the rails.

Burns has a rebuilding job on his hands to get the Bruins back to the Stanley Cup finals, where they have not been since 1990. He does have the foundation of the franchise in workhorse defenseman Ray Bourque, a life-long Bruin.

Boston's last Cup triumph was in 1972. That Cup, like the one in 1970, featured the uplifting play of a young defenseman named Bobby Orr, who first arrived on the scene in 1966-67,

**Lost Cup: For the first time in his career, Ray Bourque learned about not qualifying for the play-offs. The future Hall of Fame defenseman has yet to play for a Stanley Cup winner in 18 seasons.**

after the Bruins had missed the playoffs for six straight seasons of a streak that would eventually reach eight years.

On May 10, 1970, Orr, arguably the best defenseman ever until his knees gave out after ten years with Boston, left his personal imprint on the team's first Cup win in 29 years, scoring the winning goal against St. Louis Blues netminder Glenn Hall.

### Founder members

One of the original six NHL teams, the Bruins started play in the 1924-25 season. They had several glittering performers grace their roster in ensuing years—notably tough guy defenseman Eddie Shore, right winger Dit Clapper and center Milt Schmidt. But they had only three Stanley Cups to their credit before Orr, slick center Phil Esposito and (Chief) Johnny Bucyk combined their talents for the two Cups in the early 1970s. Orr was the first NHL defenseman to win the scoring championship, achieving the feat in 1969-70. Esposito won five scoring titles in just over eight seasons with Boston. In 1968-69, he became the first NHL player to compile more than 100 points in a season.

**Short Fame: Sheldon Kennedy's courage in telling the truth about being abused as a junior player far outshone his on-ice 18 points in 1996-97. He was released in the off-season.**

## ★ ROLL OF HONOR ★

| | |
|---|---|
| Conference/Division | **Eastern/Atlantic** |
| First Season | **1924-25** |
| Honor roll | **29 straight winning seasons** |
| Home rink/Capacity | **Fleet Center/17,565** |
| Stanley Cups: | **5 (1929, 1939, 1941, 1970, 1972)** |

**Playing Record**

| | W | L | T | Pts |
|---|---|---|---|---|
| Regular Season | 2306 | 1800 | 706 | 4883 |
| Playoffs | 228 | 242 | | |

## Despite mishaps and wrangles, a tough work ethic and great goaltending took the Sabres to the top of their division.

Their top scorer—Derek Plante—led the team with a mere 53 points. Pat LaFontaine, the Sabres only proven offensive star, appeared in 13 games before a severe concussion ended his season, and perhaps his career. At one point, the $4 million scoreboard inside the Marine Midland Arena, the team's new headquarters, crashed to the ice a few hours before a game.

And while the team was scrapping for points on the ice, there was a tug of war in the executive offices, as general manager John Muckler and coach Ted Nolan spent the season struggling for power. Eventually, both emerged losers as the Sables dismissed Muckler and did not renew Nolan's contract at the end of the season. Darcy was hired as GM and he brought in former Sabre Lindy Ruff to replace Nolan as head coach.

### Working to success

Instead of falling on its sabre, the team was probably the biggest surprise in the league, posting a 40-30-12 record to finish atop the Northeast Division and third in the Eastern Conference—a marked improvement over the 1995-96 season.

**Bargain Buy: Mike Peca, acquired in the trade that sent Alexander Mogilny to the Vancouver Canucks, was fourth in scoring on the Sabres with 49 points (20 goals) in 1996-97, and won the Frank Selke Trophy as the league's top defensive forward.**

The Sabres' formula for success was relatively simple: a tremendous work ethic, Nolan's blue-collar style, and goaltender Dominik (The Dominator) Hasek usually stopping everything in sight.

Hasek, a two-time Vezina Trophy winner, faced 2,177 shots, the most in the league, and recorded the top save percentage—.930—in a true MVP-caliber performance. But while Hasek was the major story of the regular season, he also 'dominated' the sports pages in the playoff round—making headlines after straining his knee in the third game of the team's opening-round series against Ottawa.

Backup goaltender Steve Shields, who had appeared in only 13 regular-season games, now emerged as the Sabres best post-season player. His puck-stopping ability took the team past Ottawa before its playoff run ended in the next round against the Philadelphia Flyers.

"We've grown together as a team," said Sabres right-winger Rob Ray. "We don't have any individuals out there. We don't have a go-to guy other than Dominik. It makes things easier."

### Flashy past

The Sabres were once one of the NHL's flashiest offensive teams. The franchise scored a major coup months before it took to the ice for the first time in the 1970-71 season. Through a stroke of luck—the spin of a numbered wheel—the Sabres got the first draft pick ahead of their expansion cousin, the Vancouver Canucks.

George (Punch) Imlach, the wily former Toronto Maple Leafs coach who was the Sabres first coach and general manager, plucked a rangy, swift-skating magician named Gilbert Perreault from the junior ranks. The high-scoring center was an anchor for more than a decade, especially when teamed with youngsters Rick Martin and Rene Robert to form the French Connection line. Perreault and Martin still rank 1-2 in club history for goals scored, with 512 and 382, respectively. The trio powered the Sabres to the Stanley Cup final in 1975, where they lost to Philadelphia in six games: a sobering end to their best season—they had a franchise-high 113 points in winning their first Adams Division title.

The Sabres have never got closer to a Stanley Cup title, despite the promise of the Scotty Bowman era in the early 1980s.

Bowman, a five-time Cup winner as coach of the Montreal Canadiens, did however become the winningest NHL coach while in Buffalo. He surpassed Dick Irvin's 690 career coaching wins on December 19, 1984.

**Big Chance: With center Pat LaFontaine sidelined owing to concussion, center Derek Plante led the Sabres in scoring with a relatively modest 53 points. That total, though, included a career-high 27 goals for Plante.**

## ★ ROLL OF HONOR ★

| | |
|---|---|
| Conference/Division | **Eastern/Northeast** |
| First Season | **1970-71** |
| Honor roll | **Reached Stanley Cup final, 1974-75** |
| Home rink/Capacity | **Marine Midland Arena/18,500** |
| Stanley Cups | **0** |

### Playing Record

| | W | L | T | Pts |
|---|---|---|---|---|
| Regular Season | 1004 | 797 | 331 | 2339 |
| Playoffs | 67 | 88 | | |

# CALGARY FLAMES

## Despite a disappointing season, the Flames still believe in the excitement of young, unsung, and underrated talent.

With their destiny in their own hands, the Calgary Flames stumbled down the stretch last spring, winning only two of their final ten games—seven of which were in the friendly confines of the Saddledome—and they missed the Stanley Cup playoffs for only the second time in their 17-year history.

The last ten games were a microcosm of the entire season for the Flames, who by their own admission are in a rebuilding stage: the lack of offense placed enormous pressure on the defense and goaltending, and there were simply too many leaks to plug.

"What it came down to is that we all didn't do enough," said center Dave Gagner, whose 27 goals ranked second on the team to Theoren Fleury, who notched 29. "It's tough when, as a team, you're only scoring two goals a game."

Team captain Fleury, whose 67 points led the club, was a lightning rod for much of the criticism by fans and the media, who noted that Fleury's output was 29 points lower than the previous season and his lowest for a full season since his rookie year, in 1989-90.

"What's written about me, I take personally, and I don't agree with it," said the diminutive (five foot six) but feisty Fleury, who seemed to be worn down by the punishment he absorbed on the ice.

### Right on

As a team, the Flames managed only 214 goals—San Jose was the lone club to have a worse offensive performance. Joining Gagner and Fleury as the only players to top 20 goals were German Titov, eye-catching rookie right-winger Jarome Iginla—who tired due to the longer NHL season—and center Marty McInnis, an addition following a trade that sent Robert Reichel to the New York Islanders.

Both four-year performer Trevor Kidd and rookie Dwayne Roloson, signed three years ago as an undrafted free agent, posted a goals-against average of just under 3.00, although Kidd, in particular, drew some criticism for his inconsistent play.

Despite the disappointing end to the 1996-97 season, Flames management feels it is on the right course, rebuilding the franchise with young talent that is both unsung and underrated. "That's the way we've chosen to do business," said Calgary general manager Al Coates. "People can identify with exciting young teams."

Exciting was a word used in 1972, when the Flames' franchise got its start—in Atlanta. It was the NHL's first venture into the Deep South of the United States, an experiment that lasted seven years after Georgia businessman Tom Cousins was granted a franchise.

Former Montreal Canadiens star and legend Boom Boom Geoffrion, served as coach and showman in the early years, wooing fans in an accent as sweet as a Georgia peach. Fans would flock to the 15,000-seat rink known as The Omni to watch Geoffrion direct an ice

**Whizz Kid:** Just 20 years old, rookie forward Jerome Eginla scored 21 goals and 50 points in 1996-97 for the Flames, one of the team's few bright spots in a dismal season.

symphony with performers such as goaltender Daniel Bouchard and flashy forwards Jacques Richard, Eric Vail and Guy Chouinard.

### Moving Flames

Alas, the novelty soon wore off. Geoffrion was gone by 1975, and so was the franchise five years later, purchased by Vancouver real-estate magnate Nelson Skalbania, and transferred to Calgary.

It was a humble beginning in the Flames' new abode, the 7,000-seat Stampede Corral, where the club remained until moving into the 20,000-seat Saddledome in 1983.

The Flames would win one Stanley Cup, two Conference titles and two best-overall crowns over the next 15 years. (Badger) Bob Johnson arrived from the University of Wisconsin to coach the Flames in 1982. Johnson, who coined the phrase, "It's a great day for hockey," took the Flames to the Stanley Cup final in 1985-86.

Three years later, with wisecracking Terry Crisp at the helm, Calgary won its first Cup, becoming the first visiting team to do so against the Canadiens at the venerable Montreal Forum. Fittingly, it was the final bow for Lanny McDonald, the bushy-lipped co-captain who had come to epitomize the heart and soul of the team.

**Mighty Mite:** Theoren Fleury is the league's smallest player but he may well have the biggest heart, also.

## ★ ROLL OF HONOR ★

| | |
|---|---|
| Conference/Division | **Western/Pacific** |
| First Season | **1972-73 (Atlanta); 1980-81 (Calgary)** |
| Honor roll: | **First overall in 1987-88, 1988-89** |
| Home rink/Capacity | **Canadian Airlines Saddledome/20,000** |
| Stanley Cups: | **1 (1989)** |

### *Playing Record*

| | W | L | T | Pts |
|---|---|---|---|---|
| Regular Season | 925 | 756 | 295 | 2145 |
| Playoffs | 11 | 14 | | |

# CAROLINA HURRICANES

## With a move to North Carolina, and a tough new name, the franchise hopes to shake off the jaded Whalers reputation.

It was somehow fitting that forward Kevin Dineen scored the game-winning goal, and goaltender Sean Burke had a starring role in the final game of the NHL franchise known as the Hartford Whalers, last April 13.

Dineen, who had two turns of duty in Hartford, spanning nine years, was one of the most popular players in the history of the franchise. The often beleaguered Burke has been a mainstay in the Hartford goal for the last five seasons, and the final win in Hartford was the 100th of his Whalers' career.

### Rejuvenating move

But the puck now stops in North Carolina, more specifically at the 21,500-seat Greensboro Coliseum, the temporary home of the transplanted franchise—to be known as the Carolina Hurricanes—as it awaits the completion of a new facility in West Raleigh, expected for the 1999-2000 season.

Peter Karmanos, the Compuware Corporation head who bought the Whalers from the Connecticut Development Authority in 1994, made the decision to move the franchise, citing three-year operating losses in Hartford of about $45 million.

The North Carolina region is a new territory for the NHL, but Keith Primeau, the Hurricanes hulking forward who came to Hartford last year following a major trade with Detroit for Brendan Shanahan and Paul Coffey, said the move "has to be a rejuvenation for a lot of guys."

Left-winger Geoff Sanderson isn't in need of rejuvenation. He has consistently been the team's biggest offensive threat. Discounting the strike season of 1994-95, Sanderson has a four-season goal-scoring average of 39 goals. Primeau had 26 goals last year and showed signs of joining Sanderson as a major offensive force.

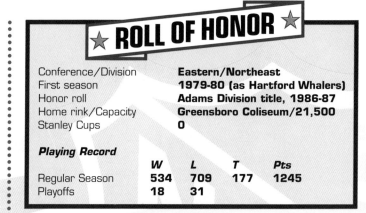

**Draft Pick: Nikos Tselios, a highly regarded prospect on defense is a cousin of another superb NHL defenseman, Chris Chelios, of the Chicago Blackhawks.**

### Frustrating misses

Hartford was one of four World Hockey Association teams who joined the NHL in 1979—Winnipeg, Quebec and Edmonton were the others.

While Hartford had a core of fans which were loyal to the end, the lack of a winning tradition was often a source of frustration. The club finished first in its division only once—in 1986-87—and, that season aside, it never ended higher than fourth place. When the Whalers were eliminated on the final weekend last season, it marked the tenth time in their 17 years in Hartford that the team missed the Stanley Cup playoffs and the eighth straight time it finished below .500. Only once did they advance beyond the first playoff round.

Hartford's first NHL season featured the Howe family—the legendary Gordie and sons Mark and Marty—whom the Whalers had signed to a WHA contract two years earlier. Gordie, a 50-year-old grandfather, played in all 80 games in 1979-80, scoring 15 goals and collecting 41 points, inspiring his young teammates to a playoff berth before retiring at the end of the season.

The player who has most marked the Whalers' history is center Ron Francis. He spent all of the 1980s with the club and remains the leader in most of the franchise's offensive categories. Francis collected 821 points and 264 goals in 714 games as a Whaler.

The Compuware group had a successful formula with their youth and junior hockey operations, and they have been trying to adhere to the same blueprint with the Whalers, a philosophy that is likely to continue in Carolina. General manager Jim Rutherford and head coach Paul Maurice were both members of that Compuware program. Maurice became the youngest head coach in professional sports when he replaced Paul Holmgren behind the Hartford bench in November 1995. He had been highly successful with the Detroit Junior Red Wings, where he compiled a 86-38-8 record in two years.

**Golden Goals: Power forward Keith Primeau contributed 26 goals for Hartford in 1996-97. He also played for Team Canada during the World Cup of Hockey, and at the World Hockey Championship.**

## ★ ROLL OF HONOR ★

| | |
|---|---|
| Conference/Division | **Western/Central** |
| First season | **1926-27** |
| Honor roll | **28 straight playoff berths since 1968-69** |
| Home rink/Capacity | **United Center/20,500** |
| Stanley Cups | **3 (1934, 1938, 1961)** |

**Playing Record**

| | W | L | T | Pts |
|---|---|---|---|---|
| Regular Season | 1965 | 2048 | 734 | 4664 |
| Playoffs | 188 | 214 | | |

# CHICAGO BLACKHAWKS

## *Although rarely an NHL champion, the talent-rich Blackhawks remain a legitimate contender in almost every season.*

I t was a tight fit but the Chicago Blackhawks squeezed into the final Western Conference playoff spot on the final weekend of the 1996-97 season, the 28th straight year the team has qualified for post-season play. With the Boston Bruins missing the playoffs last season, the Blackhawks' 28-year streak is now the longest in major professional sports.

Maintaining their string was of some solace to the Blackhawks, who were dispatched in the opening round of the playoffs by Colorado for the second straight year, despite a valiant six-game fight which saw the club decimated by injuries.

The goal-starved 'Hawks scored 50 fewer goals in 1996-97, a decline that can be traced to the loss of free agents Joe Murphy and Bernie Nicholls, the trading of Jeremy Roenick and a season-long slump by sophomore Eric Daze, whose output fell to 22 goals from 30 in his rookie year.

Much of the offense was generated by veteran right-winger Tony Amonte, who produced a career-high 41 goals, helped by center Alexei Zhamnov, a pre-season arrival from Phoenix in the Roenick trade. While Zhamnov demonstrated proven playmaking ability, his 20-goal output was his lowest in five NHL seasons.

Defensively, perennial all-star Chris Chelios and veteran Steve Smith both had their effectiveness reduced by injuries, while seasoned Gary Suter had an off-year. Conversely, Keith Carney, who had been up and down in the Buffalo system before joining Chicago two years ago, turned into the Blackhawks' steadiest defenseman in 1996-97.

### Trade for hope

Still, the Blackhawks might have missed the playoffs if not for a late-January trade engineered by general manager Bob Pulford, who sent disgruntled goaltender Ed Belfour to San Jose for defenseman Michal Sykora, winger Ulf Dahlen and netminder Chris Terreri. All three players contributed down the stretch as the Blackhawks were 16-10-5 following the trade.

"That trade turned our season around," said Chicago coach Craig Hartsburg. "It cleared the air in our dressing room and brought in three guys who were happy to play for the Chicago Blackhawks."

Stanley Cups have been few and far between for the Chicago Blackhawks, who joined the NHL back on September 25, 1926.

At the time, their first head coach was a man named Pete Muldoon, who would lose the job after one abysmal season. But he didn't go gently. He is alleged to have placed a curse on the team, saying it would never finish first because it had treated him so ignominiously.

**Hawks' Sniper: Jeremy Roenick averaged 47 goals a season in the early 1990s for Chicago.**

**Best in the Business: Chris Chelios has won the Norris Trophy as the NHL's best defenseman with both the Montreal Canadiens and Chicago Blackhawks.**

The Muldoon curse lasted 40 years, as Chicago didn't finish first until the 1966-67 season. In Stanley Cup play, the Blackhawks have escaped the curse only three times—they won in 1934, 1938 and 1961.

### Talent vs curse

Yet, it is a franchise which has been blessed with some wonderful talent who, before moving into the spacious United Center in the 1994-95 season, played at raucous Chicago Stadium.

Bobby Hull, the 'Golden Jet' who shellshocked goaltenders with his patented slap shot, became the first NHLer to score more than 50 goals in a season, in 1966. Stan Mikita, the gifted center immortalized in the Hockey Hall of Fame, sparkled for 21 seasons, scoring 541 goals, second to Hull's 604. Both Hull and Mikita are regarded as the unofficial 'inventors' of the curved stick.

Then there was 'Mr. Goalie', Glenn Hall, who introduced the butterfly style of goaltending much in vogue today.

After Hall, it was Tony (O) Esposito making some history— his 15 shutouts in 1969-70 are a modern-day single-season NHL record.

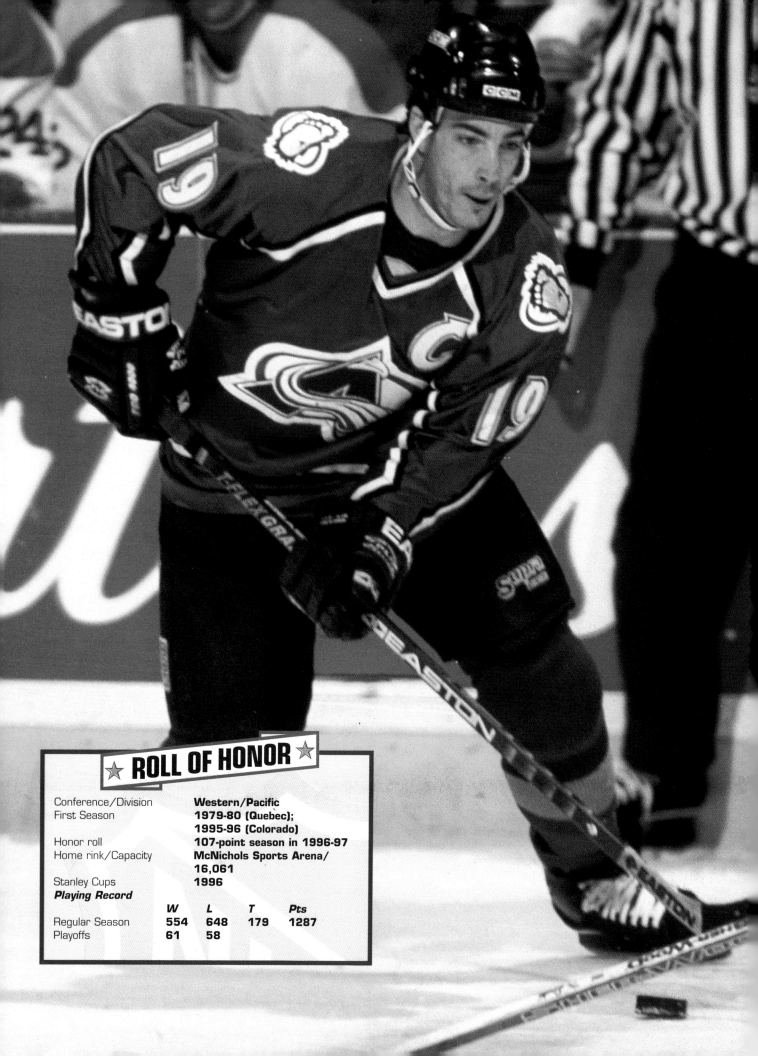

## ★ ROLL OF HONOR ★

| | | | |
|---|---|---|---|
| Conference/Division | Western/Pacific | | |
| First Season | 1979-80 (Quebec); 1995-96 (Colorado) | | |
| Honor roll | 107-point season in 1996-97 | | |
| Home rink/Capacity | McNichols Sports Arena/ 16,061 | | |
| Stanley Cups | 1996 | | |

**Playing Record**

| | W | L | T | Pts |
|---|---|---|---|---|
| Regular Season | 554 | 648 | 179 | 1287 |
| Playoffs | 61 | 58 | | |

# COLORADO AVALANCHE

To win consecutive Stanley Cups is never easy but the Avalanche gave it a good shot last season, compiling the best record in the regular schedule and reaching the Western Conference final before losing to the Detroit Red Wings.

In the end, not even the inspired play of the two Mr. Stanley Cup Playoffs—goaltender Patrick Roy and forward Claude Lemieux—could produce the NHL's first repeat champions since 1992, when the Pittsburgh Penguins achieved the feat.

## Testament to depth

Capturing the regular-season title with 107 points—three more than Dallas and New Jersey—was a remarkable achievement by the Avalanche, considering that Joe Sakic and Peter Forsberg, the team's 1-2 punch at center, and Lemieux missed a combined 71 games because of injuries.

Forsberg, the silky-smooth Swede, still managed to lead the team in points with 86 in just 65 games, and Sakic was second, collecting 74 points in 65 games, although his 22 goals were the lowest full-schedule output of his nine-year career. Lemieux, meanwhile, typically reached his peak in the playoffs, scoring 13 goals in 17 games. Lemieux has 70 career playoff goals in 172 games.

Staying ahead of the pack despite the numerous injuries was a testament to the depth of the Avalanche. Center Adam Deadmarsh, a second-round, 1993 draft pick, when the Avalanche were the Quebec Nordiques, blossomed into a team-leading, 33-goal scorer and an outstanding two-way performer. Keith Jones, obtained from Washington in a trade which saw Colorado part with hardrock forward Chris Simon, scored 25 goals, while Eric Lacroix, the son of Colorado general manager Pierre Lacroix, contributed 18.

When defenseman Uwe Krupp was sidelined following back surgery, youngsters such as Aaron Miller, Jon Klemm and Eric Masse stepped into the breach to lend a hand to linchpin Sandis Ozolinsh—the team's third-leading point-getter with 68, including 23 goals—and the steady Adam Foote.

Roy, who showed no signs of slipping, was a fortress, keeping the team in games they might have had no business winning.

## Checkered history

This is NHL Part 2 in Colorado, and, it's been a spectacular sequel thus far. Unlike 1976-77, when Colorado inherited the mediocre Kansas City Scouts, the region enticed the Quebec Nordiques, a rising NHL power whose owners felt they could no longer financially survive without a revenue-generating new rink in Quebec City. Nordiques president Marcel Aubut and his ownership group sold the franchise to COMSAT, an entertainment company headed by Charlie Lyons, in the summer of 1995. That returned the NHL to Colorado, without a franchise after the Rockies moved and became the New Jersey Devils in 1982.

**Quiet Superstar: Joe Sakic quietly, unassumingly accumulates his points every season, like clockwork.**

**Skandinavian Speeder: As a player in the Swedish Elite League, Peter Forsberg was known as the best player not in the NHL. Now he's one of the best players in the league.**

One of four World Hockey Association teams absorbed by the NHL in 1979, the Nordiques made the playoffs seven straight years after their initial season. But as star players aged and key draft picks failed to deliver, lean times arrived for the Nordiques. The club missed the playoffs for five straight seasons.

In 1991, No. 1 draft pick Eric Lindros refused to sign with Quebec, setting off a year-long battle that culminated in the Nordiques' trading him to both the New York Rangers and Philadelphia Flyers. An arbitrator had to intervene, awarding him to the Flyers.

The trade was seemingly a turning point for the franchise. Among the players Quebec acquired was Forsberg, who signed a long-term contract last season, ensuring that he will be as much a part of the Colorado scenery as the Rocky Mountains.

## ★ ROLL OF HONOR ★

| | |
|---|---|
| Conference/Division | **Western/Central** |
| First season | **1967-68 (Minnesota); 1993-94 (Dallas)** |
| Honor roll | **Finished with franchise-best 104 points in 1996-97** |
| Home rink/Capacity | **Dr. Pepper Star Center/16,924** |
| Stanley Cups | **0** |

**Playing Record**

| | W | L | T | Pts |
|---|---|---|---|---|
| Regular Season | 891 | 1090 | 377 | 2159 |
| Playoffs | 89 | 98 | | |

# DALLAS STARS

## Star-crossed Stars combined talented newcomers with experienced players to make the season a solid step forward.

The success of the Dallas Stars in the 1996-97 NHL season is a classic example of what can happen when everyone is on the same page, adhering to a well-planned system that stresses teamwork and sticking to the basics.

Despite having only one player tally more than 53 points—center Mike Modano notched 83, including 35 goals—the Stars posted their best record in franchise history. The team's 104 points— a 48-26-8 record—tied New Jersey for second place in the overall standings, and had Dallas won a showdown against Colorado on the final weekend of the regular season, it would have finished first overall. Still, it was a quantum leap over the previous season, when the Stars managed only 66 points and failed to make the playoffs.

That turn of events induced general manager Bob Gainey to make some adjustments. He signed free agents Pat Verbeek and Dave Reid, as well as goaltender Arturs Irbe as a backup to veteran Andy Moog, and acquired offensive-oriented defenseman Sergei Zubov to inject some life into a moribund power play.

### Vigor renewed

The newcomers combined with the Stars' interesting collection of experienced, character-steeped and grinding players. This group included four-time all-star Joe Nieuwendyk (who rebounded from injuries to score 30 goals), Brent Gilchrist, Guy Carbonneau, Benoit Hogue and seasoned defensemen such as Craig Ludwig, Darryl Sydor and Grant Ledyard, who joined with four-year man Derian Hatcher to help the Stars post the league's third-best goals-against mark. Moog was superb as the last line of defense, recording a 2.15 goals-against average.

"We put a real value on everyone's contribution," said Hitchcock, the second-year coach whose 'team-first' philosophy at Kamloops, BC, had made him one of the most successful coaches in the history of the Western Junior League.

The Stars' character was exemplified by their road record— the team's 23 wins in enemy rinks tied it with Colorado and Phoenix for the NHL lead in that category.

It was a loss in a key home game—the seventh game of the Western Conference final against Edmonton—that ended the Stars' Stanley Cup run last spring. It might have been a different scenario had Oilers goaltender Curtis Joseph not made a highlight-film stop on Nieuwendyk in the seventh-game overtime session.

**Lone Star Star: In Mike Modano, the Dallas Stars have a capstone player; now both they and he have a dependable supporting cast.**

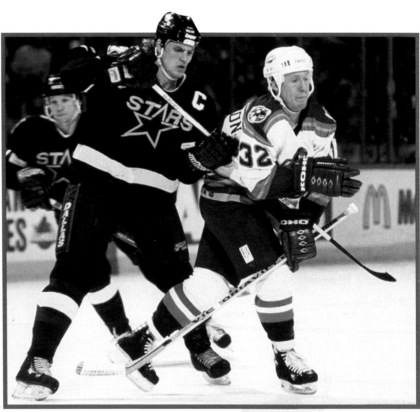

**Wheelhorse Defenseman: When Dallas general manager Bob Gainey looks at hulking defenseman, Kevin Hatcher, he must see quite a bit of Larry Robinson, Gainey's Hall of Fame teammate in Montreal.**

### Tragic start

The franchise, which has operated in Dallas since 1993, burst on the NHL scene in 1967-68, along with five other expansion brethren. It was the Minnesota North Stars back then, but early tragedy would make star-crossed a more appropriate description.

On January 13, 1968, about halfway through the North Stars' inaugural season, a helmetless Bill Masterton struck his head violently on the ice and died in hospital from brain injuries two days later. It was the first and, to this day, the only NHL on-ice death.

Bill Goldsworthy was the North Stars' first big goal-scorer. He was the first player from a post-1967 team to score 250 goals, 48 of which came in the 1973-74 season.

The North Stars made the Stanley Cup final in both 1981 and 1991, losing to the New York Islanders and Pittsburgh Penguins, respectively. The North Stars' tremendous playoff run in 1991 temporarily revived lagging fan interest in Minneapolis but in 1993 Norm Green, who had become the team owner three years earlier, moved the franchise to Dallas.

Dropping the North from their nickname, the Stars were the first NHL club in Texas and the sixth in the United States 'Sun Belt'.

# DETROIT RED WINGS

*The Red Wings' multinational array of speed, skill and all-around hockey talent finally broke the long hiatus in Stanley Cup wins.*

The Red Wings entered the 1996-97 Stanley Cup playoffs without the fanfare of the previous two years, a fact which defenseman Niklas Lindstrom noted, "took a lot of the pressure off us."

Relieved of the burden of high expectations, the Red Wings finally removed the albatross which had hovered around the franchise's neck since 1955, the year of its last Stanley Cup victory. By beating Philadelphia in the final, the Red Wings ended the second-longest Stanley Cup drought in league history— 54 years for the New York Rangers being the longest.

Losers to New Jersey in the 1994-95 Stanley Cup final, and ousted by eventual-champions Colorado in the Western Conference final the following year, the Red Wings maintained a low profile last spring, finishing with the third-best record in their conference and fifth-best overall.

## Quiet run to victory

But quietly, head coach Scotty Bowman, who coached Stanley Cup winners in Montreal and Pittsburgh and became the first NHL coach to earn 1,000 victories with a February 8, 1997 win against Pittsburgh, assembled a squad that found the winning combination.

It was a collaboration worthy of the United Nations. There was the Russia Five, a group comprised of 1994 Hart Trophy winner Sergei Fedorov, a 30-goal performer; Igor Larionov, the former center of Russia's famed KLM (Krutov-Larionov-Makarov) line; speedy forward Slava Kozlov, and rugged defensemen Vladimir Konstantinov and Viacheslav Fetisov.

Added to this quintet was Canadian-born power forward Brendan Shanahan, who led the team in short-handed, power-play and game-winning goals, as well as total goals (47) and points (88) after his early-season acquisition from Hartford. Steve Yzerman, also a Canadian and a Red Wing for his entire 14-year career, added 85 points for a career total of 1,340, second only to Gordie Howe on the club's all-time list.

Sweden's contribution came from Lidstrom, the team's fourth-best point-getter and a power-play catalyst; and 18-goal man Tomas Sandstrom. Massachusetts-born forward Doug Brown was a strong representative of the United States.

The goaltending duo of Chris Osgood and Mike Vernon divided the heroics, with the former a regular-season standout—a 2.30 average—and the latter, a surprise starter in the playoffs and a glittering performer.

The Stanley Cup triumph achieved the goal of pizza-company honcho Mike Ilitch, who purchased the stale, struggling NHL franchise in 1982, when the once-mighty team was often sarcastically called the Dead Things.

## Red hot past

The Red Wings were the NHL powerhouse in the first half of the 1950s, winning four Stanley Cups in six years.

That was the era of the Production Line of (Gordie) Howe,

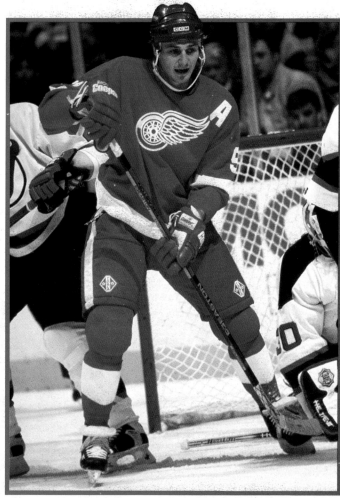

**First Among Equals:** The flashiest player in Detroit's five-man unit is undoubtedly Sergei Fedorov, a two-way superstar.

(Ted) Lindsay and (Sid) Abel, defensive stalwarts Red Kelly and Bob Goldham, icy-veined Terry Sawchuk in goal and Jolly Jack Adams at the managerial helm.

Until Wayne Gretzky came along a few decades later, Howe was the NHL's leading career goal-scorer with 801, all but 15 of them coming with Detroit. His linemate Lindsay is regarded by many as the toughest customer of all time. Abel, who went on to coach the Red Wings, was the set-up man on the line.

Sawchuk was impenetrable in goal, recording 85 shutouts with Detroit and an NHL record 103 in his career. The numbers brought Sawchuk an election to the Hall of Fame, one of 46 people associated with the Red Wings who have earned such an honor.

**Stevie Y:** Yzerman is the elder statesman of the superb Red Wings, with a career points-total second only to Gordie Howe.

## ★ ROLL OF HONOR ★

| | |
|---|---|
| Conference/Division | **Western/Central** |
| First season | **1926-27 (Cougars); 1930-31 (Falcons); 1932-33 (Red Wings)** |
| Honor roll | **Seven straight regular-season titles (1948-49 to 1954-55)** |
| Home rink/Capacity | **Joe Louis Arena/19,275** |
| Stanley Cups | **8 (1936, 1937, 1943, 1950, 1952, 1954, 1955, 1997)** |

### Playing Record

| | W | L | T | Pts |
|---|---|---|---|---|
| Regular Season | 2028 | 1975 | 743 | 4799 |
| Playoffs | 192 | 192 | (prior to final series) | |

## ★ ROLL OF HONOR ★

| | |
|---|---|
| Conference/Division | **Western/Pacific** |
| First season | **1979-80** |
| Honor roll | **5 Cups in first 11 seasons** |
| Home rink/Capacity | **Edmonton Coliseum/17,111** |
| Stanley Cups | **5 (1984, 1985, 1987, 1988, 1990)** |

### Playing Record

| | W | L | T | Pts |
|---|---|---|---|---|
| Regular Season | 692 | 552 | 177 | 1561 |
| Playoffs | 125 | 67 | | |

# EDMONTON OILERS

**Edmonton Kiddie Korps are reviving the fortunes of the Oilers as GM Glen Sather retools a former dynasty.**

Don't look now but the Edmonton Oilers are back as a force to be reckoned with. They still have a ways to go to match the powerhouse Oilers that won five Stanley Cups in the1980s, but there's no doubt that general manager Glen Sather's re-tooling and rebuilding have the team headed in the right direction.

After spending the previous four years wandering in the wilderness when it came to participation in the playoffs, the Oilers not only qualified for post-season play last spring, they pulled one of the major upsets. The plucky young Oilers, seeded seventh in the Western Conference, ousted the No. 2-seeded Dallas Stars on a seventh-game overtime goal by Todd Marchant in the opening playoff round.

The Oilers then fell in five games to the Colorado Avalanche, which served to point out that Edmonton's rebuilding process isn't quite finished. But Sather, the architect of the team of the 1980s, continues to lay a solid foundation for the late 1990s.

## Shrewd deals

He's accomplished that in several ways. Team scoring leader Doug Weight (82 points) came in a trade with the New York Rangers four years ago. Gritty left-winger Ryan Smyth, who notched a team-leading 39 goals, was Sather's second-round pick in the 1994 draft. Forward Andrei Kovalenko, a surprising 32-goal performer, was obtained in a pre-season trade with Montreal for hardrock Scott Thornton.

Curtis Joseph, acquired from St. Louis in the summer of 1995, appeared in 84 games last season and was hailed as a miracle man in getting the Oilers past Dallas. That same trade brought promising young defenseman Mike Grier. Boris Mironov, one of the club's steadiest defenseman, arrived in a 1994 trade with Winnipeg for Dave Manson, a deal that also landed Edmonton center Mats Lindgren.

Marchant, who tied a Stanley Cup playoff record with three short-handed goals, joined the Oilers following a 1994 trade to the New York Rangers for the aging Craig MacTavish.

This group of players, along with others such as center Jason Arnott, forwards Rem Murray and Joe Hulbig and defensemen Kelly Buchberger, Dan McGillis, and veteran Luke Richardson—if he can be re-signed—figure to keep the Oilers on an upward spiral.

"There's a great sense of resiliency in this team," remarked Sather. "These kids have grown up a lot in one season."

## Camelot on ice

The Edmonton franchise didn't join the NHL until 1979—one of four World Hockey Association franchises to do so—but it surely made up for lost time. In five years, the Oilers built a powerhouse that produced five Stanley Cups in seven years, between 1983-84 and 1989-90. They were successful because a superb nucleus of players came of age together, and a coach and Sather displayed a green thumb in developing the vast talent on hand. "In the 1980s it was Camelot," recalls Oilers owner Peter Pocklington. "It was almost surreal. We were always on a roll."

The supporting cast sometimes changed but the main actors did not. There was Wayne Gretzky, arguably the finest player to lace on skates, menacing Mark Messier, crafty Jari Kurri, multi-dimensional Glenn Anderson, the steady Kevin Lowe on defense and the unflappable Grant Fuhr in goal.

The shock trade of Gretzky to the Los Angeles Kings in 1988 signalled the impending demise of Camelot, it wasn't the end of the Oilers' spring skate with the Stanley Cup. Messier, Anderson, Kurri, Fuhr and Lowe were around for one last hurrah, in 1988-89.

**Oiler on the Rise: Jason Arnott's enormous potential is only one piece in Edmonton's strategy of resilience.**

**Carrying his Weight: On the post-dynasty Oilers, Doug Weight is the scoring star.**

## ⭐ ROLL OF HONOR ⭐

| | |
|---|---|
| Conference/Division | **Eastern/Atlantic** |
| First season | **1993-94** |
| Honor roll | **Most points (83) by first-year team (1993-94)** |
| Home rink/Capacity | **Miami Arena/14,703** |
| Stanley Cups | **0** |

### Playing Record

| | W | L | T | Pts |
|---|---|---|---|---|
| Regular Season | 129 | 115 | 52 | 310 |
| Playoffs | 13 | 13 | | |

# FLORIDA PANTHERS

## *Injuries and fatigue resulted in anemic offense and a truncated fourth-year Panthers' Stanley Cup playoff run.*

Through the first four months of the 1996-97 season, the Florida Panthers closely resembled the previous year's upstarts who had reached the Stanley Cup final before conceding hockey's Holy Grail to the Colorado Avalanche.

In fact, the Panthers boasted the best record in the Eastern Conference for a brief time in mid-February. But at that point, the team went into a tailspin as injuries and fatigue mounted. Florida won only one of its next 11 games and, unlike a year earlier, entered the playoffs at a low ebb, rather than a peak. The result was a quick, five-game, first-round exit against the healthier, better-prepared New York Rangers.

"The difference from the previous year was that we didn't stay as injury-free," admitted right-winger Scott Mellanby, whose 27 goals were second on the club to the 29 notched by veteran Ray Sheppard. "You can't really have the nagging injuries we had and be in a position to get back to the finals."

### Lost power

Among key performers who missed 20 or more games because of injuries were defenseman Ed Jovanovski, centers Rob Niedermyer, Brian Skrudland, and Martin Straka, and forward Johan Garpenlov. Overcoming such a depletion in personnel would have been difficult for any team, but especially so for the Panthers, whose forte is a grinding, smothering style with each player a vital cog in the wheel.

The Panthers continued to excel in goal, as the air-tight tandem of John Vanbiesbrouck and Mark Fitzpatrick combined for a 2.39 goals against average, behind only New Jersey, Detroit and Dallas. But the strong netminding wasn't enough to overcome the anemic offense in the playoffs, during which the Panthers managed only ten goals in five games.

While the Panthers have a number of veterans on their roster, including center Kirk Muller, a late-season acquisition from the Toronto Maple Leafs, the club also has talented youngsters such as Niedermyer and Czech forward Radek Dvorak, Florida's No. 1 selection and the 10th overall in the 1995 entry draft.

Panthers coach Doug MacLean says Niedermyer, who had 14 goals in 60 games, is "a great two-way center with unlimited potential."

Florida general manager Bryan Murray lists one of his priorities as adding depth to the organization through the draft, which has brought such players as Niedermyer, Jovanovski and Dvorak

### Brash rats

Owned by Wayne Huizenga of the Blockbuster Video empire, the Panthers were something of a blockbuster themselves in 1993-94, the season they joined Tampa Bay as the NHL's expansion entries from the Sunshine State. Under renowned hockey tactician Roger Neilson the Panthers became the most successful first-year NHL

**The Stopper:** Great goaltending from John Vanbiesbrouck helped the Florida Panthers play respectable hockey from Year 1.

**Not-So-Powerful Panther: Injuries sadly curtailed big Ed Jovanovski's punishing body checks.**

team, collecting 83 points and narrowly missing a spot in the Stanley Cup playoffs.

The Panthers came achingly close to a playoff berth in the strike-shortened 1994-95 season, adhering to the same smothering style and solid goaltending by Vanbiesbrouck, the first pick in the 1993 expansion draft. But Panthers management, headed by Bill Torrey, who shaped the New York Islanders' dynasty in the early 1980s, decided a coaching change was required and Neilson was replaced by MacLean, a product of the Detroit Red Wings system.

MacLean modified the neutral-zone trap during the 1995-96 season, favoring a mix of offense and defense, and it vaulted the Panthers to a dramatic seventh-game Conference final triumph over Pittsburgh and a hard-fought six games before succumbing to Colorado in the final.

**A lackluster season for the Kings proves that the building of a playoff contender is a long-term endeavor.**

**E**ver candid, Kings coach Larry Robinson was unequivocal when explaining why Los Angeles missed the playoffs for the fourth straight season in 1996-97. "Our talent level isn't up to where some of the other clubs are," explained Robinson, who saw his club make only a smidgen of progress in his second year at the helm. By finishing with a 28-43-11 mark the Kings won four more games than the previous year but also had three more losses.

Once the season ended, the Kings dipped into their past in an effort to improve their future by naming Dave Taylor, a five-time all-star in a 17-year playing career with Los Angeles, as the new general manager, replacing Sam McMaster.

The Robinson-Taylor management team is hoping to rebuild the Kings into a contender by 1999, when the club is scheduled to forsake the 16,000-seat Great Western Forum, where the average crowd was 12,000 last season, for a 20,000-seat complex in downtown Los Angeles.

## Cup drought

Robinson, a Hall of Fame defenseman with the Montreal Canadiens, said defense is the position which the Kings must bolster if they are to climb in the standings. Help is needed for veterans Dimitri Khristich and Rob Blake. Ironically, Khristich was the team's top offensive performer with 56 points, including 19 goals. Only center Ray Ferraro, with 25, had more goals.

Injury-plagued center Yanic Perreault, a 25-goal man a year earlier, had his season and, consequently, his production sliced in half. Kevin Stevens, one of the league's top snipers with Pittsburgh in the early 1990s, had his second straight sub-par season, managing 14 goals in 69 games.

Only the San Jose Sharks scored fewer than the 214 goals notched by the Kings, who are hoping for increased production from the likes of Russian forwards Vladimir Tsyplakov and Vitali Yachmenev, and Finland native Kai Nurminen.

The Kings are still without a crown, almost 30 years after Canadian-born entrepreneur Jack Kent Cooke engineered the NHL's West Coast expansion by establishing a franchise in Los Angeles. The crown almost materialized in 1993, when the Kings imbued their fans with a fever reminiscent of the California gold rush by reaching the Stanley Cup final for the first time. Alas, they fell in five games to the Montreal Canadiens.

## LA stars

The franchise has had its share of jewels. One of them was Marcel Dionne, a diminutive but Houdini-like center who was acquired in a trade with Detroit after the 1974-75 season. He skated his way into the Hall of Fame, scoring 550 of his 731 career goals—third-best in NHL history—as a member of the Kings. Along the way, Dionne inherited Charlie Simmer and Dave Taylor as linemates, and the Triple Crown Line, as they were dubbed, were the scourge of the league for several seasons.

**Man of the Future: Finnish defenseman Aki-Petteri Berg has the kind of talent teams build winning franchises around.**

The Dionne era ended in 1987, when he was dealt to the New York Rangers. But in true Hollywood fashion another superstar arrived on the set just over a year later. Fellow by the name of Wayne Gretzky. The NHL's marquee player arrived from Edmonton in a blockbuster trade.

While Gretzky revived sagging hockey interest in Los Angeles, the Kings got no closer to their first Stanley Cup triumph than the dramatic 1992-93 final against Montreal.

**On the Rebound: Injuries have stifled the development of Kings' defenseman Rob Blake, a 20-goal scorer three seasons ago.**

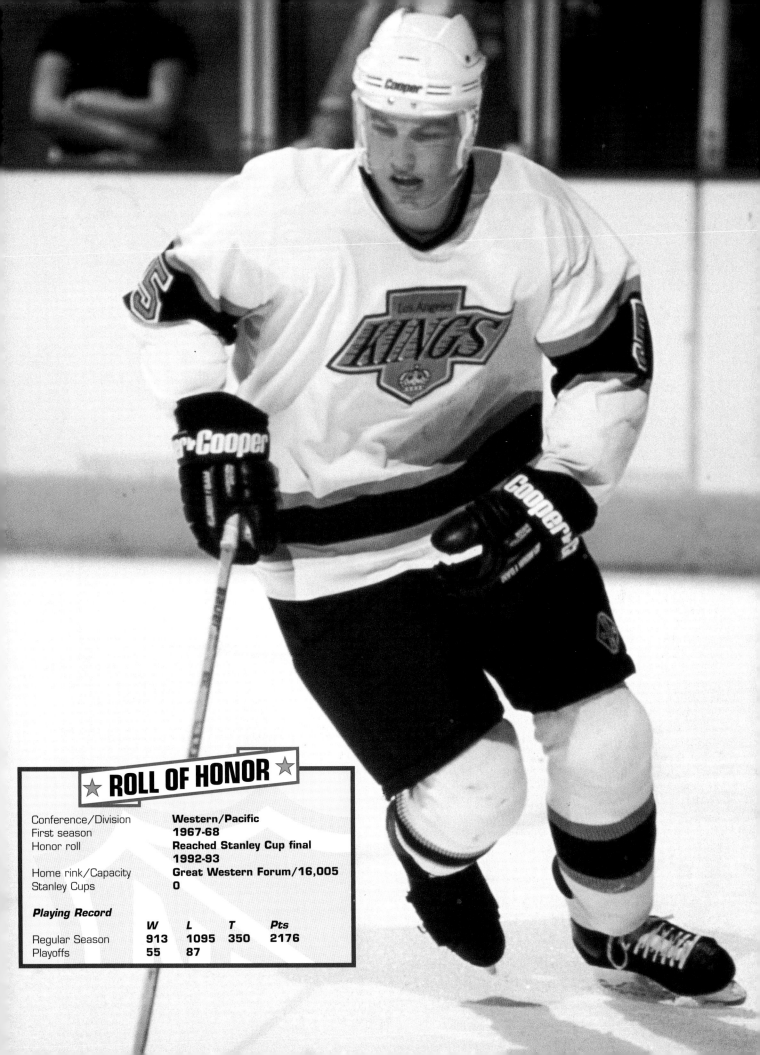

## ★ ROLL OF HONOR ★

| | | | | |
|---|---|---|---|---|
| Conference/Division | **Western/Pacific** | | | |
| First season | **1967-68** | | | |
| Honor roll | **Reached Stanley Cup final** | | | |
| | **1992-93** | | | |
| Home rink/Capacity | **Great Western Forum/16,005** | | | |
| Stanley Cups | **0** | | | |

**Playing Record**

| | W | L | T | Pts |
|---|---|---|---|---|
| Regular Season | 913 | 1095 | 350 | 2176 |
| Playoffs | 55 | 87 | | |

## ⭐ ROLL OF HONOR ⭐

| | |
|---|---|
| Conference/Division | **Eastern/Northeast** |
| First season | **1917-18** |
| Honor Roll | **Record for most consecutive Stanley Cup titles (5)** |
| Home rink/Capacity | **Molson Centre/21,361** |
| Stanley Cups | **24 (1916, 1924, 1930, 1931, 1944, 1946, 1953,1956, 1957, 1958, 1959, 1960, 1965, 1966, 1968, 1969,1971, 1973, 1976, 1977, 1978, 1979, 1986, 1993)** |

*Playing Record*

| | W | L | T | Pts |
|---|---|---|---|---|
| Regular Season | **2610** | **1593** | **769** | **5989** |
| Playoffs | **377** | **243** | | |

**The Canadiens hopes of entrusting the torch to a crop of talented, young players, have been sorely tested in a below-par season.**

Uneasy lies the head of the coach of the Montreal Canadiens—especially when the NHL's most successful team isn't wearing the crown, or at least taking a run at the Stanley Cup. In a tumultuous and injury-plagued 1997 season, the Canadiens squeezed into the eighth and final Eastern Conference playoff spot on the next-to-last day of the regular season. They lasted only five games against New Jersey, the second straight year the team failed to get past the first round.

A few days later, Mario Tremblay, in his first full year as head coach, resigned, delivering a stinging attack on a few of his media adversaries in the process. Tremblay became the fifth coach in 12 years to depart the pressure-cooker of guiding the fortunes of a franchise that is under intense media and public scrutiny.

While the debate continues to rage about the merits of Tremblay as a coach—a job he inherited when Jacques Demers was fired four games into the 1995-96 season—injuries were a contributing factor as the Canadiens finished below .500 for the second time in three years.

While Shayne Corson, Marc Bureau and defenseman Vladimir Malakhov all missed significant playing time, the absence of shifty center Saku Koivu for 32 games might have made the difference between finishing eighth and fifth in the conference.

## Disappointing mediocrity

Durable right-winger Marc Recchi was the team's most consistent performer, leading the club with 34 goals, and his 80 points were one fewer than team leader Vincent Damphousse. Goaltending was and continues to be a subject of controversy, with Jocelyn Thibault—obtained in the colossal Patrick Roy trade with Colorado a year earlier—still playing tentatively and now being pushed by rising prospect Jose Theodore.

In their first full season in the glamorous Molson Centre, the Canadiens posted a mediocre 17-17-7 home record, a far cry from the years at the Forum, where visiting teams were often intimidated by the building's status as a hallowed hockey shrine.

No team has to deal with higher expectations from its loyal followers than the Canadiens—and that's because of the winning tradition of the Club de Hockey Canadien. With 24 Stanley Cups, they are the most successful major professional sports franchise. By comparison, the New York Yankees have won 23 World Series and the Boston Celtics have 16 National Basketball Association crowns. The Canadiens have 11 more Cup triumphs than their closest pursuer, the Toronto Maple Leafs.

**Little Big Man: As a rookie, Saku Koivu scored 20 goals and won a strong following with the Canadiens.**

Leading Man: A native Montrealer, Vincent Damphousse is the on-ice leader for the young, harassed Canadiens.

## Torch of Glory

Little did J. Ambrose O'Brien realize when he founded the team on December 4, 1909 that it would gain world-wide renown for its hockey prowess—in fact, he sold the club a year later. But by 1926 Canadiens players such as Newsy Lalonde, Aurele Joliat, Joe Malone, Georges Vezina and Howie Morenz were stars.

The late 1950s saw an unmatched five consecutive Stanley Cups, as the team responded to an excerpt from the John McRae poem *In Flanders Fields*—"To you from failing hands we throw the torch. Be Yours to Hold it High" which has been a fixture in the dressing room since 1952. No one grabbed the torch with as much gusto as Maurice (Rocket) Richard, the team's career goal-scoring leader with 544. An icon in Quebec, Richard's suspension for striking a linesman, touched off a riot by fans at the Forum on March 17, 1955.

The string of Stanley Cups started the following the year as Jean Beliveau, Dickie Moore, Boom Boom Geoffrion, Doug Harvey, Jacques Plante and Maurice's kid brother Henri led a star-studded cast coached by Toe Blake, who would win eight Cups in 13 seasons behind the bench.

With Scotty Bowman at the helm, and such performers as Jacques Lemaire, Guy Lafleur, Larry Robinson and Ken Dryden, the Canadiens added four straight Stanley Cups between 1975-76 and 1978-79.

# NEW JERSEY DEVILS

New Jersey coach Jacques Lemaire's mastery of the neutral trap strategy won the Devils their first conference crown.

P atience. Intensity. Neutral-zone trap. Tight defense. Awesome goaltending. Mention the New Jersey Devils and these words and descriptions are likely to be used in the conversation. You won't find too many Devils listed among the league's top scorers.

In fact, if you exclude Doug Gilmour, who arrived from Toronto in a late-season trade, the team's top point-getter was left-winger Bobby Holik, with a career-high 62 points. John MacLean, Bill Guerin and Dave Andreychuk all topped Holik's 23 goals with 29, 29 and 27 respectively.

But you don't have to read far down the list to find a New Jersey connection in matters of defense. Goaltender Martin Brodeur, for example, led all NHL goaltenders with a 1.88 goals-against average and ten shutouts in 67 games last season. As a team, the Devils posted the league's lowest goals-against average—2.18. And several players, including Andreychuk and defensemen Scott Stevens and Ken Daneyko, were deep into the plus side of the plus-minus statistics which, essentially, reflect a player's ability as a two-way performer.

**Franchise Defenseman: Scott Stevens anchors a rock-solid defense in New Jersey.**

## Lemaire's trap

While Devils coach Jacques Lemaire did not invent the neutral trap—a system that basically clogs the area between the two blue lines and stifles the offensive threats of opposing teams— he is a master at implementing the strategy.

"Jacques always has a good game plan," says Gilmour, who scored seven goals and added 15 assists in 20 regular-season games after a February trade in which the Maple Leafs parted with the tough and talented center (along with defenseman Dave Ellett) for a trio of young prospects. "It's a very patient game and you've got to play that way for 60 minutes."

The Devils needed the final 60 minutes of the regular season to clinch the Eastern Conference title, with a win over Philadelphia. Not only was it the franchise's first conference crown, it was the first time the Devils finished first in their division. But the season ended sourly for the newly crowned champs, when the arch-rival New York Rangers, buoyed by the sensational goaltending of Mike Richter, ousted the Devils in five games in the conference semifinal.

## From funnies to champs

Few remember that the New Jersey Devils were once the Kansas City Scouts, and only vaguely that they were the Colorado Rockies, a club that John McMullen and his group purchased in 1982 and moved to the New Jersey Meadowlands.

Some might recall that the Devils were almost as dreadful as the Scouts and Rockies in their early years in New Jersey. In fact, after a 1983 game in which Edmonton routed New Jersey 11-4, Oilers superstar Wayne Gretzky likened the Devils to Mickey Mouse.

Until 1988, the Rockies-Scouts-Devils had qualified for a playoff berth only once in 13 seasons, and had one playoff-game victory—by Colorado in 1977-78.

But the first taste of post-season play as the Devils was memorable as they reached the Wales Conference championship before losing to Boston in seven games.

The Devils did not make the conference final again until 1994. That ended in heartbreak, when Stephane Matteau's overtime goal in the seventh game sent the New York Rangers, rather than New Jersey, to the Stanley Cup final.

But under Lemaire, part of eight Stanley Cup championships as a player with Montreal, the Devils embarked on a 1994-95 playoff run in which it lost only four of 20 games, culminating in a four-game sweep of the favored Detroit Red Wings for the first Stanley Cup in the history of the franchise.

**Goalie Prodigy: Martin Brodeur has won the Calder Trophy as top rookie and backstopped his team to a Stanley Cup. He's only 25.**

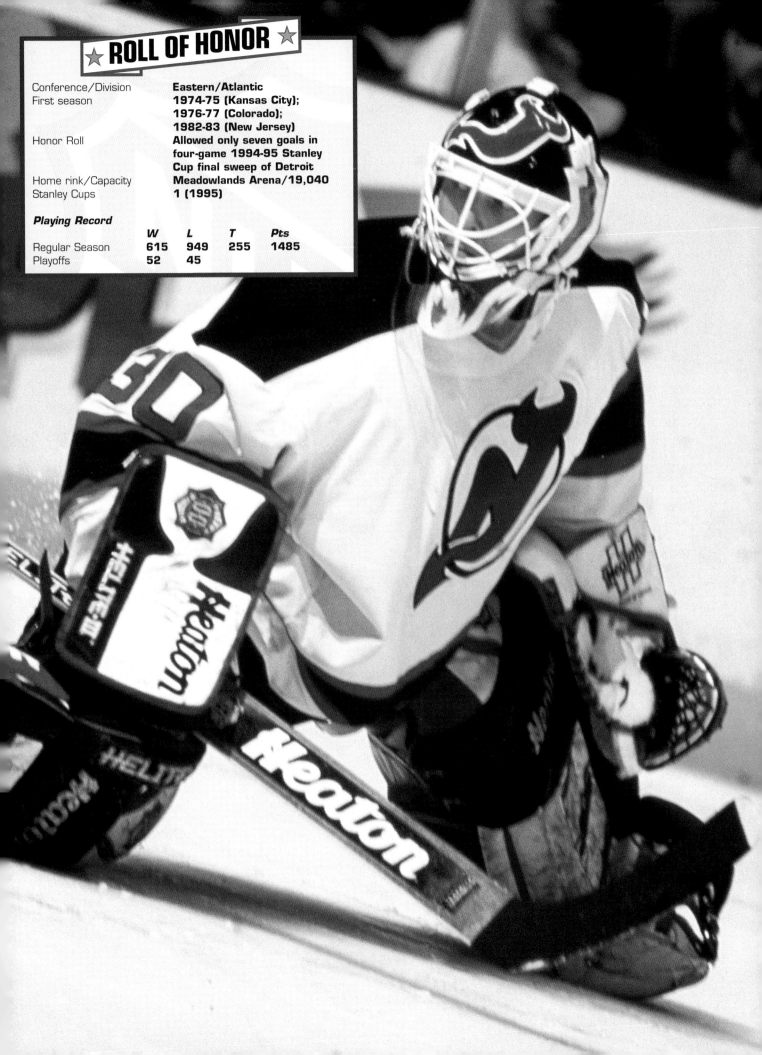

### ★ ROLL OF HONOR ★

| | |
|---|---|
| Conference/Division | **Eastern/Atlantic** |
| First season | **1974-75 (Kansas City);** |
| | **1976-77 (Colorado);** |
| | **1982-83 (New Jersey)** |
| Honor Roll | **Allowed only seven goals in** |
| | **four-game 1994-95 Stanley** |
| | **Cup final sweep of Detroit** |
| Home rink/Capacity | **Meadowlands Arena/19,040** |
| Stanley Cups | **1 (1995)** |

**Playing Record**

| | W | L | T | Pts |
|---|---|---|---|---|
| Regular Season | 615 | 949 | 255 | 1485 |
| Playoffs | 52 | 45 | | |

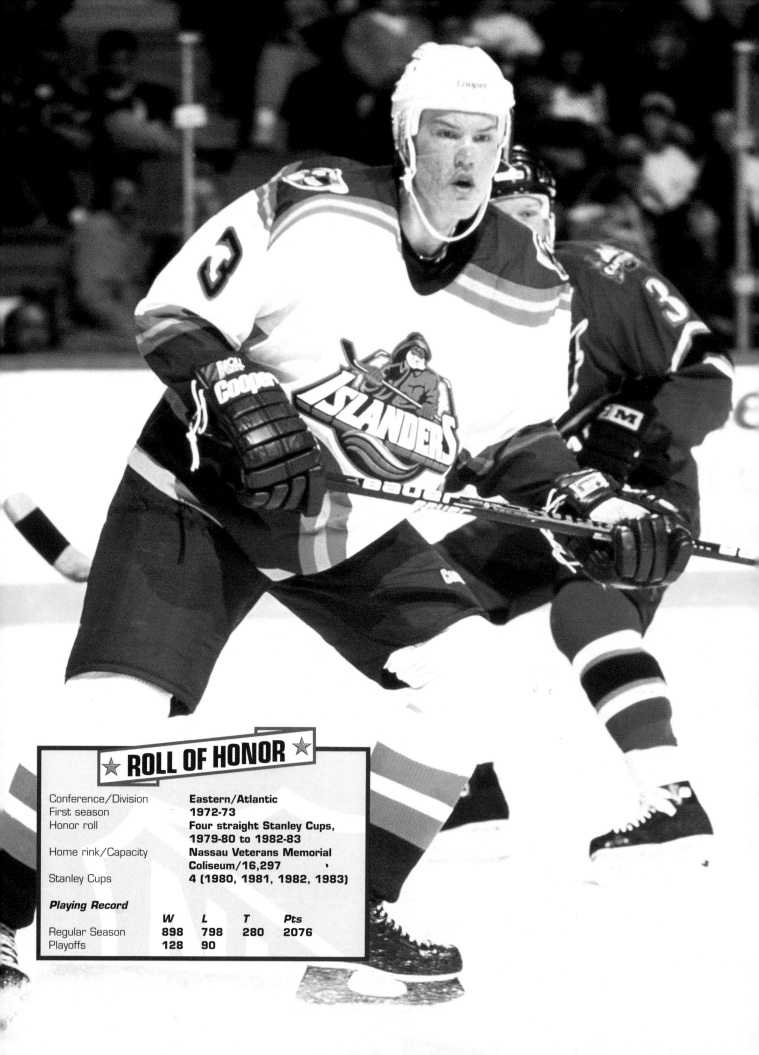

## ★ ROLL OF HONOR ★

| | |
|---|---|
| Conference/Division | **Eastern/Atlantic** |
| First season | **1972-73** |
| Honor roll | **Four straight Stanley Cups, 1979-80 to 1982-83** |
| Home rink/Capacity | **Nassau Veterans Memorial Coliseum/16,297** |
| Stanley Cups | **4 (1980, 1981, 1982, 1983)** |

**Playing Record**

| | W | L | T | Pts |
|---|---|---|---|---|
| Regular Season | 898 | 798 | 280 | 2076 |
| Playoffs | 128 | 90 | | |

# NEW YORK ISLANDERS

## Blessed with a cluster of impressive youngsters, the Islanders are a promising work-in-progress.

Rome wasn't built in a day, and the same can be said for the rebuilding process of the New York Islanders, the NHL dynasty of the early 1980s. But while the Islanders missed the Stanley Cup playoffs for the third straight time last season, it's obvious that the pieces are starting to fall into place.

The Islanders won seven more games than they did during the 1995-96 season, and they remained in the playoff hunt until the final week. They dramatically cut their goals-against totals to 250 from a gaudy 315 a year earlier, helped immeasurably by the arrival of defenseman Bryan Berard and the development of goaltender Tommy Salo, who also played a key role in Sweden's silver medal at the World Championships last spring.

Berard, who turned 20 last March, was the No. 1 pick in the 1995 entry draft, but refused to sign with the Ottawa Senators, who traded him to the Islanders in January, 1996. Berard collected 48 points as one of the NHL's top rookies in 1996-97.

### Boy soldiers

Berard is one of several fresh faces that figure to raise the Islanders—the NHL's smallest team, and second-youngest last year—to contending status. This group includes forwards Niklas Andersson and Todd Bertuzzi, and defensemen Bryan McCabe and Kenny Jonsson.

Crafty Czech Zigmund Palffy, a 48-goal performer in 1996-97, is almost a greybeard among the youngbloods, and he's only 25. Travis Green and Bryan Smolinski, both considered as veterans on the young squad, had 23 and 28 goals respectively.

And the future seems even rosier for the Rick Bowness-coached team since the Islanders had two of the first selections in the entry draft last June.

"I think our team needs to get bigger, deeper on the wings and deeper down the middle (at the center position), and we need some leadership in the dressing room," said Islanders general manager Mike Milbury in analyzing his up-and-coming club.

The Islanders' plight in recent years is a reminder of the franchise's humble beginnings, after joining the Atlanta Flames as a new league member in the 1972-73 season.

### Torrey magic

The Islanders managed only 12 victories and 30 points in their fledgling season but they improved dramatically from then on, as astute general manager Bill Torrey, who'd been an executive with the expansion California Seals, started weaving his magic. Torrey hired Al Arbour as head coach following the 1972-73 season. One week later, he drafted Denis Potvin, a gifted young junior defenseman. At the draft table the following year, Torrey grabbed a bruising forward named Clark Gillies, and a shifty center named Bryan Trottier.

**On the Move:** A smooth skater and a gifted offensive player, Kenny Jonsson is one of a cluster of talented young defensemen on the Island.

The combative Billy Smith, a little-known goaltender Torrey had selected in the 1972 expansion draft, suddenly became a key component in the building process. In the 1977 draft, Torrey plucked a wiry, high-scoring forward named Mike Bossy from the Quebec Major Junior League and the last building block was virtually in place.

By the 1979-80 season, these five players led an Islanders charge that displaced the Montreal Canadiens as the dominant NHL force. The Canadiens were seeking a fifth straight Cup when the upstart Islanders breezed through four series, including a six-game victory over Philadelphia in the final, for the first of four consecutive Stanley Cup championships.

The Islanders narrowly missed matching the Canadiens' record five straight Cups. They reached the final in 1983-84, only to lose to the Edmonton Oilers.

It was a wonderful run while it lasted. Trottier became New York's all-time points leader with 1,353 and Bossy, forced into premature retirement because of an aching back, topped the goal-scoring list with 573.

**Scoring Whiz:** In Zigmund Palffy, the Islanders have a bona fide NHL sniper.

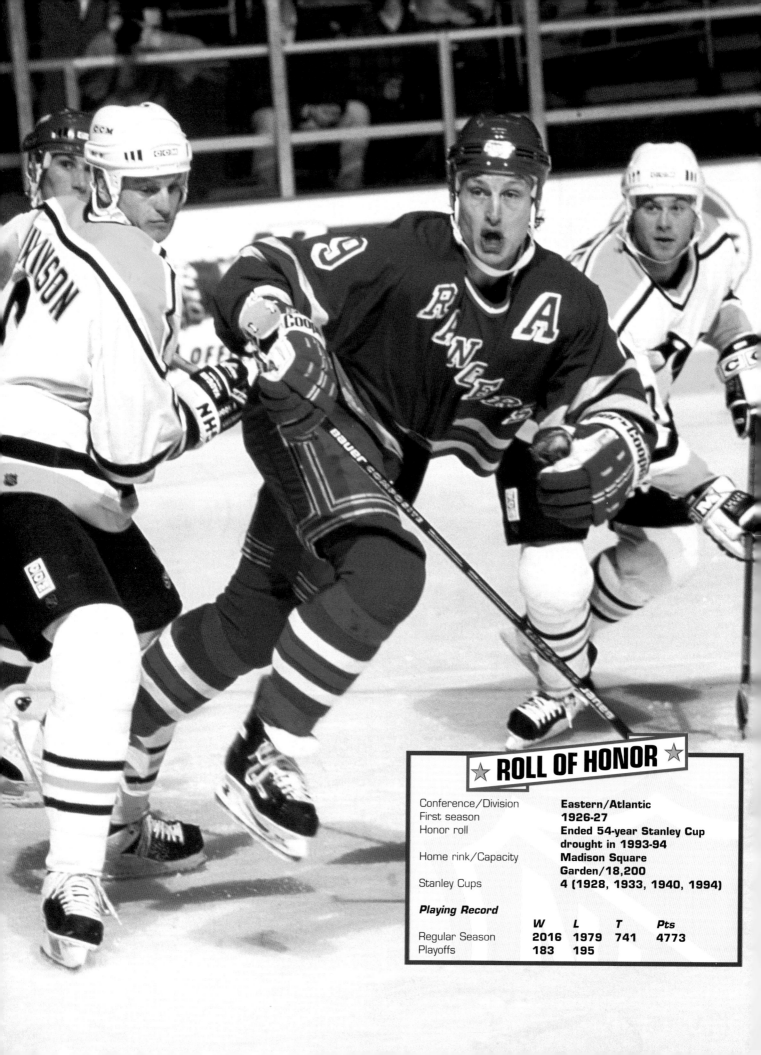

## ★ ROLL OF HONOR ★

| | |
|---|---|
| Conference/Division | **Eastern/Atlantic** |
| First season | **1926-27** |
| Honor roll | **Ended 54-year Stanley Cup drought in 1993-94** |
| Home rink/Capacity | **Madison Square Garden/18,200** |
| Stanley Cups | **4 (1928, 1933, 1940, 1994)** |

**Playing Record**

| | W | L | T | Pts |
|---|---|---|---|---|
| Regular Season | 2016 | 1979 | 741 | 4773 |
| Playoffs | 183 | 195 | | |

## Inspired by newly-signed Wayne Gretzky, the Rangers caught fire in the Stanley Cup playoffs.

**W**hen Wayne Gretzky signed as a free agent with the Rangers in the summer of 1996, his long-time friend and teammate Mark Messier predicted that Gretzky would "elevate some players to a place where they had never been before."

For a while last spring it seemed that place would be the pinnacle of NHL achievement—a Stanley Cup triumph. Spurred by Gretzky, Messier, Esa Tikkanen—another former Cup-winning Oiler—and goaltender Mike Richter, the Rangers rebounded from a mediocre regular season to skip past Florida and arch-rival New Jersey before losing to Philadelphia in the Eastern Conference final.

Injuries to four forwards, combined with nagging ailments for Gretzky and defenseman Brian Leetch, and the physical punishment dished out by the Flyers, ended the run for the Rangers, whose strong content of former Oilers prompted some people to sarcastically dub them "Edmonton East".

### Roster of talent

Turning back the clock, the 36-year-old Gretzky led the team with 97 points, including 25 goals. The latter total might have been higher, but Gretzky went through the longest goal-scoring drought of his career—21 games—before finally connecting against Hartford in a February 21 game.

Messier matched his age by scoring a club-leading 36 goals and center Adam Graves, rebounding from a mediocre season, followed closely behind with 33 goals.

Leetch was his usual tower of strength, both defensively and offensively, collecting 78 points, including 20 goals. Niklas Sundstrom and well-seasoned Luc Robitaille were the other 20-goal scorers, and speedy forward Alexei Kovalev, a hero from the Rangers' 1994 Cup triumph, would easily have topped that total, but his run was ended at mid-season by a shattered knee.

Richter, whose stellar play helped the United States entry capture the World Cup last fall, again showed why he is among the NHL's elite goaltenders, posting a 2.68 goals-against average, while Glenn Healy—a 2.61 mark for 23 games—continued to be one of the top backup netminders.

Still, despite having a roster laden with experience and championship credentials, the Rangers spent the first half of the season under the .500 mark. They finished the regular schedule with a 38-34-10 mark before catching fire in the playoffs.

### From Cup to Cup

Success in the playoffs hasn't been a Rangers hallmark. No NHL team has won a Stanley Cup one year after joining the league, as the Rangers did in 1928, but no team has gone without a Stanley Cup for 54 years, as the Rangers did before striking paydirt in 1993-94.

In the early years, Madison Square Garden echoed with

**Little Mess: Rugged and skilful, Adam Graves has learned his NHL lessons well from his mentor, Messier.**

**West Coast Moose: After six seasons in New York, Mark Messier signed with the Vancouver Canucks during the off-season.**

exhortations for scoring star Frank Boucher, brothers Bill and Bun Cook and Lester Patrick, the club's first coach and general manager. In the second game of the 1928 Stanley Cup finals, the 44-year-old Patrick was pressed into service as the team's goaltender. He allowed only one goal, the Rangers won in overtime, and Patrick was forever etched in the club's history.

Another brother combination—Mac and Alex Shibicky—joined with future Hall of Famer Neil Colville to lead the Rangers to their 1940 Cup triumph.

While the Rangers' Cup drought continued, the club made the playoffs nine straight years, starting in 1966-67.

The Rangers, who lost to Montreal in the 1978 final, wouldn't get another chance until 1994 in the final against Vancouver.

The Cup-clinching goal in Game 7 of the final came from Messier, a five-time Cup winner with Edmonton and one of several acquisitions made by Rangers general manager Neil Smith in building his championship squad.

# OTTAWA SENATORS

"**N**obody will be laughing at the Senators any more." Veteran defenseman Steve Duchesne uttered the line in the euphoria of Ottawa's clinching its first-ever Stanley Cup playoff berth on the next-to-last day of the 1996-97 regular-season schedule. And it was Duchesne who sent the Senators to post-season play by scoring with four minutes to play, ending a 0-0 duel against the Buffalo Sabres.

For long-suffering Ottawa fans, who along with the players had been the butt of jokes because the Senators were the NHL's most futile team since joining the league in 1992, there were tears of joy, rather than frustration. The 77 points compiled by the Senators last season was a 36-point improvement over the previous year.

The Senators promptly drew Buffalo in the opening round of the playoffs last spring and extended the series to seven games before gallantly bowing out.

"The season was a learning situation for our club," said Jacques Martin, in his first full season as Ottawa's head coach. "We learned how to handle pressure situations. We got a lot better in the second half."

### Flowering strength

Indeed, the Senators posted the Eastern Conference's fourth-best record in the second half, going 19-15-7. The team needed a strong second half, because it was nine games under .500 at the halfway mark, after spending a fair amount of time in last place in the overall standings.

Season-ending injuries only a handful of games into the schedule to key defensemen Sean Hill and Stan Neckar didn't faze the young Senators. Duchesne lifted his game a notch and rookie Wade Redden, a former No. 2-overall draft pick of the New York Islanders, settled in like a seasoned pro.

Center Alexei Yashin, embroiled in a bitter contract dispute with management the previous year, blossomed into a 35-goal performer, leading the team. Speedy Swedish forward Daniel Alfredsson, the NHL's top rookie in 1995-96, shook off early signs of the sophomore jinx and finished with 71 points—including 24 goals—ten points more than the previous season.

In goal, when first-stringer Damian Rhodes was sidelined with a leg injury in late February, Ron Tugnutt, a well-travelled backup, stepped into the breach and was sensational down the stretch, enabling Ottawa to finish with a rush, and nestle into seventh place in the Eastern Conference.

### Walking the plank

While last season was a huge ray of sunshine for the Senators, there have been plenty of stormy moments in their brief history. Mel Bridgman, the club's first general manager was fired immediately after the Senators' maiden season of 24 points—second-lowest in NHL history for a minimum 70-game schedule. The first-

**Swedish Sharpshooter: Daniel Alfredsson's multi-talented game helps give Ottawa fans hope for a promising future.**

year Senators also tied an NHL record with only one road victory.

The abysmal record gave Ottawa the first draft choice in 1993, and the Senators grabbed Quebec Junior League scoring whiz Alexandre Daigle. Signed to a whopping five-year, $12 million contract, Daigle struggled his first two seasons, before notching 26 goals in 1996-97, second-highest on the club.

Yashin, meanwhile, missed three months in 1995-96 before a settlement was reached in his contract dispute. In the interim, the popular Rick Bowness—Ottawa's head coach from Day One—was fired, and key administrative personnel such as former NHL tough guy John Ferguson left the organization in frustration.

Sexton, too, eventually walked the plank, replaced by Pierre Gauthier, a rising executive with the San Jose Sharks, whose first move was to sign Yashin to a five-year deal. He then dumped interim coach Dave Allison and brought in the seasoned Martin.

**Big Shoulders: The Ottawa Senators are hoping talented center Alexei Yashin can carry their franchise to the playoffs again.**

## ★ ROLL OF HONOR ★

| | |
|---|---|
| Conference/Division | **Eastern/Atlantic** |
| First season | **1967-68** |
| Honor roll | **Consecutive Stanley Cups, 1974-75** |
| Home rink/Capacity | **CoreStates Center/19,500** |
| Stanley Cups | **2 (1974, 1975)** |

***Playing Record***

| | W | L | T | Pts |
|---|---|---|---|---|
| Regular Season | 1174 | 818 | 366 | 2714 |
| Playoffs | 144 | 121 | (before final series) | |

# PHILADELPHIA FLYERS

A season that started on a low pitch ended on a high note for the Flyers in 1996-97. Center Eric Lindros, arguably the most dominant player in the NHL, watched from the sidelines for the first 23 games, waiting for his injured right groin to heal. In his absence, the Flyers compiled a very ordinary 12-10-1 record.

But shortly after Lindros returned, the Flyers, particularly the No. 1 line of Lindros and wingers John LeClair and Mikael Renberg, started to hum on all cylinders.

The Flyers went on to amass 103 points in regular-season play—matching their total of the previous season—finishing just a point behind New Jersey for the Eastern Conference title. But the Flyers quickly erased the disappointment in the Stanley Cup playoffs, defeating Pittsburgh, Buffalo and the New York Rangers to advance to the final round—against Detroit—for the first time since 1987.

## Laying down the law

Somewhat reminiscent of the Broad Street Bullies—the nickname for the intimidating Flyers teams which ruled the NHL in the mid 1970s—the 1996-97 club used its size, especially that of the Lindros-LeClair-Renberg trio to lay down the law.

"Our motto has just been to get the puck to the net, get some traffic there, and get some rebounds," explained LeClair, one of four 50-goal scorers in the NHL last season, the second straight year he reached that plateau. LeClair led the team with 97 points, despite missing the 23 games, while Renberg, Rod Brind'Amour and Trent Klatt all topped the 20-goal mark.

Chris Therien was a pleasant surprise on the defense corps, as was Lithuanian-born Dainius Zubrus at right wing. The only 1996 first-round draft selection to spend all of last season in the NHL, Zubrus contributed several key goals in the Stanley Cup playoffs.

Despite their success, the Flyers continued to have goaltender controversy. Veteran Ron Hextall was in and out of favor for much of the season. He split the duties with Garth Snow, who was knighted No. 1 to start the playoffs, but Hextall worked his way back into the job during the Eastern Conference final.

## Intimidating force

There's always been something special about the Flyers, one of the six expansion teams to join the NHL for the 1967-68 season. Six years later, they became the first expansion team to win the Stanley Cup, an exploit repeated in 1974-75. The Flyers of that era were tough and talented, attributes exemplified by acknowledged on-ice leader Bobby Clarke, who today is the Flyers' president and general manager.

Enforcers Dave (The Hammer) Schultz, Bob (Hound Dog) Kelly and Don Saleski did plenty of body-thumping. The Flyers' bruising defense corps of Andre (Moose) Dupont, the Watson brothers—Joe and Jim—and Ed Van Impe dished out more bitter medicine.

But the Flyers, under coach Fred Shero, were much more than brawn. They had a 50-goal man in Rick MacLeish, another in Reggie Leach, who in 1975-76 notched 61 goals, only the second NHLer to reach that mark. And they had Bill Barber, whose 420 goals in 903 games as a Flyer remain the career best on the club.

In goal, Bernie Parent, traded to Toronto in 1971 and re-acquired two years later, won the Conn Smythe Trophy as the most valuable performer in the Stanley Cup playoffs in both 1974 and 1975, the first player to accomplish the feat.

Amid the triumphs, there was also tragedy. Barry Ashbee, one of the Flyers' best defensemen, had his career ended in 1974 after being struck in the eye by a puck, and Vezina Trophy winner Pelle Lindberg was killed in an automobile accident at the height of his goaltending career in 1985.

**Big Man on Campus: dominant Eric Lindros missed 23 games through injury, but returned to inspire.**

**Legionaire of Doom: Teamed with Lindros and John Leclair, Swedish star Mikael Renberg is an offensive force in Philadelphia.**

# PHOENIX COYOTES

## The Jets left a proud legacy in Winnipeg; the Coyotes must work hard to build one in Phoenix.

They had the NHL's top sharpshooter in 52-goal performer Keith Tkachuk. Right-winger Mike Gartner, the fifth-highest goal-scorer in league history, moved four goals shy of 700 with a 32-goal effort. And third-year goaltender Nikolai Khabibulin came into his own, posting seven shutouts and a 2.83 goals against average, appearing in all but ten of the team's 82 games.

In other words, there were several sparkling developments as the transplanted Winnipeg Jets left the frozen Canadian prairies for the sun-baked desert of Phoenix. But, in the end, the result wasn't much different than it was during the 17 seasons the franchise was in Winnipeg.

The Coyotes did have the franchise's best regular season since 1992-93, qualifying for the Stanley Cup playoffs with a 36-35-11

record, fifth-best in the Western Conference. But a seventh-game defeat against the Anaheim Mighty Ducks in post-season play marked the sixth straight opening-round elimination for the Jets-cum-Coyotes and the 12th time in 14 playoff appearances in which the club didn't move into the second round.

### Still underachievers

Phoenix general manager Bobby Smith, who played for 11 different coaches during his 15-year NHL career, reacted to the early exit by firing head coach Don Hay, who had been hired the previous summer by his predecessor John Paddock following an impressive stint as the coach of Kamloops in the Western Junior League.

Inconsistent play, especially at their new digs, the America West Arena, kept the Coyotes from shaking the same tag as underachievers that the team had when it was based in Winnipeg. The Coyotes were only 15-19-7 in front of the home crowd, the fourth-worst home record in the league. That didn't keep fans away from the building, however. The Coyotes averaged 15,604 fans in the 16,210 seat arena, a 38 percent attendance boost over the team's last season in Winnipeg.

Heading into the 1997-98 season, the Coyotes have center Jeremy Roenick coming back from a knee injury that prematurely ended his season in Game 6 of the playoffs. They also enter the new season with high hopes that Deron Quint, their first choice in the 1994 draft, will start to approach the talent of Oleg Tverdovsky, the former No. 1 pick of the Mighty Ducks who is now the Coyotes' anchor on defense.

### Shaping influence

The Coyotes' NHL roots are in Winnipeg, where the Jets entered the league in 1979. While not very proficient in the NHL, the club was instrumental in the evolution of European players and, so, had much to do with shaping the style and substance of the game.

While Swedish stars Ulf and Kent Nilsson, and Anders Hedberg from the WHA years didn't accompany the Jets to the NHL, Europeans such as Willy Lindstrom and and Lars-Erik Sjoberg carried the torch. The Jets also had NHL scoring great Bobby Hull for 18 games that first season, before trading him to Hartford.

As the 1980s unfolded, two players emerged as the cornerstones of the franchise. Dale Hawerchuk, a rangy center who was the No. 1 overall pick in the 1981 NHL draft, was the team's leading scorer for the next nine years, a remarkable stretch that made him the team's all-time leader in goals (379) and points (929).

Thomas Steen, of Sweden, wasn't a prolific scorer. But he combined toughness, speed and grace for 14 seasons with the Jets, making him the club's longest-serving player. There wasn't a dry eye in the Winnipeg Arena when the Jets retired Steen's No. 25 in a ceremony following the 1995 season.

**Shifty Coyote: Alexei Zhamnov's skills were often overshadowed with the Winnipeg Jets by his former teammate, Teemu Selanne.**

**Leader of the Pack: Keith Tkachuk, a 50-goal scorer in 1995-96, is the on-ice leader of the Coyotes in their second year in Phoenix.**

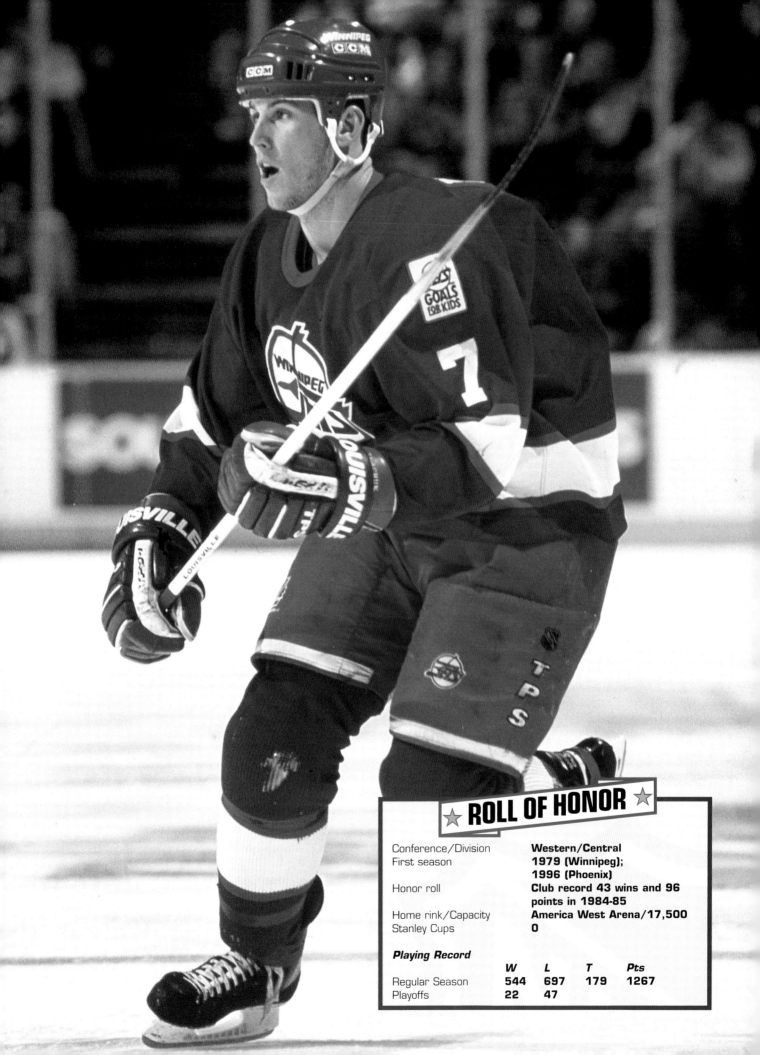

## ★ ROLL OF HONOR ★

| | |
|---|---|
| Conference/Division | **Western/Central** |
| First season | **1979 (Winnipeg);** |
| | **1996 (Phoenix)** |
| Honor roll | **Club record 43 wins and 96** |
| | **points in 1984-85** |
| Home rink/Capacity | **America West Arena/17,500** |
| Stanley Cups | **0** |

### Playing Record

| | W | L | T | Pts |
|---|---|---|---|---|
| Regular Season | 544 | 697 | 179 | 1267 |
| Playoffs | 22 | 47 | | |

# PITTSBURGH PENGUINS

## Mario Lemieux's retirement leaves the Penguins with a formidable void to fill in order to secure their NHL future.

Two years ago, the Pittsburgh Penguins had to go through a half-season—the schedule started in January because of the players' strike—without superstar center Mario Lemieux, as he recovered from Hodgkin's disease. The team kept its head above .500 but didn't get beyond the Eastern Conference semifinals in the playoff round.

Lemieux returned to win the NHL scoring title in each of the last two seasons. But now, the Penguins are back on the LAM (Life After Lemieux). This time it's for good, since Lemieux, who revived a sagging Pittsburgh franchise during a 745-game, 613-goal career (in regular-season play), has retired. And no one is quite certain how the Penguins will react to the absence of the Hall-of-Fame bound wizard who was instrumental in bringing consecutive Stanley Cups to Pittsburgh at the start of the 1990s.

"Not being able to challenge people one-on-one the way I could a few years ago, that's a part of my game that's been missing," Lemieux said, in explaining why he was bowing out at the age of 31. "I can't seem to beat anybody one-on-one anymore... that's why I'm stepping out."

One-On-One Dazzler: A swift skater and one of the strongest on his skates in hockey, Jaromir Jagr is probably the best one-on-one player in the NHL, and a key to Pittsburgh's future.

### To fill a void

Despite a 50-goal, 122-point season by Lemieux in 1996-97, the Penguins finished sixth overall in the Eastern Conference standings, with a 38-36-8 record. They lasted only five games in the opening playoff round against the younger, hungrier and more physical Philadelphia Flyers.

It's a dilemma for Penguins general manager Craig Patrick, who took over the coaching reins when he relieved Eddie Johnston of such duties late in the season. Patrick must not only bolster the team's offense following the loss of Lemieux, but he needs to bolster the defensive corps, after the club finished next-to-last in goals-against average at 3.38.

Goaltending seemed the least of the Penguins' worries a few weeks into last season. After a 2-9 start, the team went on a 20-4-2 roll, largely because young Patrick Lalime was recalled from the minors, and set an NHL record for netminders by going undefeated—14-0-2—in his first 16 games.

Some of Patrick's wheeling and dealing following the bad start also reaped dividends. Defensemen Darius Kasparaitis, Jason Wooley and Fredrik Olausson were among the new arrivals who combined with Lalime to shore up the Penguins' defense.

But Lalime eventually cooled off and a nagging late-season groin injury to Jaromir Jagr—who is to shoulder a big load with Lemieux gone—affected the team's production down the stretch, especially since Lemieiux, Jagr and Ron Francis had performed so well as a line.

### Bolstering a center

The history of the Penguins did not start on June 9, 1984, the day they selected Lemieux as the top pick in the NHL entry draft—but the fortunes of the franchise improved dramatically as of that date. Gradually, general manager Patrick assembled strong support for Lemieux. Jagr, a gifted Czechoslovakian was grabbed in the 1990 entry draft, two-way center Francis was obtained in a trade with Hartford, and rangy Larry Murphy was added to the defense corps to clear the goal crease for netminder Tom Barrasso.

Two great hockey minds joined the Penguins for the 1990-91 season—(Badger) Bob Johnson as coach and Scotty Bowman as director of player development. Together, the former Stanley Cup-winning duo made the Penguins, out of the playoffs in seven of the previous eight seasons, into sudden Stanley Cup champions.

Bowman made it two straight Cups in 1992 when he relieved Johnson as coach at the start of that season. Johnson died of cancer several weeks later and fans honored his memory in a candlelight ceremony at the Civic Arena.

Simply the Best: Sublime is the most appropriate word to describe Mario Lemieux's extraordinary talent—now lost to the Penguins.

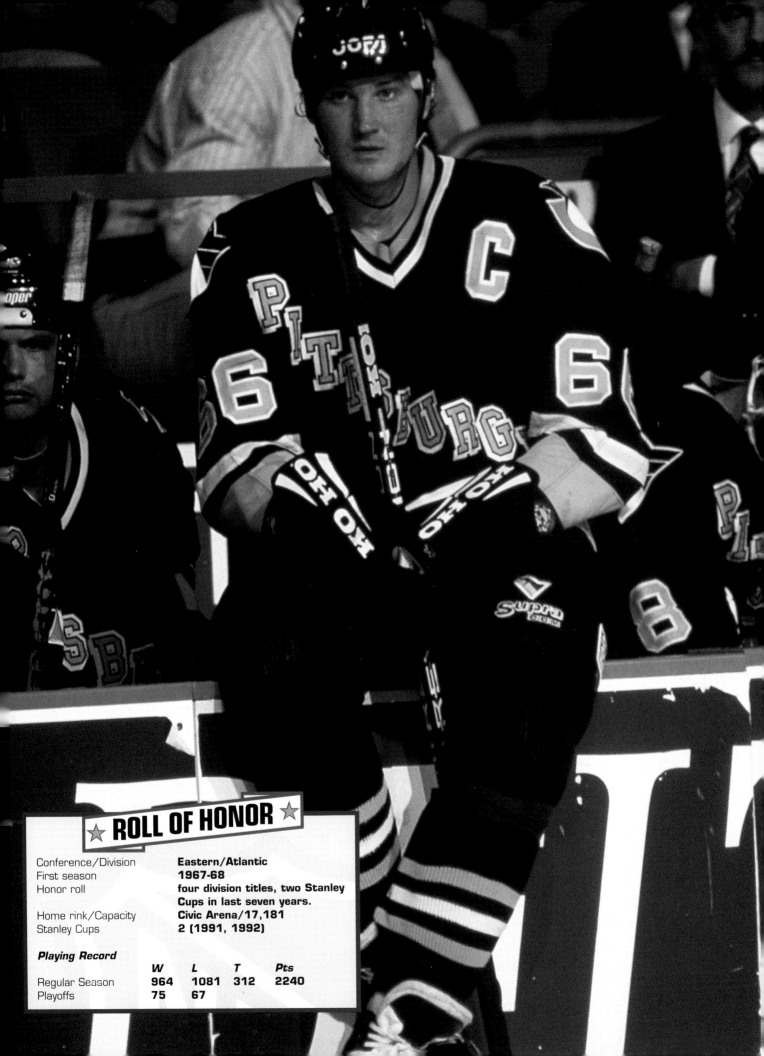

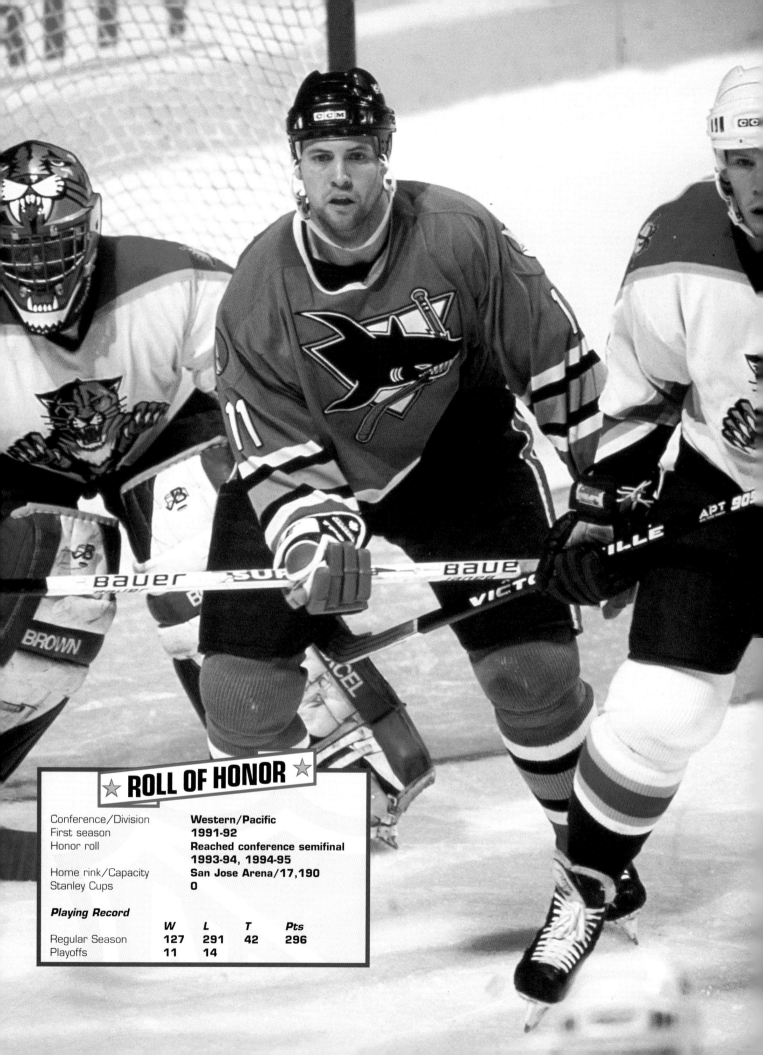

## ⭐ ROLL OF HONOR ⭐

| | |
|---|---|
| Conference/Division | **Western/Pacific** |
| First season | **1991-92** |
| Honor roll | **Reached conference semifinal 1993-94, 1994-95** |
| Home rink/Capacity | **San Jose Arena/17,190** |
| Stanley Cups | **0** |

**Playing Record**

| | W | L | T | Pts |
|---|---|---|---|---|
| Regular Season | 127 | 291 | 42 | 296 |
| Playoffs | 11 | 14 | | |

# SAN JOSE SHARKS

## The Sharks, a promising young franchise, saw their bite suffer from a marked lack of discipline last season.

Fans continued to fill the San Jose Arena to the rafters last season, but for the fifth straight year the hometown Sharks failed to reach the .500 mark, ending the regular season with a 27-47-8 record. Only one point separated the Sharks from the Boston Bruins, the last-placed team in the overall standings.

Despite the lowly finish, the sellout crowds in San Jose had much to cheer about in 1996-97, a year in which the NHL all-star game finally came to the city, after the players' strike forced its postponement in San Jose in 1995.

### Talent vs discipline

There was the heartwarming comeback of forward Tony Granato, whose career was thought to be over when he developed a blood clot in his head after falling into the boards while playing for the Los Angeles Kings a year earlier. Not only did Granato rebound from major surgery, he signed with the Sharks as a free agent, notched 25 goals and was selected to participate in the all-star game.

Further encouragement was the emergence of 20-year-old Jeff Friesen, the Sharks' first-round pick in the 1994 draft and the cornerstone of the team's re-construction process. The speedy Friesen started the season as a third-line winger and gradually moved up to first-line center, scoring 28 goals and collecting 60 points, second on the team in both categories to rugged right-winger and linemate, Owen Nolan. Viktor Kozlov, 22, the third member of the top line, is showing continued progress, after the Sharks made him their first-round draft selection in 1993.

Contrasting with up-and-comers such as the first-line threesome, the Sharks' defensive and goaltending corps is largely a veteran group, with the much-injured Al Iafrate, Doug Bodger, Todd Gill and Marty McSorley the anchors behind the blueline last season. Veteran netminders Ed Belfour—an unrestricted free agent following the season—and Kelly Hrudey were solid in goal.

A major deficiency, however, was the Sharks lack of on-ice discipline. They led the league in penalty minutes, putting a strain on the team's penalty-killing units and

prompting veteran forward Bob Errey to remark, "This is one of the least-disciplined teams I've seen."

The breakdown in discipline was apparently a contributing factor in the rather surprising post-season announcement that the team was relieving first-year head coach Al Sims of his duties.

"The fit was not right for the future of this team," explained Sharks general manager Dean Lombardi.

### Killer sharks

San Jose joined the NHL for the 1991-92 season, 17 months after the league granted permission to George and Gordon Gund to sell the Minnesota North Stars in return for the rights to an expansion team in San Jose.

A first order of business was to come up with a nickname for the new club. A contest was devised, and Sharks won out. The nickname is fitting for a franchise that has frequently struck without warning and shattered the Stanley Cup aspirations of the old guard. Ask the Detroit Red Wings, a strong Cup contender in 1993-94 who were ripped by the Sharks in the first round, losing in an emotion-charged seventh game. San Jose was in only its third season, and had managed only 11 victories in an 84-game schedule the previous year.

The Sharks, whose team colors of Pacific teal, gray, black and white were an instant merchandising hit, pulled another major surprise in 1994-95, eliminating the second-seeded Calgary Flames in seven games in the opening round of the Western Conference playoffs.

**Deadly Shark: The Sharks pried Owen Nolan from the Colorado Avalanche two seasons ago and he twice led San Jose in scoring.**

**Sleeping Giant: Despite injuries and orientation problems Viktor Kozlov, a gifted and sizeable center from Russia, has made steady progress.**

# ST. LOUIS BLUES

## Management changes and great players failed to achieve a decisive turnaround in a lackluster season.

A mid the upheaval of the 1996-97 season, there were at least a few positive developments for the St. Louis Blues. They ended the season with a three-game winning streak which put them into the Stanley Cup playoffs for the 18th straight season, the second-longest streak in the NHL, next to the 28 by the Chicago Blackhawks.

Veteran center Pierre Turgeon was highly productive after the Blues obtained him in a trade with Montreal, rookie center Jim Campbell was a revelation, and venerable goaltender Grant Fuhr made a tremendous comeback from a career-threatening knee injury.

### Early elimination

But, all things considered, 1996-97 was a lost season for the Blues, largely because arch-rivals Detroit dispatched them in six games in the opening round of the playoffs. The Red Wings had also ousted St. Louis a year earlier, in the second round.

That elimination was under the iron-fisted rule of Mike Keenan, who was handed the dual job of coach and general manager in the summer of 1994. In the next two-and-a-half seasons, Keenan moved all but two players out of St. Louis, and had a deteriorating relationship with some of the players he brought in.

Finally, last December, Blues ownership dismissed Keenan and team president Jack Quinn, restoring Ron Caron as interim general and naming Colorado Rockies assistant coach Joel Quenneville as the new head coach. The Blues responded to the patient, development-oriented Quenneville by winning seven of the first ten games under

his tutelage. But they quickly leveled off and needed a season-ending spurt to finish sixth in the Western Conference, only two points ahead of Edmonton and Chicago. Following the season, Quinn hired former Rangers' player personnel wizard Larry Pleau as the Blues' GM.

Turgeon, obtained early in the season from the Canadiens for forward Shayne Corson and defenseman Murray Baron, paced the team with 85 points. Sharpshooter Brett Hull topped the team in goals with 42, one fewer than the previous season.

Campbell notched 23 goals in 68 games and was a rookie-of-the-year candidate, while Fuhr was his workhorse self, appearing in 73 games and compiling a 2.72 goals-against average.

### Sentimental favorites

In their early years, the Blues, a product of the NHL's 1967 expansion, provided every hockey fan with a trip down memory lane, drafting or signing many of the heroes of their youth—Glenn Hall and Jacques Plante in goal, Doug Harvey, Al Arbour and Jean-Guy Talbot on defense, center Phil Goyette and diminutive forward Camille Henry. The first year, the Blues even coaxed former Montreal Canadiens great Dickie Moore and his aching knees out of retirement.

Teaming up with young snipers such as Red Berenson, Gary Sabourin and Frank St. Marseille, the old-timers were sprightly enough to get the Blues into the Stanley Cup final in each of the club's first three seasons, winning the West Division regular-season title in two. They were sentimental favorites in each of the Stanley Cup finals but, despite a gritty effort, they were swept two straight years by Montreal and by Boston in 1969-70. Scotty Bowman, launching a Hall-of-Fame coaching career, was behind the Blues' bench for the latter two seasons.

The Blues haven't returned to the Stanley Cup final since, despite a number of talented performers. Brett Hull, acquired in a 1988 trade, emerged from virtual obscurity to become the Blues' career goal-scoring leader, including 86 goals in 1990-91, a single-season output topped only by Wayne Gretzky. The latter became Hull's teammate for the last few weeks of the 1995-96 season, after the Blues obtained his services in an unsuccessful bid to reach the Stanley Cup final.

He Shoots, He Scores: Brett Hull's blazing slap shot and unobtrusive style make him a stealthy sniper.

**Sturdy Veteran:** Traded from the Montreal Canadiens to the Blues, Pierre Turgeon's skills quickly meshed with those of sniper Brett Hull. Turgeon led the Blues with 85 points, including 26 goals and 59 assists playing on-line with the Golden Brett.

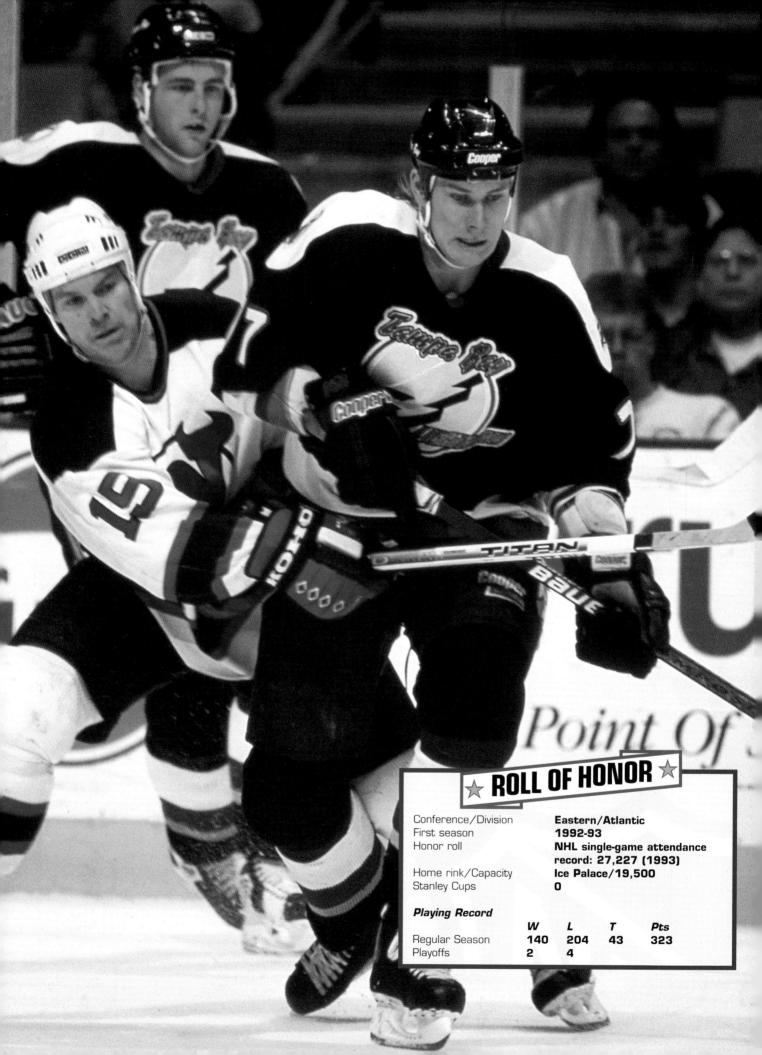

## ★ ROLL OF HONOR ★

| | | | | |
|---|---|---|---|---|
| Conference/Division | **Eastern/Atlantic** | | | |
| First season | **1992-93** | | | |
| Honor roll | **NHL single-game attendance record: 27,227 (1993)** | | | |
| Home rink/Capacity | **Ice Palace/19,500** | | | |
| Stanley Cups | **0** | | | |

### Playing Record

| | W | L | T | Pts |
|---|---|---|---|---|
| Regular Season | 140 | 204 | 43 | 323 |
| Playoffs | 2 | 4 | | |

# TAMPA BAY LIGHTNING

## After making the playoffs for the first time in 1995-96, Tampa failed to build on that first brush with playoff success.

Lightning did not strike twice when it came to the fortunes of Tampa Bay's NHL franchise last season. A year earlier, the overachieving Lightning dramatically clinched the first Stanley Cup playoff berth of its four-year existence on the next-to-last day of the regular season. But, the scenario was reversed in 1996-97, as the underachieving Lightning was denied a post-season spot when Ottawa and Montreal earned the last two positions on the penultimate day of the regular schedule.

After the promise the team displayed in 1995-96, Tampa Bay finished last season with 14 fewer points, even though several Lightning personnel insisted it iced a better team in 1996-97. On paper, at least, some of the Lightning's problems could be traced to an anemic offense. As a team, it produced 217 goals, only six more than San Jose, which had the league's lowest output.

### Woes and plusses

Losing center Brian Bradley, ordinarily a 25-goal man, for almost 50 games because of a shattered wrist, certainly didn't help the cause. Bradley was able to contribute only seven goals. Right-winger Alexander Selivanov, who married the daughter of Lightning general manager Phil Esposito, fell to 15 goals, from 31 a year earlier. The season-long absence of goaltender Darren Puppa because of a severe back injury compounded the Lightning's woes.

On the plus side, rangy center Chris Gratton, the team's first selection in the 1993 draft, came of age, leading the team with 62 points, including 30 goals, almost double his output of the previous season. Eighteen-year veteran Dino Ciccarelli, ten years older than the 21-year-old Gratton, defied his age by connecting for a team-leading 35 goals.

Amid the disappointment of missing the playoffs was much more sobering news for the Lightning—veteran center John Cullen was diagnosed with lymphoma, a form of cancer, late in the season and left to undergo treatment.

While the Lightning has gradually been working some of its recent top draft picks such as center Daymond Langkow into the lineup, the team has maintained continuity behind the bench, where Terry Crisp, currently the longest-serving NHL coach, presides.

Esposito, among others, is convinced that last year's shortfall was merely a blip on the screen. "I think we're close—real, real close—to being a superb hockey team," declared Esposito.

### Big box office

While the Lightning's five seasons have produced ups and downs in the standings, the team was a record-setter at the box office. Because it moved in its second season into the ThunderDome, with the largest seating capacity in the league, the team drew more than 23,000 fans several times, including an NHL record 27,227 for its 1993-94 home opener against state-rival Florida Panthers.

**Future Star: Rugged winger Chris Gratton gives the Lightning size, strength and scoring—and led the team in points last season.**

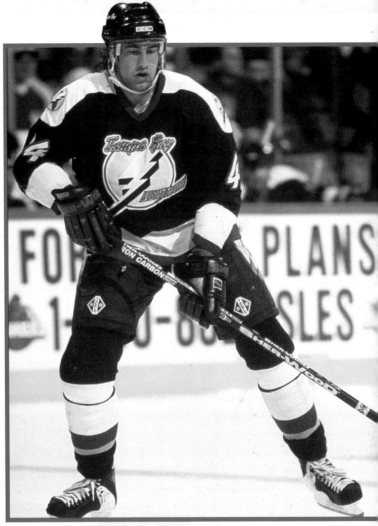

**Blueline Stalwart: Defenseman Roman Hamrlik is a budding star and the linchpin of Tampa's defensive corps.**

The Lightning left the Dome after the 1995-96 season, and now frequently play in front of a capacity crowd at the 19,500-seat Ice Palace in downtown Tampa. One player who didn't move to the new building was goaltender Manon Rheaume. But she remains a part of the club's early history, as the first woman to play one of the four professional major sports in North America. Rheaume was signed by Phil Esposito and invited to training camp in 1992. She made one appearance in an exhibition game, making seven saves in a 20-minute period before joining a Tampa Bay minor league affiliate.

Esposito hasn't been idle as an executive. He grabbed Gratton and defensemen Roman Hamrlik and Mike McBain in the entry draft, signed left-winger Rob Zamuner as a free agent and, last year, acquired serviceable veterans Jeff Norton, Jamie Huscroft and goaltender Rick Tabaracci to bolster the team's defense.

"I think our club has improved in a big way," said Zamuner.

## ★ ROLL OF HONOR ★

| | |
|---|---|
| Conference/Division | **Central/Western** |
| First season | **1917-18** |
| Honor roll | **Only NHL team to rally from 3-0 games deficit in Stanley Cup final** |
| Home rink/Capacity | **Maple Leaf Gardens/15,746** |
| Stanley Cups | **13 (1918, 1922, 1932, 1942, 1945, 1947, 1948, 1949, 1951, 1962, 1963, 1964, 1967)** |

### *Playing Record*

| | W | L | T | Pts |
|---|---|---|---|---|
| Regular Season | 2129 | 2121 | 722 | 4980 |
| Playoffs | 210 | 230 | | |

## As a legacy of success recedes into history, the Leafs introduce young blood to build a winner.

The Leafs won their 1996-97 opener and they closed out the season with a victory over Calgary. But, as head coach Mike Murphy noted, in a burst of understatement, "we had a little bit of trouble in between."

It was trouble with a capital T, as the club slipped to a 30-44-8 record to finish 23rd in the 26-team league and out of the Stanley Cup playoffs for the first time since 1992.

The winds of change swept through Toronto last year, and plenty of Leafs fell in its wake. It was a process that started months before the season-opener, as aging veterans Todd Gill, Mike Gartner and Dave Gagner were moved out in favor of fresher legs.

Later, as the March trading deadline approached and the Leafs slipped further from playoff contention, center Doug Gilmour, once the anchor of the team but the subject of season-long trade rumors, was shipped to New Jersey, along with 33-year-old defenseman Dave Ellett. Center Kirk Muller, another player whose warranty had seemingly expired, was sent to the Florida Panthers. The moves further pared the payroll and cleared the way for a rebuilding job.

### In with the new

Budding youngsters arrived in their place—Leafs of the future, such as center Steve Sullivan and defensemen Alyn McCauley and Jason Smith. With Mats Sundin, the club's linchpin contributing a team-leading 41 goals, rookie Sergei Berezin impressively adding 25, and goaltender Felix Potvin returning to form after months of unsettling trade rumors, the Leafs approached respectability in the last two and a-half months, finishing only a game under .500 for that stretch.

It gave Leafs president and general manager Cliff Fletcher, who missed the playoffs for only the second time in 22 years as the GM of an NHL team, some reason for optimism. But he, too, was shaken by the winds of change. He resigned in late May, after he was told of plans by Leafs' ownership to bring in a new general manager and have Fletcher concentrate solely on his duties as team president.

Hall of Fame goaltender Ken Dryden was made president, with the mandate to "bring a Stanley Cup to Toronto." As a player, Dryden was on six Stanley Cup winners with Montreal.

"The way our team looked at the end of last season was a lot better than the way we played up until Christmas," said Murphy, who will be helped by the return of defenseman Mathieu Schneider, absent for more than half of last season following groin surgery.

### Colorful heroes

The Leafs, who have won 13 Stanley Cups—second only to the 24 hoisted by Montreal—are steeped in history, with colorful personnel such as (Happy) Day; (King) Clancy; (Turk) Broda;

**Nimble as a Cat: Goaltender Felix Potvin led the Maple Leafs to the Stanley Cup semifinals in 1993.**

**Luxury Swede: Mats Sundin's size, speed and scoring prowess have made him a prized commodity in the NHL.**

(Busher) Jackson; (Teeder) Kennedy; (Punch) Imlach; and 'The Big M' among those who proudly wore the Maple Leaf, emblematic of the franchise that joined the NHL in 1927.

The Leafs' most satisfying Cup was the one in 1942, when they became the only NHL club to overcome a 3-0 deficit in games in a Stanley Cup final, against Detroit. They were the first team to win three straight Cups, between 1947-49, and again won three consecutive times 1962-64; but the 1967 Cup triumph was their last.

The Cup-less interval has had great performers, notably Darryl Sittler, defenseman Borje Salming, and forward Wendel Clark.

It was Sittler who on February 7, 1976, scored six goals and added four assists in Toronto's 11-4 rout of Boston. Sittler's ten points are still a single-game NHL record.

# VANCOUVER CANUCKS

## Canucks architect Pat Quinn's hopes for the Bure-Mogilny pairing have been spoilt two years in a row.

One Russian Rocket—Pavel Bure—was grounded for 19 games because of injuries. Another Russian Rocket—Alexander Mogilny—fell from a 55-goal output to 31. Linchpin Trevor Linden tore knee ligaments and missed almost a half-season. Veterans Esa Tikkanen and Russ Courtnall openly complained about new head coach Tom Renney and were later traded.

These were all key events which added up to a dismal 1996-97 season for the Canucks, who missed the playoffs for the first time in seven years with a 35-40-7 record, amid reports that bad dressing-room chemistry was a contributing factor in the team's demise.

### Collective responsibility

With Bure, Mogilny and Linden all declining from their previous production, it was left to left-winger Martin Gelinas, a former Los Angeles Kings first-rounder who is proving to be a late bloomer, to pick up the slack. Gelinas established career highs with 35 goals —to lead the team—and 68 points.

One of the Canucks' most consistent players in the final month was another apparent late-bloomer—forward Lonny Bohonos, who scored eight goals in 16 games following his recall from the minors early in March. Veteran Jyrki Lumme was a pillar on defense.

Renney, who was hired by the Canucks following an outstanding career with Kamloops, a Western Junior League team, and the Canadian national team, admitted that he might have tried to overcoach in his maiden NHL season. But Vancouver general manager Pat Quinn said it was a collective, rather than an individual failing that sank the team.

When the season ended, the Canucks had 15 players eligible to become either restricted or unrestricted free agents, leading to speculation that there could be a number of familiar faces missing when the Canucks open the 1997-98 season with a new team logo— a stylized Orca whale, which ties in to their corporate operations— the club is owned by Orca Bay Sports and Entertainment.

### Burly original

But the guy whose name keeps turning up as the franchise torch-bearer is Pat Quinn. He's an original Canuck, a burly defenseman selected in the 1970 expansion draft, when Vancouver, a new entry that year along with Buffalo, started to stock its franchise. As a player, Quinn left after two seasons, but he

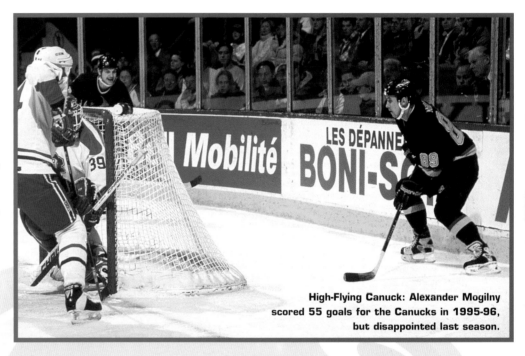

**High-Flying Canuck: Alexander Mogilny scored 55 goals for the Canucks in 1995-96, but disappointed last season.**

returned as general manager in 1987 and later added coaching duties.

Once Quinn returned behind the bench he became the most successful skipper in team history, fashioning a .554 winning percentage between 1992-95. After winning a division title in 1992-93, Vancouver advanced to the Stanley Cup final for only the second time in its history the following year. The first was in 1981-82, when goaltender Richard Brodeur and forward Stan Smyl were instrumental in a stunning upset of Chicago in the Conference championship.

The Canucks spent many of their early years in the shadow of the Sabres, their expansion cousin who, on the spin of a wheel, got the first choice in the NHL entry, and selected center Gilbert Perreault. That left Vancouver with defenseman Dale Tallon, who would not be quite the impact player as Perreault was.

But Vancouver, with Andre Boudrias leading the team in scoring for the second straight year, won its first Smythe Division title in 1974-75, the same year Buffalo was first in the Adams Division.

The signature phrase of Frank Griffiths, the patriarch of the family who formed the Canucks and were its long-time owners, was "2 points", the number awarded to a team for each victory. The two points were easier to come by once Quinn arrived as the GM in 1987.

He engineered an aggressive rebuilding plan, starting with the selection of Linden in the 1988 entry draft and adding another cornerstone—the Soviet League star Bure—in the 1989 draft.

**Captain Canuck: Veteran center Trevor Linden brings grit and skill to the Vancouver lineup, but has been beset by injury.**

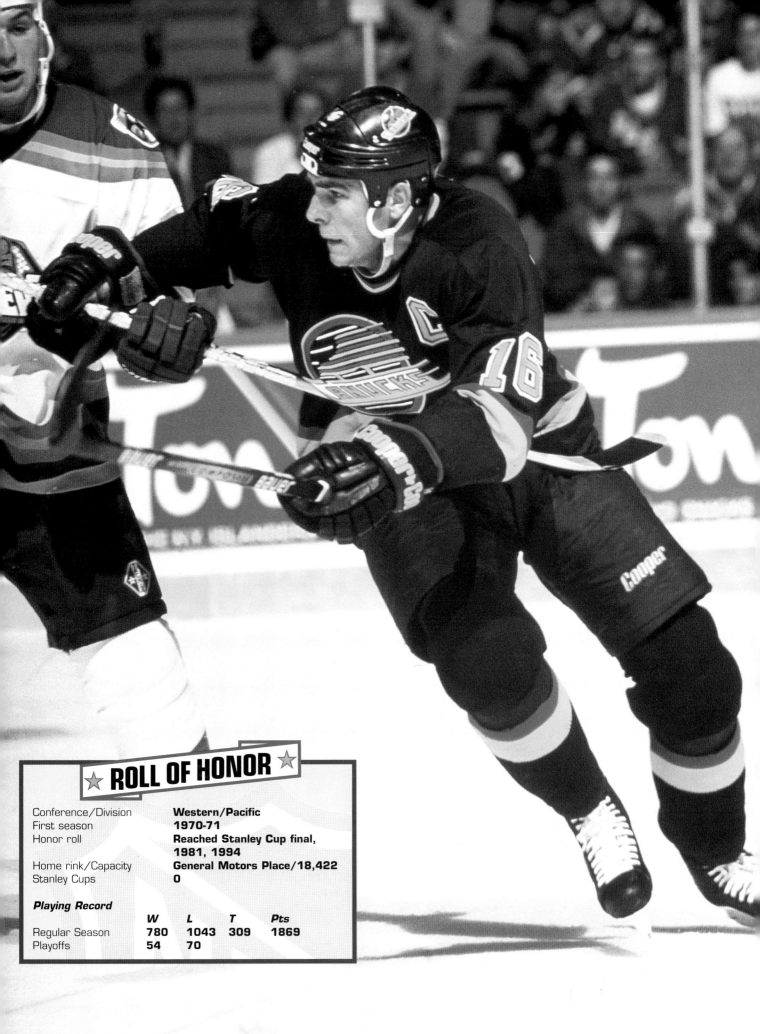

## ★ ROLL OF HONOR ★

| Conference/Division | **Western/Pacific** | | | |
|---|---|---|---|---|
| First season | **1970-71** | | | |
| Honor roll | **Reached Stanley Cup final, 1981, 1994** | | | |
| Home rink/Capacity | **General Motors Place/18,422** | | | |
| Stanley Cups | **0** | | | |

**Playing Record**

| | W | L | T | Pts |
|---|---|---|---|---|
| Regular Season | 780 | 1043 | 309 | 1869 |
| Playoffs | 54 | 70 | | |

# WASHINGTON CAPITALS

The best-laid plans can sometimes go awry. Just ask former Washington Capitals general manager David Poile. In an attempt to ensure the Capitals would reach the Stanley Cup playoffs for the 15th straight year—every year since he'd been the GM—Poile made a number of personnel moves that seemed favorable. He signed free agent defenseman Phil Housley, acquired hardrock forward Chris Simon and promising Russian forward Andrei Nikolishin.

When the club still hadn't solidified a playoff spot as the March trade deadline approached, Poile pulled off a blockbuster trade with the Boston Bruins. He sent goaltender Jim Carey and a pair of prospects for three disgruntled but seasoned performers—center Adam Oates, forward Rick Tocchet and goaltender Bill Ranford.

The Mask: Goaltender Jim Carey gave the Capitals the championship goaltending they have lacked in recent years, but was traded to Boston by GM David Poile.

## Bad deal

Alas, the injury bug which bit the Capitals all season, didn't spare the new arrivals, and all but Oates added to man-games lost because of various mishaps. Some of the injuries were downright bizarre—forwards Steve Konowalchuk and Pat Peake were shaken up when their car was struck by another vehicle while they were leaving the parking lot of the US Air Arena. Only venerable Dale Hunter, the 36-year-old center whose feisty style invites retaliation, played the full 82-game schedule.

To shorten a sad story, the Capitals missed the playoffs by two points, and Poile paid for the shortfall with his job a few weeks after the season ended. "The injuries had a big effect on us," said Washington forward Kelly Miller. "I've never seen that many key players go down with injuries."

Peter Bondra, who managed to stay healthy for all but five games, led all Capitals goal-scorers with 46 goals. That represented more than 21% of the team's output, since no other player who was with the team for the entire season got more than Konowalchuk's 17 goals.

Right from the start of its NHL existence, the only way was up for the Capitals. It could not have gotten any lower for a team that joined the NHL as an expansion franchise in 1974-75 and proceeded to set all kinds of modern-day league records for futility. Most of the records are still in the book, more than two decades later.

But that first year? "It was demoralizing and depressing, but you tried not to have a defeatist attitude," remembers Doug Mohns, an NHL veteran. The 1974-75 Capitals established a record for the fewest points—21—in a 70-game season. Their .131 winning percentage remains the lowest in NHL history. They managed only one victory on the road. In one stretch they lost 17 games in a row, still a record. They went through three coaches, allowed an all-time record 446 goals and one of its goaltenders—Michel Belhumeur (which translated from French means good humor)—appeared in 35 games and was the winning goaltender in none.

## Out of the pit

But climb the Capitals did—incrementally at first as Guy Charron arrived as a bonafide scorer and, finally, beyond the .500 mark and into the playoffs for the first time in 1982-83. That coincided with the arrival of David Poile. Under Poile the Capitals had only two seasons under .500, and captured one Patrick Division title, in 1988-89.

Key draft picks such as sparkplugs Mike Gartner, Bobby Carpenter and Ryan Walter joined with defensemen Scott Stevens, Larry Murphy and Rod Langway—the latter pair coming after big trades with Los Angeles and Montreal—to continue Washington's rise from rags to respectability.

**Capital Gain: Peter Bondra continued his fine, young career in 1996-97, leading his weakened team with 46 goals.**

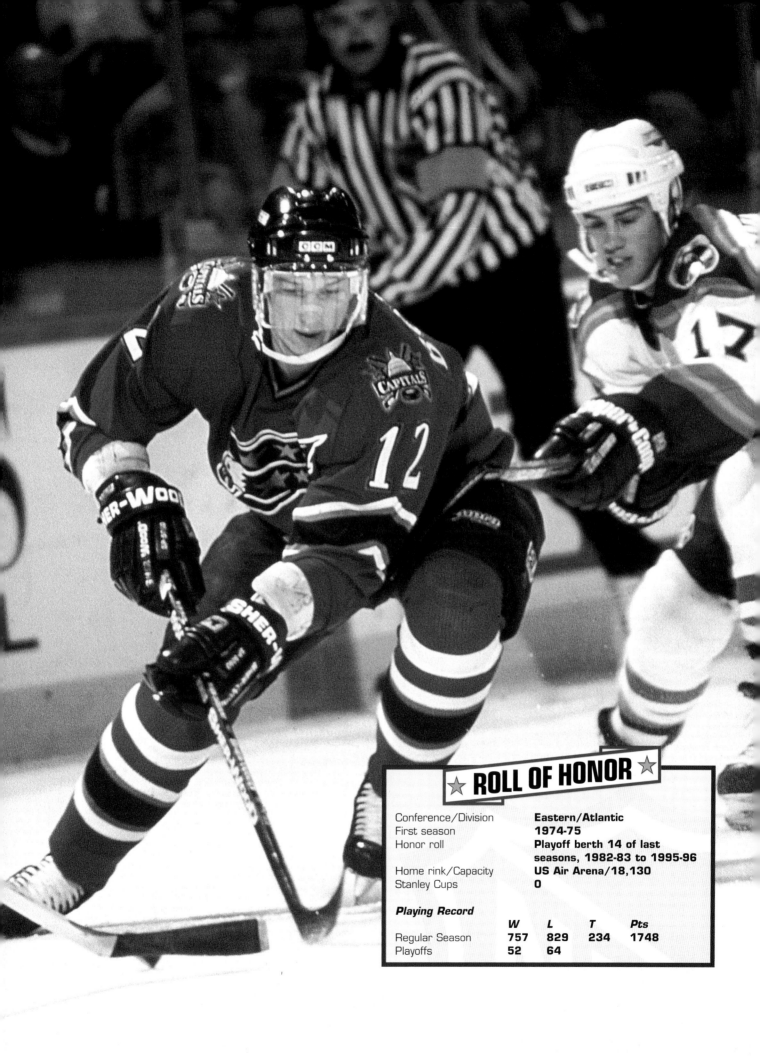

## ⭐ ROLL OF HONOR ⭐

| | |
|---|---|
| Conference/Division | **Eastern/Atlantic** |
| First season | **1974-75** |
| Honor roll | **Playoff berth 14 of last seasons, 1982-83 to 1995-96** |
| Home rink/Capacity | **US Air Arena/18,130** |
| Stanley Cups | **0** |

### *Playing Record*

| | W | L | T | Pts |
|---|---|---|---|---|
| Regular Season | 757 | 829 | 234 | 1748 |
| Playoffs | 52 | 64 | | |

# NHL
# EXPANSION

**W**hen the National Hockey League Board of Governors granted four new expansion franchises, to be phased in by the year 2000, it capped a decade-long project to de-regionalize the sport of hockey in the United States. The project has succeeded beyond the NHL's wildest expansion dreams since it doubled in size from six to 12 teams in 1968.

"Our basic goal is to strengthen the league long term," said NHL commissioner Gary Bettman. "We want to do everything possible to make sure this house we're building has the strongest possible foundation.

"We're delighted with the four new franchises that have been awarded. By the year 2000, we'll be in 21 U.S. markets, a big increase (from 12 in 1990)."

The four new franchises, officially granted on June 25, are: Nashville, Atlanta, Columbus, Ohio and St. Paul, Minnesota. Nashville will begin play in the 1998-99 season, Atlanta will ice a team in 1999-2000, while both St. Paul and Columbus will enter the league for real in the 2000-2001 season.

The NHL has indeed traveled a long way from the Original Six.

Here are thumbnail sketches of the four new franchises:

## NASHVILLE

| | |
|---|---|
| Owner | **Craig L. Leipold and SC Johnson family** |
| Home rink/Capacity | **Nashville Arena/20,840 64 luxury suites/1,800 club** |
| Nickname | **Not selected** |
| Population | **2.1 million** |
| First Season | **1998-99** |
| History | **Minor-league Nighthawks currently playing in Nashville** |

## ATLANTA

| | |
|---|---|
| Owner | **Turner Broadcasting** |
| Home rink/Capacity | **New 20,000 seat arena scheduled to open in fall 1999** |
| Nickname | **Thrashers** |
| Population | **4.3 million** |
| First Season | **1999-2000** |
| History | **NHL expansion Flames played here from 1972-1980** |

## MINNEAPOLIS/ST. PAUL

| | |
|---|---|
| Owner | **Robert O. Naegele, Jr.** |
| Home rink/Capacity | **New arena planned to open in 2000** |
| Nickname | **Not selected** |
| Population | **3.8 million** |
| First Season | **2000-01** |
| History | **Expansion North Stars operated from 1967-68 until 1993-94** |

## COLUMBUS

| | |
|---|---|
| Owner | **John H. McConnell** |
| Home rink/Capacity | **New 18,500 seat arena scheduled to open in 2000** |
| Nickname | **Not selected** |
| Population | **1.95 million** |
| First Season | **2000-01** |
| History | **Minor-league team, the Chill (East Coast League) currently operating.** |

# HOCKEY HEROES

I t's a truism in professional team sports that collective play wins championships. It's no less true that fans come out to watch the stars of the game, to marvel at their virtuosity, as much as to root for a winner.

Across its 79-year history the National Hockey League has produced and continues to produce as richly varied a cast of sporting legends as any professional league in the world.

Each generation of fans, it turns out, has its Golden Age; each new wave of player talent leaves behind indelible memories of sporting brilliance that resonate forever in the collective imagination.

Some of the memories are passed down, like the legend of One-Eyed Frank McGee, who once scored 14 goals—eight of them consecutively—in a Stanley Cup game, a 23-2 drubbing of Dawson City by the Ottawa Silver Seven. McGee's nickname was no joke—he lost an eye when he was struck there by the butt end of a hockey stick.

Keen hockey fans, even the young ones, know of Frank Nighbor, who perfected the poke check, of Fred (Cyclone) Taylor, said to have scored a key Stanley Cup goal while skating full speed backwards, of Joe Malone, who once scored 44 goals in a 20-game season.

They certainly know the story of Lester Patrick, the coach of the New York Rangers, who in a 1928 Stanley Cup game, shed his jacket, shirt and tie and put on the goalie pads, and replaced the injured Lorne Chabot. The Rangers won the game and, later, the Cup.

Patrick was surely one of many stars of his era. The NHL of the 1920s and 1930s boasted names like Syl Apps, Ace Bailey, King Clancy, Clint Benedict, the first goalie to wear a mask, and Howie Morenz, known as the Stratford Streak, and the most electrifying player of his time.

## What's my line?

The 1930s, 1940s and 1950s were famous for the marvelous forward lines that made hockey magic. The Toronto Maple Leafs had the Kid Line, with Gentleman Joe Primeau flanked by Harvey (Busher) Jackson and Charlie Conacher. The Boston Bruins featured the Kraut Line—Milt Schmidt, Bobby Bauer and Woody Dumart.

**Ice Hard: It is hard to find a weakness in the Colorado Avalanche lineup, which combines speed, skill, size and toughness right through the lineup.**

The Montreal Canadiens delivered the Punch Line, with 'Elegant' Elmer Lach centering for Maurice (Rocket) Richard and Hector (Toe) Blake, The Old Lamplighter. Richard was the first to score 50 goals in 50 games, the first to reach 500 goals.

And Detroit, the automobile center of America, assembled the Production Line, with Sid Abel centering for Gordie Howe and Terrible Ted Lindsay, as tough and mean a player as he was skilled.

Stars like Rocket Richard, Henri (Pocket Rocket) Richard, Jean Beliveau, Jacques Plante, Doug Harvey, Dickie Moore and Bernard (Boom Boom) Geoffrion took the Montreal Canadiens to the Stanley Cup finals for ten straight years in the 1950s. They won six Cups, including a record five in a row.

In the early 1960s, goaltender Glenn Hall, defenseman Pierre Pilotte, and fowards Stan Mikita and Bobby Hull, The Golden Jet, made the Chicago Blackhawks a feared opponent.

### Stars on ice

The Toronto Maple Leafs, blending the talents of aging stars such as Bob Baun, Tim Horton and Johnny Bower with the emerging brilliance of Frank (The Big M) Mahovlich and Davey Keon, won three straight Stanley Cups.

Sublime individual feats remained a constant as the NHL expanded, first from six to 12 teams in 1968, then to 14 and 18, on up to its current 26-team membership.

Guy Lafleur's six straight 50-goal, 100-point seasons with the Montreal Canadiens in the 1970s; Mike Bossy saying he would match Richard's 50 goals in 50 games, then going out and doing it in 1981; Denis Potvin breaking the legendary Bobby Orr's goal-scoring and points records. The stars, indeed, keep on coming.

In the 1980s, sprightly Wayne Gretzky kept coming and coming, like a bad dream, his opponents thought. Here was Gretzky, scoring 92 goals, bagging 212 points, both records in 1982, winning the scoring championship by 65-point margin. There was Greztky, winning seven straight scoring titles, breaking the all-time scoring marks of Gordie Howe, leading the Edmonton Oilers to four Stanley Cups in five years.

And suddenly, The Great One had a rival—Mario Lemieux, The Magnificent One, who scored 85 goals and added 114 assists for 199 points in 1989.

As the NHL entered the 1990s, the league's galaxy of stars had become truly international, with names like Jaromir Jagr, Sergei Fedorov, Pavel Bure, Alexander Mogilny, Peter Forsberg and Teemu Selanne taking their place in the pantheon.

As spectacular as the NHL's stars have been for close to 80 years, the best, it seems reasonable to suggest, is yet to come.

**Jaunty Jaromir:** With the retirement of the incomparable Mario Lemieux, the Pittsburgh Penguins will look to Jaromir Jagr to shoulder a larger burden.

74

# The Bruins' Workhorse
# RAY BOURQUE

**B**obby Orr was the ultimate Bruin of the late 1960s and 70s, and Ray Bourque has been Mr. Bruin in the 1980s and 90s. Like Orr, Bourque is a defenseman with sublime offensive skills, capable of changing the tempo of a game on his own. Like Orr, Bourque arrived in the NHL as an élite player who made an immediate impact.

## ICE TALK

"THERE'S NO WAY I'LL LET PEOPLE DOWN BY NOT GIVING EVERYTHING I'VE GOT OR NOT SHOWING UP AND PLAYING HARD. I FEEL EVERYONE SHOULD FEEL THAT WAY. THAT'S JUST MY MAKEUP."

*RAY BOURQUE*

**Bruins' Big Shooter: A perennial All-Star, Bourque thrilled Boston fans at the 1996 game when he scored the winning goal.**

In his rookie season, Bourque scored 17 goals and added 48 assists for 65 points, an NHL record (since broken) for points by a rookie defenseman. Not surprisingly, Bourque was named rookie-of-the-year in the NHL and was named a first-team NHL all-star, establishing a nearly annual NHL tradition. He has been the best defenseman of his era, winning the James Norris Trophy five times in his career.

### Boston centerpiece

In an era of unprecedented player movement—Wayne Gretzky has played for four NHL teams—Bourque has been a fixture in Boston, where he has been the centerpiece player for 18 seasons. He's also been a workhorse on rebuilding Bruins teams that win through the brilliance of Bourque and a handful of others, and the relentless hard work of the supporting cast. None works harder than Bourque, though. He routinely plays 25-30 minutes a game.

Bourque has scored more than 20 goals in a season nine times, including a 31-goal performance in 1983-84, when he totaled 96 points, the most in his career. He also posted a plus-minus record that season of plus 51. That means Bourque was on the ice for 51 more goals by his own team at even strength than the Bruins' opponents scored, a barometer of his effectiveness at both ends of the ice.

A quiet leader who prefers to let his on-ice performance speak for itself, Bourque was named co-captain (with Rick Middleton) of the Bruins at the beginning of the 1985-86 season. He has been the lone captain there since 1988.

In 1995-96, on a Bruins team bothered by injuries to stars like Cam Neely and others, and struggling under a rookie coach, Bourque

found himself speaking up in the dressing room more than he normally wants to. Fearful of hurting his teammates' feelings, he had to force himself to prod the Bruins to perform better.

"It's not something that was easy for me to do," he says. "I had to grow into that role off the ice. On the ice, it's (leading by example) always been easy."

The prodding obviously helped. In danger of missing the playoffs, the Bruins lost just six of their final 19 games to qualify for the Stanley Cup tournament for the 29th straight season.

### Tough times

Bourque and the Bruins had a rougher go in 1996-97, though. After leading all defensemen in 1995-96 with 80 points, Bourque slipped to 50 points and the Bruins failed to make the playoffs for the first time in 30 seasons.

It was a rare absence from the Stanley Cup tournament for the classy defenseman. Since he joined the Bruins, they have twice advanced to the Stanley Cup finals and twice made it to the Eastern Conference finals (semifinals). His 146 points, including 34 goals, in 162 playoff games demonstrate that his level of play does not diminish any in the post-season. The absence of a Stanley Cup championship on his impressively packed résumé is hardly through any fault of his own.

## CAREER RECORD

**Personal**

| | |
|---|---|
| Birthplace/Date | Montreal, Quebec/12-28-60 |
| Height/Weight | 5-11-215 |

**Awards**

| | |
|---|---|
| Calder Memorial Trophy | 1980 |
| First All-Star Team | 1980, 1982, 1984-85, 1987-88, 1990-94, 1995-96 |
| James Norris Memorial Trophy | 1987-88, 1990-91, 1994 |
| King Clancy Memorial Trophy | 1992 |

**NHL Career** — 18 seasons Boston Bruins

**Playing Record**

| | Games | Goals | Assists | Points | PIM |
|---|---|---|---|---|---|
| Regular Season | 1290 | 362 | 1001 | 1363 | 953 |
| Playoffs | 162 | 34 | 112 | 146 | 135 |

## New Jersey's Goalie of the 1990s
### MARTIN BRODEUR
From minor-league goalie to NHL-best claimant in just two years—that's brilliance.

F ate helped goaltender Martin Brodeur get a skate in the door as the No. 1 goaltender with the New Jersey Devils, but his stellar play and nothing but has kept him there.

**Circus Save: Brodeur's spectacular goaltending carried the Devils to the 1995 Stanley Cup. At 25, his best years are ahead of him.**

The year before Brodeur emerged as one of the best young goalies in the National Hockey League, the Devils' goaltending combination consisted of Chris Terreri and Craig Billington, both solid veteran goaltenders.

But Billington was shipped to Ottawa in a trade that brought Peter Sidorkiewicz to New Jersey. Sidorkiewicz, it turned out, had not recovered from a severe shoulder separation and was not ready for the 1993-94 training camp. Enter Brodeur, a promising minor-league goalie at the time.

Brodeur's play was so good as a rookie that he eased Terreri out of the No. 1 job. Brodeur played in 47 games, posted a won-lost-tied record of 27-11-8 and a regular-season goals-against average of 2.40.

As impressive as his regular-season performance chart was, Brodeur was even more brilliant in the playoffs. He posted an 8-9 won-lost mark in the Stanley Cup tournament, with a sparkling goals-against average of 1.95 as he backstopped the Devils to the Eastern Conference Finals.

## Devils' Cup

By this time, Brodeur had not only supplanted Terreri as the top goalie in the Devils organization, he had staked a claim as the best goaltender in the NHL—period.

Brodeur played 40 of the 48 games for New Jersey in the lockout-shortened 1994-95 season, going 19-11-6 with a 2.45 goals-against average in regular-season play.

His playoff performance was spookily brilliant. He played in all 20 of the Devils' playoff games, winning 16, three of them by shutout. All three shutouts came in the Devils' first-round victory over the Boston Bruins, and produced this unlikely linescore for Brodeur: a 4-1 won-lost record; an 0.97 GAA and a .962 save percentage.

The wonder is that the Bruins won a game at all, facing goaltending that stingy.

Brodeur's brilliance carried the Devils' to their first-ever Stanley Cup victory, but it was winger Claude Lemieux who won the Conn Smythe Trophy as the top playoff performer, as he scored 13 goals in New Jersey's playoff run.

## Rink rat

There was a certain resonance about Brodeur playing so well and winning a Stanley Cup on a team coached by Jacques Lemaire, a brilliant center with the great Montreal Canadiens teams of the 1960s and 70s. Lots of Canadian kids are rink rats, but Brodeur grew up hanging around the Montreal Forum, where his father, Denis, was the team photographer for the Canadiens. Brodeur had been just 14 when Devils teammates Stephane Richer and Claude Lemieux had helped the Canadiens win the Stanley Cup in 1986.

In 1994-95, Brodeur was indisputably The Goalie in New Jersey. The Devils traded Terreri and handed the backup role to Corey Schwab. That role was a bit part, really, since Brodeur played in 77 of the team's 82 regular-season games, including 44 straight starts, as the Devils fought for inclusion in the Stanley Cup playoffs the entire second half of the season.

## NHL CAREER RECORD

**Personal**

| | |
|---|---|
| Birthplace/Date | Montreal, Quebec/ 5-6-72 |
| Height/Weight | 6-1/205 |

**Awards**

| | |
|---|---|
| NHL All-Rookie Team | 1994 |
| Calder Memorial Trophy | 1994 |

**NHL Career** — 4 seasons New Jersey Devils

**Playing Record**

| | Games | Wins | Losses | Ties | GAG |
|---|---|---|---|---|---|
| Regular Season | 235 | 119 | 67 | 39 | 2.25 |
| Playoffs | 48 | 29 | 19 | 0 | 1.84 |

# Vancouver's Rocket
# PAVEL BURE

Back after a traumatic injury, he looked set to continue his high-scoring career with the Canucks, but disappointment loomed.

After Pavel Bure's first game with the Vancouver Canucks, the media nicknamed him the 'Russian Rocket' and his brilliant rookie season touched off Pavelmania among the long-suffering Canucks fans.

In Bure, the Canucks finally had landed a superstar to build a true contender around.

The 5-foot-10, 187-pound right winger certainly arrived in Vancouver with pedigree. He first dazzled North American hockey people at the World Junior Championships in Anchorage, Alaska in 1989-90. Playing on a line with Sergei Fedorov and Alexander Mogilny, Bure scored eight goals and added six assists for 14 points to help the USSR win the gold medal in that tournament. He was named the tournament's top forward.

The following year, he helped the Soviets win gold at the World Hockey Championships. He starred for both the junior and senior men's teams in 1990-91 also, helping the juniors win a silver medal and the senior men win the bronze.

### Bure frenzy

The Canucks had drafted Bure in the sixth round of the 1989 entry draft, only to have then-NHL president John Ziegler rule him ineligible. The decision was reversed more than a year later, clearing the way for Bure to join the Canucks.

Three years after Bure was named rookie-of-the-year in the Soviet National League, he scored 34 goals for the Canucks and won the Calder Trophy as the top freshman in the NHL—and

| CAREER RECORD | | | | | |
|---|---|---|---|---|---|
| **Personal** | | | | | |
| Birthplace/Date | Moscow, USSR/3-31-71 | | | | |
| Height/Weight | 5-10/187 | | | | |
| **Awards** | | | | | |
| Calder Memorial Trophy | 1992 | | | | |
| First All-Star Team | 1994 | | | | |
| **NHL Career** | 6 seasons Vancouver Canucks | | | | |
| **Playing Record** | Games | Goals | Assists | Points | PIM |
| Regular Season | 346 | 203 | 185 | 388 | 282 |
| Playoffs | 60 | 34 | 32 | 66 | 72 |

created a frenzy among Vancouver hockey supporters.

In 1992-93, Bure scored 60 goals and added 50 assists for 110 points, becoming the first Canuck ever to score as many as 50 goals and reach 100 points in a season.

Bure snapped off another 60-goal season in 1993-94, slipping to 47 assists and 107 points. He then led all playoff goalscorers with 16, leading the Canucks to the Stanley Cup final, which they lost in a seven-game thriller to the New York Rangers.

Bure negotiated a rich new contract in the midst of the playoff run, which pushed some noses out of joint. Bure obviously had learned that leverage matters in the free enterprise system, another indicator that he was a quick study in adapting to North American life and the NHL.

Some thought the swift, creative Bure too slight to withstand the inevitable physical pounding NHL forwards are subjected to. Owing to his total commitment to his sport, Bure spent his first summers in North America adhering to a severe fitness regimen overseen by his father, Vladimir, a former swimmer and three-time Olympian for the Soviet Union.

### Russian Rocket stalls

Unfortunately, Bure's last two NHL seasons have been disrupted by injuries. Off to a slow start in 1995-96, with seven goals and 13 points in his first 15 games, Bure's season ended early after he was checked by Chicago Blackhawks defenseman Steve Smith. Bure caught a skate in a rut and suffered a torn anterior cruciate ligament in his right knee.

There were early fears that the injury would cut short his pro career, but by season's end Bure was skating again, elevating the hopes of his fans.

They were to be disappointed.

Injuries forced him out of 19 games in 1996-97, when he scored 23 goals and added 32 assists for 55 points. Not surprisingly, the Canucks fortunes sagged as well. They failed to make the playoffs in 1996-97 under new head coach Tom Renney. Obviously, when the Rocket fizzles, so do the Canucks.

**Pavelmania!: The charismatic Bure touched off a fan frenzy in his rookie season, but injuries have marred his performance of late.**

## Defenseman with (Flyers) Wings

*After the Oilers, the Penguins, the Kings, the Red Wings, and the Whalers, the Flyers are now enjoying his high-speed fluid play.*

# PAUL COFFEY

One great shining moment illustrates Paul Coffey's arrival as a world-class defenseman. It was in the 1984 Canada Cup (now World Cup) tournament final—in overtime. Coffey was the only defenseman back on a two-on-one break by Russian forwards Vladimir Kovin and Mikhail Varnakov.

Just inside the Canadian blue line, Coffey went to one knee, used his stick to intercept a pass and, in one motion, swept to his feet and launched a Canadian rush into the Soviet zone. Mike Bossy scored on the play, deflecting a Coffey shot.

It was pure hockey brilliance—thwarting the opposition at one end and scoring on them at the other. It also answered some of the critics who pigeon-holed the swift, impossibly smooth-skating Coffey as a one-way points machine, but a disaster in his own end.

That tournament appearance came after Coffey's fourth National Hockey League season with the talent-laden Edmonton Oilers, in which he scored 40 goals and added 86 assists. His 126 points led not only all NHL defensemen, they placed Coffey second overall in league scoring, an eye-popping 79 points behind teammate Wayne Gretzky's 205 points. Gretzky's brilliance overshadowed Coffey's achievement.

Nonetheless, Coffey's explosive scoring ability, and his seemingly effortless skating skills prompted comparisons with legendary Bobby Orr, the prototypical 'offenseman.' Coffey enhanced his extraordinary skating skills by wearing skate boots several sizes too small and by using an elongated blade, to increase his ability to glide. But it's his ability to make plays at high speed that sets him apart, not merely his speed.

## Goal maker

In 1985-86, Coffey scored 48 goals, breaking Orr's NHL record for goals by a defenseman, and added 90 assists for 138 points, the most by a defenseman since Orr totaled 139 in 1970-71. That achievement earned Coffey his second straight James Norris Trophy as the best defenseman in the NHL, but did not cement his future with the Oilers, the NHL's dynasty of the mid-80s.

Just one season later, Coffey was traded to the Pittsburgh Penguins in a multi-player deal. Edmonton's coach and general manager, was beginning the process of turning over the club's assets—trading those the club no longer could afford for younger, less expensive talent.

The developing Penguins missed the playoffs in Coffey's first year in Pittsburgh, but he was an important part of the first of two straight Stanley Cup victories in 1990-91. He scored 24 goals that season and added 69 assists for 93 points.

A great-offense-no-defense tag continued to dog Coffey, though, and shortly after the mid-point of his fifth season, he was off to Los Angeles, to be reunited with old teammate Gretzky. Just 60 games later, Coffey was off to Detroit in another multi-player deal.

## On the road

Detroit was home for a little more than four seasons, when head coach Scotty Bowman's impatience with Coffey's defensive play resulted in a trade to Hartford.

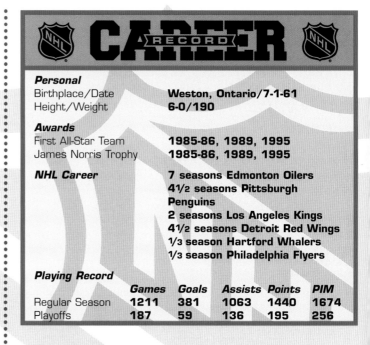

### CAREER RECORD

**Personal**

| | |
|---|---|
| Birthplace/Date | Weston, Ontario/7-1-61 |
| Height/Weight | 6-0/190 |

**Awards**

| | |
|---|---|
| First All-Star Team | 1985-86, 1989, 1995 |
| James Norris Trophy | 1985-86, 1989, 1995 |

**NHL Career**

- 7 seasons Edmonton Oilers
- 4 1/2 seasons Pittsburgh Penguins
- 2 seasons Los Angeles Kings
- 4 1/2 seasons Detroit Red Wings
- 1/3 season Hartford Whalers
- 1/3 season Philadelphia Flyers

**Playing Record**

| | Games | Goals | Assists | Points | PIM |
|---|---|---|---|---|---|
| Regular Season | 1211 | 381 | 1063 | 1440 | 1674 |
| Playoffs | 187 | 59 | 136 | 195 | 256 |

That was just a pit stop, as Coffey was later dealt to the Philadelphia Flyers just in time for their Stanley Cup stretch drive. He helped the Flyers advance to the Stanley Cup finals, but watched, disappointed, from the sidelines after a concussion knocked him out of that series after just two games.

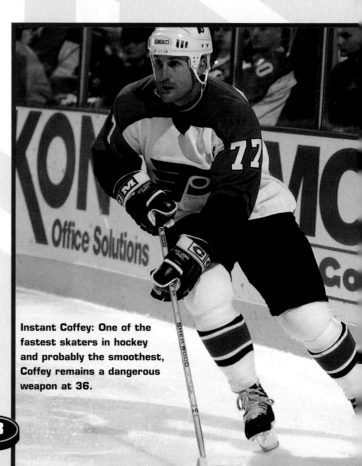

**Instant Coffey: One of the fastest skaters in hockey and probably the smoothest, Coffey remains a dangerous weapon at 36.**

*As part of the Red Wings' Russian unit this poster-boy hockey powerhouse has made a fine team great.*

## ICE TALK

*"FEDOROV IS AS GOOD AS ANYBODY IN ANY ERA SKILLWISE. FEDOROV IS ONE OF A KIND."*

*AN NHL SCOUT*

Squeeze Play: Opponents rarely contain Red Wings star Sergei Fedorov, whom many consider the best all-around player in the NHL.

When Sergei Fedorov arrived in Detroit, the Red Wings already had a No. 1 center—veteran Steve Yzerman. So Fedorov, brilliantly talented offensively, was asked to handle a big part of the defensive load. That would seem a waste. Except Fedorov applied himself to the task and, in his second season in the NHL, he was named runner-up to Guy Carbonneau for the Frank J. Selke Trophy as the league's best defensive forward.

Two years later, in 1994, he won the trophy.

He also won the Hart Trophy that year as the league's most valuable player, was named to the first all-star team and won the Lester B. Pearson Award, voted on by his peers and awarded to the league's outstanding player.

It wouldn't be a stretch to suggest that not only is Fedorov the best all-around player in hockey, but everyone in hockey knows it.

### Russian might

He came to the league with impeccable credentials. As a junior in Russia, he centered a line with wingers Pavel Bure and Alexander Mogilny—one of the most electrifying trios ever assembled.

Fedorov played four years with Central Red Army, and helped the Soviet National team win gold medals at the World Championships in 1989 and 1990.

With his speed, improvisational moves executed at full speed, and all-around game, Fedorov made an immediate impact on the NHL, leading all rookies in goals (31), assists (48) and points (79) in 1990-91. He finished runner-up to Ed Belfour in the voting for the Calder Trophy.

As exciting as his skills are, Fedorov always has understood that even star players perform best as part of an ensemble.

Luckily, his Detroit coach, Scotty Bowman, understands this also. It was Bowman who acquired veteran Russian Igor Larionov and assembled a five-man unit with Fedorov, Vyacheslav Kozlov, Viacheslav Fetisov and Vladimir Konstantinov.

The unit, used selectively by Bowman, a master strategist, performed brilliantly for the Red Wings in 1995-96. Fedorov, ever the team man, moved to right wing on the unit, ceding the center position on the line to Larionov, who centered the famous KLM (Vladimir Krutov, Larionov and Sergei Makarov) for the Soviet National team in the 1980s.

Like the five-man units in the Russian national teams, Detroit's unit stressed puck control and patience, preferring to circle back in the neutral zone, and to hold on to the puck in the offensive zone rather than try a low percentage play.

### Russian light

A crackdown on obstruction penalties by NHL officials enhanced the unit's effectiveness also. Its play, which turned an already fine Detroit team into a special one, was one of the best stories of the 1995-96 season.

Fedorov's spectacular play, sly sense of humor and good looks convinced Nike to make him their poster boy for their hockey equipment. He showcased Nike's new line of skates at the mid-season All-Star Game in Boston.

That might be the ultimate signal of Fedorov's utter assimilation into North American hockey and the NHL. He not only skates circles around his peers on the ice, he outdistances them in the arena of commercial Capitalism, also.

Talk about your Russian Revolution.

## NHL CAREER RECORD

**Personal**

| | |
|---|---|
| Birthplace/Date | Pskov, USSR/ 12-13-69 |
| Height/Weight | 6-1/200 |

**Awards**

| | |
|---|---|
| All-Rookie Team | 1991 |
| First All-Star Team | 1994 |
| Frank J. Selke Trophy | 1994, 1996 |
| Lester B. Pearson Award | 1994 |
| Hart Trophy | 1994 |

**NHL Career** — 7 seasons Detroit Red Wings

**Playing Record**

| | Games | Goals | Assists | Points | PIM |
|---|---|---|---|---|---|
| Regular season | 506 | 242 | 350 | 592 | 346 |
| Playoffs | 88 | 27 | 70 | 97 | 79 |

*Fleury has proved to the Flames that small is not only beautiful, but powerful too.*

In the hyper-macho world of the NHL, size is said to matter above all. Theoren Fleury's entire career has been a refutation of that cliché. Not outlandishly larger than the average thoroughbred jockey, Fleury—swift, skilled, creative and combative—has been a star at every level of hockey. He has forced hockey people, who don't let go of their stereotypes easily, to see past his stature and recognize the dazzling things he can do with the gifts he possesses, to forget about the things he cannot do.

As a junior star with the Moose Jaw Warriors, Fleury was an offensive machine, racking up 472 points in four seasons. In his final year as a junior, he produced 160 points, including 68 goals—and 235 minutes in penalties in the rough and tumble Western Hockey League.

He was a member of Canada's National Junior Team in 1987 and 1988, when the team won a gold medal.

Rarely has a junior player achieved more than Fleury did. Yet he was taken 166th in the NHL Entry Draft in 1987, his low selection an obvious function of his size.

### Playing big

He began his pro career in the minors playing for Calgary's Salt Lake City farm club, but by season's end that year—1988-89—he was playing for the NHL Flames in Calgary, helping them win their first Stanley Cup championship by beating the fabled Montreal Canadiens, and in the legendary Forum, to boot.

In his first full season with the Flames, he scored 31 goals, 30 being a benchmark of excellence.

The following season—1990-91—he bagged 51 goals, establishing himself as a star. He has delivered big scoring numbers every season he has played in the NHL. And playing on a team that has featured bigger, stronger players like Gary Roberts, Brett Hull and Doug Gilmour, Fleury has led the Flames in scoring five of the last seven years.

Fleury continues to shine on the international stage, as well, as he did while a junior. Twice (1990 and 1991) Fleury has played for Canada at the World Hockey Championship, helping Canada win a silver medal in 1991.

### Dream on

In September 1996, Fleury was a member of Team Canada at the inaugural World Cup of Hockey and will probably be among those seriously considered for a spot on Team Canada when the so-called Dream Teams—national teams composed of NHL stars—make their debut at the Winter Olympics in Nagano, Japan in February 1998.

For a guy considered too small early in his career, Fleury certainly has scaled impressive heights in hockey.

**Thwarted Theoren:** Injuries—his own and those of too many teammates—contributed to a sub-par season for Theoren Fleury in 1996-97, following a brilliant performance for Canada in the inaugural World Cup of Hockey.

## CAREER RECORD

### Personal

| | |
|---|---|
| Birthplace/Date | Oxbow, Saskatchewan/6-29-65 |
| Height/Weight | 5-6/160 |

### Awards

| | |
|---|---|
| NHL 2nd All-Star Team | 1995 |
| Co-winner Alka Seltzer Plus Award (league plus-minus leader) —with Marty McSorley | 1991 |
| NHL All-Star Game | 1991-92, 1996 |

### NHL Career

9 seasons Calgary Flames

### Playing Record

| | Games | Goals | Assists | Points | PIM |
|---|---|---|---|---|---|
| Regular season | 649 | 307 | 376 | 683 | 1074 |
| Playoffs | 59 | 29 | 33 | 62 | 96 |

*The Great One teams up with old mates and proves there's plenty of magic in him yet.*

# WAYNE GRETZKY

Perhaps it was inevitable that Wayne Gretzky would wind up, somehow, in New York City. The question a lot of observers had was, how much of his incomparable act remained intact. Plenty, it turned out, to the surprise of more than a few.

After all, Gretzky's quarter-season stay in St. Louis at the end of 1995-96 had been nothing but the Blues. The supporting cast was paper thin and the specter of Gretzky and Brett Hull combining to lead the Blues on a lengthy playoff run simply didn't materialize.

Joining the New York Rangers, rejoining old Edmonton Oilers teammate Mark Messier, turned out to be a far better fit. As young players, Gretzky and Messier had been the linchpins of the Oilers' Stanley Cup dynasty in the 1980s. With a stronger ensemble cast around him in New York, Gretzky was able to quietly go about his business.

Throughout his career, Gretzky has managed to be at once brilliant and unobtrusive, a rare combination.

## Studied foresight

A deceptively swift skater, preternaturally able to anticipate the game's patterns, Gretzky rarely absorbs punishing body checks. And phenomenal energy enables him to play at a high level even in a game's late stages.

He shares with Bobby Orr the gift of redefining the game, making it his own. One skill he brought to the NHL involved setting up behind the opposition's net, where he could see the entire pattern of play in the attacking zone and feed passes to onrushing teammates. His Oilers teammates called this space Gretzky's 'launching pad.'

He led them to four Stanley Cups in five years. The talent-rich Oilers sandwiched a pair of Cups around a surprise cup victory by the Montreal Canadiens in 1986.

"Nine out of ten people think what I do is instinct," Gretzky once said. "It isn't. Nobody would ever say a doctor had learned his profession by instinct; yet in my own way I've spent almost as much time studying hockey as a med student puts in studying medicine."

Gretzky became a hockey demigod in Edmonton. When Oilers owner Peter Pocklington, viewing him merely as a depreciating asset, traded Gretzky to the Los Angeles Kings in 1989, an entire country felt betrayed.

## Sunny revival

But Gretzky became something greater in Los Angeles, he was a marketer's dream. His high-profile presence made it hip to attend Kings games and re-established hockey in Southern California. That, in turn, helped sell the game to warm-weather markets such asSouth Florida, where the NHL had long yearned to penetrate.

The Rangers didn't sign Gretzky to fill Madison Square Garden —it was already full. A Stanley Cup was on general manager Neil Smith's mind when he signed Gretzky. That they fell short certainly was not Gretzky's fault. All he did in 1996-97 was rack up 97 points during the regular season, then score 10 goals and add as many assists while leading the Rangers to the Stanley Cup semifinals. The Great One is a great one still.

**Still Great: Wayne Gretzky silenced whispers of "too old" in his first season with the Rangers—and was their strongest performer during the playoffs, also.**

# NHL CAREER RECORD

**Personal**

| | |
|---|---|
| Birthplace/Date | Brantford, Ontario/1-26-61 |
| Height/Weight | 6-0/180 |

**Awards**

| | |
|---|---|
| Hart Trophy | 1980-89 |
| Lady Byng Trophy | 1980, 1991-92, 1994 |
| First All-Star team | 1981-87, 1991 |
| Art Ross Trophy | 1981-87, 1990-91, 1994 |
| Lester B. Pearson Award | 1982-85, 1988 |
| Conn Smythe Trophy | 1985, 1988 |

**NHL Career**

9 seasons Edmonton Oilers
7 1/2 seasons LA Kings
1/2 season St. Louis Blues
1 season New York Rangers

**Playing Record**

| | Games | Goals | Assists | Points | PIM |
|---|---|---|---|---|---|
| Regular season | 1335 | 862 | 1843 | 2705 | 565 |
| Playoffs | 208 | 122 | 260 | 392 | 66 |

*The son of a star has made his own goal-scoring way to the top in St. Louis.*

# BRETT HULL

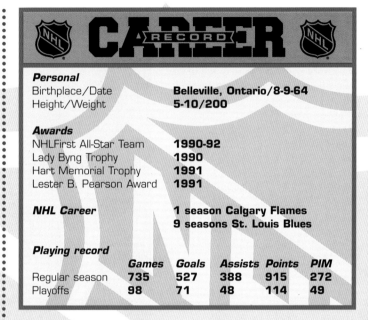

**W**hen Bobby Hull was on the ice, all eyes were on him. Brett Hull plays a different game from his dad. A labored skater, the younger Hull moves quietly around the ice, particularly in the offensive zone, circling into spaces others have left, positioning himself to accept a setup pass. He tries to draw as little attention to himself as possible, laying in the weeds, as the hockey players say. Until, that is, he unleashes The Shot.

By the time the defenders realize it is Hull who is shooting, it often is too late. Possessed of one of the fastest, hardest slap shots in hockey, Hull is a prolific but mostly unflashy scorer. He has been called the NHL's Stealth Bomber.

## Quietly to the top

Similarly, Hull insinuated himself into the NHL élite quietly. Because of his name, the NHL saw Hull coming up through the junior and college ranks, but he was not regarded as a rising star.

The Calgary Flames selected Hull in the sixth round of the 1984 entry draft, an unheralded 117th overall out of the University of Minnesota-Duluth.

In his full first NHL season—1987-88—Hull scored 26 goals in 52 games for the Flames, who traded him before season's end to St. Louis.

With the Blues, Hull was paired with Adam Oates, one of the league's

**Golden Brett: Hull has been The Franchise since he was traded to St. Louis.**

## CAREER RECORD

**Personal**

| | |
|---|---|
| Birthplace/Date | Belleville, Ontario/8-9-64 |
| Height/Weight | 5-10/200 |

**Awards**

| | |
|---|---|
| NHL First All-Star Team | 1990-92 |
| Lady Byng Trophy | 1990 |
| Hart Memorial Trophy | 1991 |
| Lester B. Pearson Award | 1991 |

**NHL Career** — 1 season Calgary Flames  
9 seasons St. Louis Blues

**Playing record**

| | Games | Goals | Assists | Points | PIM |
|---|---|---|---|---|---|
| Regular season | 735 | 527 | 388 | 915 | 272 |
| Playoffs | 98 | 71 | 48 | 114 | 49 |

top playmakers. Hull and Oates quickly became a hit.

Hull scored 41 goals and added 43 assists for 84 points in his first full season with the Blues, but that was merely the warm-up.

In 1989-90, Hull scored 72 goals to lead the NHL in goal-scoring for the first of three straight seasons. The following year his quick-release shot found the net 86 times and another 70 times in 1991-92.

Along with the goal-scoring blitz came official recognition. Hull was a first-team all-star three straight times, won the Lady Byng as the league's most sportsmanlike player and the Hart Trophy as the most valuable player.

## Ups and downs

He was named captain of the Blues, but he had made himself something more important to St. Louis—its franchise player.

The Blues traded Oates, the set-up man, to the Bruins in February 1992, but replaced him with Craig Janney, another able playmaker. Still, some of his fans were disappointed when Hull 'slumped' to 54 goals in 1992-93 and managed 'only' 57 goals in 1993-94. In the lockout-shortened 1994-95 season, Hull delivered 29 goals in 48 games, which pro-rates to 49 goals over an 82-game schedule. Strictly routine for the Golden Brett, some would say.

Head coach Mike Keenan stripped Hull of the captaincy in 1995-96. Nothing personal, he assured people. "The heck it's not personal," Hull said. "It's a complete slap in the face."

Gone, too, was the playmaking Janney, who had been traded to San Jose during the 1994-95 season. In March 1996, Keenan traded for Wayne Gretzky, the ultimate playmaker, but the Hull-Gretzky duo was shortlived. Gretzky left for New York as a free agent at season's end.

Partway through the 1996-97 season, yet another playmaking center was brought in—Pierre Turgeon.

Setting up the Golden Brett, it seems, is a limited engagement.

# JAROMIR JAGR

Jaromir Jagr is the closest thing the NHL has to a rock star. He's young (24), good-looking, and has long, unruly hair, much too long for his helmet to contain. Jagr loves to laugh, too, and who can blame him? There seems little the 6-foot-2, 208-pound forward cannot do.

"He's still so young," says former teammate Rick Tocchet. "He's going to be a force in this league for a long time."

He's already a force, has been since his rookie season in 1990-91. He made the all-rookie team that year, scoring 27 goals and adding 30 assists. He added 13 points in the Pittsburgh Cup-winning playoff run.

He is a fixture as one of the top offensive players in the league. Indeed, in 1994-95, Jagr won the scoring title with 70 points, including 32 goals in the lockout-shortened, 48-game regular season.

More important, he arrived as a mature player, having to step up and shoulder the burden of being the go-to guy for the Penguins. Teammate Mario Lemieux took the season off to recover from his bout with Hodgkin's Disease and chronic back problems.

## Record breaker

Playing the star comes effortlessly for Jagr, who has a long, fluid, deceptively swift skating stride, and he's equally fluid handling the puck. He truly creates art on ice.

"He is a master of deception," said New York Rangers goaltender Mike Richter. "If you try to anticipate with him, you'll often guess wrong. And if you just try to react, he's too fast and you get beat."

In 1995-96, Jagr lifted his artistry to new heights. He and Lemieux became the first pair of teammates in NHL history to score more than 60 goals each in a single season.

On March 28, Jagr displaced Peter Stastny from the record books when he recorded his 140th point of the season, which was also his 60th goal.

The Maestro: Many consider Jaromir Jagr the best one-on-one player in the NHL.

In 1995-96, Jagr and Lemieux separated from the scoring pack early in the season, putting on their own personal scoring race.

But the two were friendly, complementary talents, not rivals. Jagr says he never has felt overlooked, never worried that he was playing Lemieux's shadow.

"No, I never looked at it that way when we were winning the Stanley Cup," said Jagr. "As long as we were winning, nothing else mattered. It's still the same now. I don't need a lot of attention."

## Center Stage

With Lemieux retired, and classy center Ron Francis in the autumn of his outstanding NHL career, though, Jagr figures to receive more special attention than ever before.

Jagr, who potted 47 goals and added 48 assists for 95 points in 1996-97, and Petr Nedved (33-38-71,) are the undisputed leaders on the Penguins offense now.

More than ever before, the Penguins will look to Jagr's unique attributes—too fast for many defenders, too strong for others and more creative than most players, period—to lead them into a new era in Pittsburgh.

The Jaromir Jagr era.

He seems ready to shoulder a mantle that would prove too daunting for all but a few of the NHL's brightest stars.

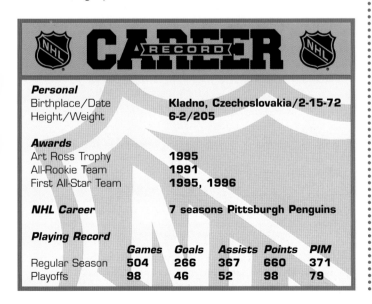

# CAREER RECORD

**Personal**

| | |
|---|---|
| Birthplace/Date | Kladno, Czechoslovakia/2-15-72 |
| Height/Weight | 6-2/205 |

**Awards**

| | |
|---|---|
| Art Ross Trophy | 1995 |
| All-Rookie Team | 1991 |
| First All-Star Team | 1995, 1996 |

**NHL Career** — 7 seasons Pittsburgh Penguins

**Playing Record**

| | Games | Goals | Assists | Points | PIM |
|---|---|---|---|---|---|
| Regular Season | 504 | 266 | 367 | 660 | 371 |
| Playoffs | 98 | 46 | 52 | 98 | 79 |

**A**nyone who glanced at the NHL scoring leaders last December 6 might have been at least a trifle surprised to see the name of Montreal Canadiens center Saku Koivu at the top of the list. But later that night, Koivu tore ligaments in his left knee, and didn't return until February. His absence only further demonstrated how much the Fabulous Finn means to the Canadiens.

Despite missing 32 games last season, Koivu still managed 56 points, including 17 goals in the 50 games in which he appeared. That was 11 points more than he had accumulated a year earlier, his rookie season with the Canadiens.

"He's so strong," says Marc Recchi, Koivu's linemate for much of last season. "People don't understand how strong he is. That's why he can go into the corners and come out with the puck."

When he's not bumping with opposing forwards and defensemen, Koivu is skipping past them, like a water bug skimming the surface of a lake. He has lifted many a discerning Montreal hockey fan out of his or her seat with his exciting style, becoming one of the more popular performers at the new Molson Center.

## Playing tough
That's precisely what Montreal management envisioned when it made the native of Turku, Finland, its first-round selection and the 21st pick overall in the 1993 NHL entry draft. Koivu apprenticed for his NHL debut by compiling 74 points

in only 45 games with TPS Turku in 1994-95, capping the season by helping Finland win the gold medal at the World Championships.

Koivu weighed only 165 pounds when the Canadiens drafted him, but a rigorous training program has since added 15 pounds to his physique, making him even more effective in the rough going.

"I always try to play aggressively," remarks Koivu. "When you go into the corners with any kind of reluctance, your body isn't ready to take a hit. When you play softly, that's when you have a tendency to get hurt."

As a youngster growing up in Turku, Koivu was a big admirer of Finnish compatriot Jari Kurri. Actually, he was fascinated by several NHL stars that he watched on tape.

"Especially Edmonton, with Kurri and Wayne Gretzky," he recalls. "I watched Mario Lemieux. But I didn't copy anyone. I just took bits here and there, and worked on them in practice."

## Heart winner
When Koivu isn't working on improving his hockey skills, he's spending time studying the French language. He already speaks Finnish, Swedish, English, and a bit of German. He's anxious to become fluent in French so he can converse with the people who hail him on the streets of Montreal.

"I have so many things I want to say, that I get a little frustrated not being able to express them," admits Koivu.

Not that he needs to win his way into the hearts of Canadiens supporters. He's already done that by his flashy play, his relentless work ethic, and his spunkiness. Koivu backs down from no one—even when he's flattened by bigger opponents. He is tough to knock down, and even when he falls, he bounces back up in the blink of an eye.

"Keeping my balance on my skates is easy for me," explains Koivu. "I'm small and I do a lot of skating drills. I work on skating on one leg for my balance."

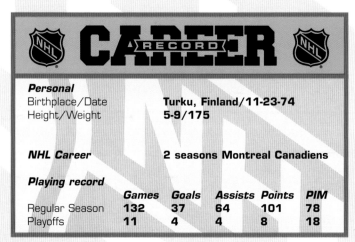

## NHL CAREER RECORD

**Personal**

| | |
|---|---|
| Birthplace/Date | Turku, Finland/11-23-74 |
| Height/Weight | 5-9/175 |

**NHL Career**      2 seasons Montreal Canadiens

**Playing record**

| | Games | Goals | Assists | Points | PIM |
|---|---|---|---|---|---|
| Regular Season | 132 | 37 | 64 | 101 | 78 |
| Playoffs | 11 | 4 | 4 | 8 | 18 |

**Hurt Finn:** Montreal's newest offensive star, Saku Koivu, started the season with flair, but missed almost half the year with a knee injury that laid him—and the Canadiens—low.

*Hungry for hockey and tough on ice, this rock-loving powerhouse excels at golf, works for good causes, and is a superb role model.*

In his days with the Montreal Canadiens, strapping left winger John LeClair was nicknamed Marmaduke, after the playful but uncoordinated comic-strip canine. "John used to fall down a lot," recalled defenseman Kevin Haller, a teammate of LeClair's both in Montreal and in Philadelphia.

"He didn't have real good balance and he wasn't strong on his skates. Now, he's totally the opposite."

Indeed, LeClair, as a member of the Flyers' Legion of Doom line with Eric Lindros and Mikael Renberg, is solid as a rock in every facet of the game. He sends opposing players scattering like bowling pins with his 6-foot-3, 225-pound frame. He has developed into one of the NHL's finest two-way forwards, while at the same time being one of its top sharpshooters, following up on a 51-goal season in 1995-96 with a 50-goal performance last season.

"He is a great two-way player," admitted Renberg. "He's strong in our zone, and along the boards. He's also a great role model for our younger players."

### Rockin' and scorin'

LeClair, the only player from the U.S. state of Vermont to make the NHL, emerged from obscurity with the Canadiens in the 1992-93 playoffs, in which Montreal surprisingly won the Stanley Cup. LeClair scored an overtime goal in both the third and fourth games of the series, which Montreal won in five games. He became the first player to score consecutive overtime game-winners in the Stanley Cup finals since Don Raleigh of the Rangers in 1950.

But LeClair could do no better than a 19-goal output the following season—matching his total of the previous year. Early in the 1994-95 season, with both LeClair and the Canadiens struggling, he was dealt to the Flyers, along with defenseman Eric Desjardins and forward Gilbert Dionne, for the high-scoring Marc Recchi.

The change in scenery had an immediate effect on LeClair. "It was a situation where I wasn't expected to score in Montreal," said LeClair, attempting to account for the transformation. "Here, they put me with Eric and Mikael right away, and it was an entirely different philosophy."

LeClair started to rock, which is an appropriate term for someone who is a huge fan of U2 and 1980s rock music, with more than 500 CDs in his collection. A tireless worker, LeClair improved his skating, refined his already booming shot, and used his imposing frame to create havoc around the net.

"My shot is hard, but a lot of times it's not how hard you shoot it, it's how quick you get it away," explained LeClair. "I think that's one of the things I've really worked on."

### Hungry Flyer

Even as a youngster, growing up in St. Albans, Vermont, which is only a one-hour drive from Montreal, LeClair would spend hour after hour whacking a tennis ball against a shed. That's when he wasn't racing to be the first person in the bathroom each morning, since there were seven people in the LeClair family.

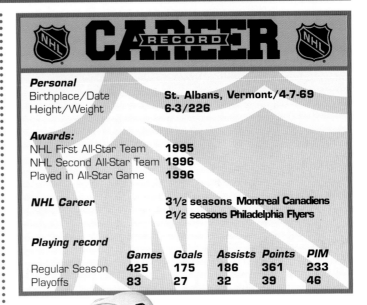

| NHL | CAREER | RECORD | NHL |
|---|---|---|---|

**Personal**

| | |
|---|---|
| Birthplace/Date | St. Albans, Vermont/4-7-69 |
| Height/Weight | 6-3/226 |

**Awards:**

| | |
|---|---|
| NHL First All-Star Team | 1995 |
| NHL Second All-Star Team | 1996 |
| Played in All-Star Game | 1996 |

**NHL Career**

| | |
|---|---|
| | 3½ seasons Montreal Canadiens |
| | 2½ seasons Philadelphia Flyers |

**Playing record**

| | Games | Goals | Assists | Points | PIM |
|---|---|---|---|---|---|
| Regular Season | 425 | 175 | 186 | 361 | 233 |
| Playoffs | 83 | 27 | 32 | 39 | 46 |

Whether it's golf, a sport at which he also excels—according to Lindros, LeClair has Babe Ruthian drives off a golf tee—or the many charitable causes in which he is involved, LeClair has a hunger to succeed.

That passion is evident even at Flyers practices. "Even in practice," remarked Flyers goaltender Ron Hextall, "John is the hungriest guy on the ice wanting to score a goal against me."

**Vermont Wonder: With a 51-goal season in 1995-96, John Leclair established himself as one of the most feared power forwards in hockey.**

# New York's Prime Mover
# BRIAN LEETCH

*In this era of transition hockey, the Smythe-decorated Texan keeps the Rangers' on top.*

A compact package combining quick acceleration and excellent straightahead speed, playmaking brilliance, a hard accurate shot and sound defensive ability, Brian Leetch is a Renaissance player—a defenseman who can do it all.

It was Leetch, lifting his game to new heights of virtuosity, who led the New York Rangers to a Stanley Cup championship in 1994, the club's first in 54 years. He led all playoff scorers with 34 points, including 11 goals. He scored five times in the seven-game final series against the Vancouver Canucks and fully earned the Conn Smythe Trophy as the most valuable performer in the post-season.

## Texas hockey

He'd become the first American-born player—and a Texan, at that— to capture the Conn Smythe.

He joined the Rangers in 1988-89, after a year with the U.S. National team, and an Olympic appearance as captain of the U.S. team. The international experience, coupled with one year with the Boston College Eagles had fine-tuned his explosive raw talent—Leetch was named rookie-of-the-year in his first NHL season.

His numbers dropped off next season, scoring 11 times and adding 45 assists, before being knocked out of action by a fractured left ankle, the first of many disruptive injuries.

But in 1990-91, Leetch re-asserted his claim to being a franchise defenseman by scoring 16 goals and adding 72 assists for 88 points, breaking Hall of Famer Brad Park's team record for most points (82) in a season by a defenseman.

In 1991-92, Leetch totaled 102 points, including 22 goals and won the James Norris Memorial Trophy as the best defenseman in the league. He won the award again in 1996-97.

Some of Leetch's best work last year, though, came before the NHL regular season. He was brilliant for Team USA as the

**On the Move: Leetch's acceleration launches him on rinklength dashes that often result in goals—by the speedy defenseman or one of his teammates.**

Americans upset Canada to win the inaugural World Cup of Hockey.

## Undeterred by injury

Injuries hit Leetch in 1992-93, when he missed 34 games with a neck and shoulder injury. Then he slipped on some ice on a Manhattan street, fracturing his right ankle, and missed the final 13 games that season. The injury was ominous for a player whose game is based on speed, but Leetch achieved a superb regular-season (23 goals, 56 assists) and sublime playoff performance.

He was also strong in the 1994-95 playoffs, generating 14 points (6 goals) in 10 games as the Rangers failed to advance beyond the second round. Since the 1993-94 season, Leetch has not missed a game, an Ironman string of 296 straight regular-season games. His reliability permitted the Rangers to trade the talented, but superfluous Sergei Zubov, and gain Ulf Samuelsson in 1995. He was also one of the reasons Wayne Gretzky signed with the Rangers as a free agent in 1996.

"As much as I've done offensively, I know that to win championships, you need defense," Gretzky said. "The Rangers have great defense. Playing with Brian Leetch was obviously part of the attraction. He reminds me of Paul Coffey."

Leetch's claim to greatness could not possibly be stamped with more authenticity than that.

## ICE TALK

*"I WOULD BEG ANYONE TO ARGUE THAT BRIAN'S NOT THE BEST TWO-WAY DEFENSEMAN IN THE NHL TODAY."*

*RANGERS TEAMMATE ADAM GRAVES*

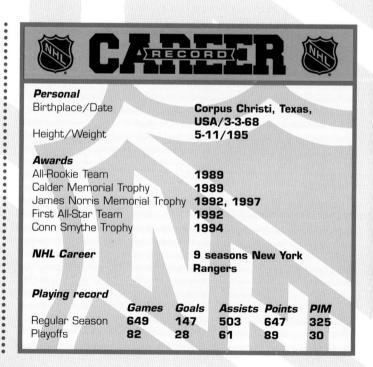

## CAREER RECORD

**Personal**

| | |
|---|---|
| Birthplace/Date | Corpus Christi, Texas, USA/3-3-68 |
| Height/Weight | 5-11/195 |

**Awards**

| | |
|---|---|
| All-Rookie Team | 1989 |
| Calder Memorial Trophy | 1989 |
| James Norris Memorial Trophy | 1992, 1997 |
| First All-Star Team | 1992 |
| Conn Smythe Trophy | 1994 |

**NHL Career**

9 seasons New York Rangers

**Playing record**

| | Games | Goals | Assists | Points | PIM |
|---|---|---|---|---|---|
| Regular Season | 649 | 147 | 503 | 647 | 325 |
| Playoffs | 82 | 28 | 61 | 89 | 30 |

*He combines the finesse of Gretzky, the size of Lemieux and the presence of Messier. Lindros' future is a no-brainer.*

An astonishing blend of fearsome physical strength, speed, skill, rink savvy and unquenchable competitive desire, 6-foot-4, 229-pound center Eric Lindros moved with ridiculous ease up the hockey ladder—junior to international competition to the NHL.

## ICE TALK

**"HIS SOLE FOCUS IS GETTING HIS TEAM TO THE STANLEY CUP."**

*FORMER TEAMMATE CRAIG MACTAVISH*

While still junior age, Lindros helped Canada win the gold medal at the Canada Cup. During that tournament, Lindros knocked rugged Ulf Samuelsson out of action with a devastating body check that was routinely easy for him.

Before he had played an NHL game he had served notice that he was going to be a force. He has lived up to his advance billing.

### The Legion of Doom

Injuries reduced his effectiveness in his first two seasons—yet he still scored 85 goals and chipped in 87 assists in 126 games. Much of that production came while playing on a line with Mark Recchi and Brent Fedyk, both since traded. The line, called the Crazy Eights, was an instant hit in Philadelphia, where fans quickly warmed to Lindros.

But he really hit his NHL stride in 1995 when Flyers coach Terry Murray grouped him with 6-foot-2, 220-pound left winger John Leclair and 6-foot-1, 218-pound right winger Mikael Renberg. As talented as any trio in the league and certainly the best combination of skill and sheer physical power, the line was christened The Legion of Doom.

Lindros totaled 70 points, including 29 goals, in 46 games in 1994-95, tying Pittsburgh's Jaromir Jagr for the points lead, but losing the scoring title, on the final day of the shortened season, because Jagr scored three more goals.

Lindros and the Legion led the Flyers to the club's first division title since 1987 and first playoff berth since 1989. The Flyers lost in the conference final to the New Jersey Devils, the eventual Stanley Cup champions.

The strong performance by Lindros earned him the Hart Trophy as the most valuable player in the NHL, a mantle he assumed with a degree of unease.

**The Big Guy: Lindros defines the team impact player—he can hurt opponents with his size, strength, speed, rink savvy, and his considerable skill.**

"The more people you have carry the game, the better the game's going to be," Lindros said. "When everybody carries it together, it makes it stronger... We've got some great people to carry this game."

### Quebec's loss

Few would appear to have a greater upside potential than Lindros, whose leadership abilities were recognized early in Philadelphia, where he was named captain of the Flyers at 21.

In 1995-96, both Lindros and Leclair took serious runs at 50-goal seasons—Lindros finished with 47, Leclair with 51. The Flyers challenged the Penguins and the New York Rangers for first place overall in the Eastern Conference all season long.

At 24, Lindros has finally grown comfortable with the dominant role foreseen for him when the Quebec Nordiques drafted him first overall in 1991. He refused to report to the Nordiques, forcing a trade to the Flyers, who drained their organizational depth chart to land Lindros, sending eight players and $15 million to the Nordiques.

Nothing anyone could offer the Flyers could pry Lindros away now.

"He's a great player who's going to be greater," said Flyers general manager Bobby Clarke. "I think he started out terrific and he's progressing at the proper rate. He'll be better next year and even better the year after that."

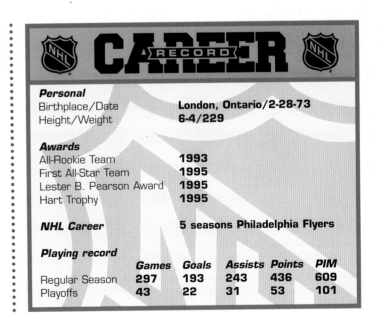

# CAREER RECORD

| Personal | | | | |
|---|---|---|---|---|
| Birthplace/Date | London, Ontario/2-28-73 | | | |
| Height/Weight | 6-4/229 | | | |

| Awards | | | | |
|---|---|---|---|---|
| All-Rookie Team | 1993 | | | |
| First All-Star Team | 1995 | | | |
| Lester B. Pearson Award | 1995 | | | |
| Hart Trophy | 1995 | | | |

| NHL Career | 5 seasons Philadelphia Flyers | | | |
|---|---|---|---|---|

| Playing record | Games | Goals | Assists | Points | PIM |
|---|---|---|---|---|---|
| Regular Season | 297 | 193 | 243 | 436 | 609 |
| Playoffs | 43 | 22 | 31 | 53 | 101 |

Speed defines some hockey players, strength others, still others personify skill. Mark Messier displays ample amounts of all three qualities, but to understand his essence, you start with the glare.

When Messier gets that look, his teammates get into formation behind him and opponents blanch just a little. The glare could translate into a game-breaking goal, a skilful passing play, a bone-rattling body check or even a well-timed, lethal elbow to an opponent's jaw. Messier is the ultimate hockey player: big, fast, strong, skilful and junkyard-dog mean.

The former captain of the New York Rangers is above all an incomparable on-ice leader, the capstone player on any team he has played for. He was a central player on five Edmonton Oilers teams that won the Stanley Cup, a leader on three Canadian teams that won the Canada Cup and indisputably the central force that carried the Rangers to the Stanley Cup in 1994, their first championship in 54 years.

In July, the Vancouver Canucks, hoping Messier could lift them from chronic underachiever status to contender, signed him to a three-year deal worth a reported $20 million. Few could command that kind of money at 36 years of age. But then, few have Messier's portfolio.

### Trail of a giant

He has won two Hart Trophies as the league's most valuable player, one Conn Smythe Trophy as the best individual performer in the playoffs and two Lester B. Pearson Awards as the most outstanding player in the league, as voted on by his peers.

## NHL CAREER RECORD

**Personal**

| | |
|---|---|
| Birthplace/Date | Edmonton, Alberta/1-18-61 |
| Height/Weight | 6-1/205 |

**Awards**

| | |
|---|---|
| First All-Star Team | 1982-83, 1990, 1992 |
| Conn Smythe Trophy | 1984 |
| Hart Trophy | 1990, 1992 |
| Lester B. Pearson Award | 1990, 1992 |

**NHL Career**

12 seasons Edmonton Oilers
6 seasons New York Rangers

**Playing record**

| | Games | Goals | Assists | Points | PIM |
|---|---|---|---|---|---|
| Regular Season | 1272 | 575 | 997 | 1468 | 1572 |
| Playoffs | 236 | 109 | 186 | 295 | 244 |

His individual performance chart reveals impressive statistics: one 50-goal season; six seasons of 100 points or more; more than 100 playoff goals and almost 300 post-season points; a record 13 playoff shorthanded goals.

But the true measure of Messier seems to be how teams he plays for perform. In 1990-91, Edmonton was 29-20-4 (won-lost-tied) with Messier in the lineup, just 8-17-2 without him. In the 1991 Canada Cup, Team Canada coach Mike Keenan extended an eligibility deadline to make room on the team for Messier. Canada won the tournament that year. In 1984, with the Wayne Gretzky Oilers, it was he who won the Conn Smythe Trophy as the most valuable player in the Stanley Cup playoffs as Edmonton won its first Cup in history.

### No rash promise

The most celebrated illustration of Messier's leadership abilities came before Game 6 of the 1994 Stanley Cup semifinals against the New Jersey Devils.

The Devils held a 3-2 series lead, but Messier told a TV audience he guaranteed a victory by the Rangers in Game 6. He backed it up by scoring the hat trick as the Rangers won the game 4-2, sending the series to a seventh game in Madison Square Gardens which the Rangers won in double overtime, the third of three games decided in a second overtime period. Not since New York Jets quarterback Joe Namath guaranteed a Super Bowl victory over the Baltimore Colts in 1969 had a New York sporting hero been so brash, then backed up his boast. Messier's guarantee had profound resonance for New York hockey fans.

The Rangers would need seven games to dispatch a determined and talented Vancouver Canucks team, but the most vivid Stanley Cup memory for many New Yorkers that year was Messier's Game 6 semifinal guarantee. For the élite few unlucky enough to be around for the 54-year duration, it probably was worth the wait.

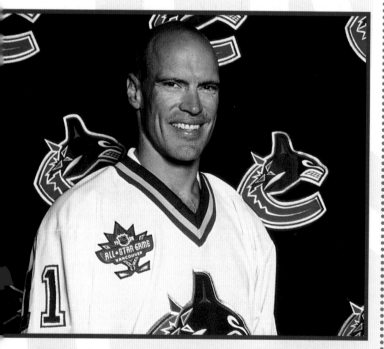

**Money Smiles:** Paying Mark Messier as much as $20 million over three years proved too rich for the New York Rangers' blood, but the Vancouver Canucks believe Messier will pump much-needed vigor into their Stanley Cup aspirations.

# MIKE MODANO

*Handsome, swift and feared as a pinpoint sharp shooter, this lad from Michigan has blossomed with the Dallas Stars.*

As a kid growing up in Livonia, Michigan, Mike Modano would spend plenty of hours in the family basement honing his hockey skills. Often, he would beg his mother to serve as a goaltender and hold up the top part of a garbage can, which Mike used as a target to develop pinpoint precision in his shooting.

The hours certainly weren't wasted. Modano went on to a brilliant junior career with the Prince Albert Raiders of the Western Junior League—232 points in only 106 games in his final two seasons—before the then-Minnesota North Stars made the 6-foot-3, 200-pound center the No. 1 pick overall in the 1988 draft.

Excluding the 1994-95 strike season, Modano has led the team—which moved to Dallas prior to the 1993 season and became the Stars—in scoring for five straight seasons. That string of success started in the 1991-92 season—his third year in the NHL—when he collected 77 points.

His biggest goal-scoring season, however, was in 1993-94 when he became the first center in the history of the franchise to score 50 goals. "I started to improve on my ability to go to the net that season," recalled Modano. "That obviously wasn't a part of my game the first few years, but the more you do it, the more you get used to it."

## Matinée idol

Modano was under a great deal of pressure to produce in the early years. The North Stars had missed the playoffs for two straight seasons prior to drafting Modano, who at the time was only the third American-born player to be selected No. 1. One year after that draft, Modano was a bonafide member of the North Stars, amassing 75 points as a rookie, including 20 points in the Stanley Cup playoffs, as the upstart North Stars went all the way to the final.

Still, Modano was a long ways from refinement. The concern for Bob Gainey, who at the time had the dual role of coach and general manager, was Modano's play in the offensive zone when he didn't have the puck. Gradually, Modano learned to let other players work the puck to him, rather than vacate a good offensive position because of his own impatience and frustration.

Modano's star continued to rise when the North Stars relocated in Dallas. More than a hockey star, he became a matinee

**Michigan Mike: The strong showing by the Dallas Stars during the 1996-97 regular season is in large part due to Mike Modano, their Franchise Player.**

idol, especially when his handsome features found their way into some of the top women's magazines, and Giorgio Armani used him as a runway model. He also became a familar sight on the golf course, taking advantage of the Dallas climate to work assiduously at reducing his handicap, which is getting close to 0.

## Sharpshooting leader

On the ice, Modano blossomed into one of the NHL's swiftest skaters and most feared sharpshooters, to the extent that one team scout remarked, "If Dallas beats you, two things probably happened: they got strong goaltending, and Mike Modano was one of the three stars."

Modano continued to flourish after Ken Hitchcock, a highly successful Western Junior League coach, took over the Stars' coaching reins in the middle of the 1995-96 season. "Too often in the past, Mike worried about things that were out of his control—like who he was playing with," said Hitchcock. "He got too wound up. There is no reason why he can't be a significant offensive force every shift of every game."

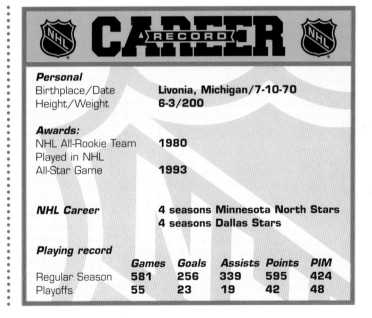

## CAREER RECORD

| Personal | |
|---|---|
| Birthplace/Date | Livonia, Michigan/7-10-70 |
| Height/Weight | 6-3/200 |

| Awards: | |
|---|---|
| NHL All-Rookie Team | 1980 |
| Played in NHL All-Star Game | 1993 |

| NHL Career | 4 seasons Minnesota North Stars |
|---|---|
| | 4 seasons Dallas Stars |

**Playing record**

| | Games | Goals | Assists | Points | PIM |
|---|---|---|---|---|---|
| Regular Season | 581 | 256 | 339 | 595 | 424 |
| Playoffs | 55 | 23 | 19 | 42 | 48 |

**Consistently brilliant, this Russian is a dangerous Canuck.**

# ALEXANDER MOGILNY

**Alex in Lotusland:** When Mogilny was traded to Vancouver, he rejoined Pavel Bure, his linemate in Russia.

The pride of Khabarovsk, Russia, knew at an early age that he had a special talent for hockey. Alexander Mogilny joined Central Red Army and legendary head coach Viktor Tikhonov at age 17 for three years.

Tikhonov formed a line around Mogilny with wingers Pavel Bure and Sergei Fedorov, one of the most explosive forward trios ever seen. As an 18-year-old, Mogilny helped his country win a gold medal at the Calgary Olympics, the youngest player ever to do so.

There seems little doubt that playing under the demanding Tikhonov helped mould Mogilny into the swift, talented winger he has become. There also is no doubt that Mogilny wanted no part of the rigid Soviet system.

### Fresh start

Mogilny defected in May 1989 and joined the Buffalo Sabres, who had drafted the 5-foot-11, 190-pound right winger in the fifth round (89th overall) of the 1989 entry draft.

Wearing No. 89—signifying his draft number and the year of his fresh start—Mogilny wasted no time proving he would make an impact on the NHL. He scored a goal for the Sabres on the first shift of his first game, 20 seconds into Buffalo's home opener against the Quebec Nordiques.

He scored 15 goals and had 28 assists in 1989-90, modest totals for a player of his talent, but understandable given the culture shock and language difficulty he was undergoing.

After back-to-back 30-goal seasons, Mogilny exploded for 76 goals in 1992-93, adding 51 assists and 127 points, seventh overall in the NHL. He scored 27 of those goals on the Sabres potent power play, one that included Pat LaFontaine, Dale Hawerchuk and Doug Bodger. In an ordinary season, Mogilny would have been a shoo-in for the first All-Star team, but in 1992-93 Teemu Selanne filled that position and Mogilny had to be content with a second All-Star team selection. In Game 3 of the Adams Division Finals against the Montreal Canadiens that spring, Mogilny suffered a fractured fibula in his right leg and ligament damage to his right ankle, a setback that seems to have slowed him little since.

### New shores

Following the lockout-shortened 1994-95 season, the Sabres traded Mogilny to the Vancouver Canucks.

The Sabres were offloading some big salaries and the Canucks, on the verge of opening the new GM Place Arena, wanted to add some flash to an already talent-rich lineup to keep the new building full.

The deal reunited Mogilny with Bure, his Central Red Army linemate, but the reunion was postponed after Bure went down with a knee injury early in the 1995-96 season, finishing him for the year.

In 1996-97, Bure again had injury trouble. Fortunately for Vancouver, Mogilny has contributed 86 goals over those two seasons, establishing himself as the undisputed offensive leader on the Canucks.

The prospect of having both Bure and Mogilny healthy for an entire season fills Canucks fans with anticipation.

## NHL CAREER RECORD

**Personal**

| | |
|---|---|
| Birthplace/Date | Khabarovsk, Russia/2-18-69 |
| Height/Weight | 5-11/187 |

**Awards**

| | |
|---|---|
| Second All-Star Team | 1993 |

**NHL Career**

6 seasons Buffalo Sabres
2 seasons Vancouver Canucks

**Playing record**

| | Games | Goals | Assists | Points | PIM |
|---|---|---|---|---|---|
| Regular Season | 536 | 297 | 327 | 624 | 237 |
| Playoffs | 37 | 15 | 24 | 39 | 26 |

## ZIGMUND PALFFY

*Flair and imagination, and a formidable score count, have made Ziggy an Islanders' star.*

Zigmund (Ziggy) Palffy is that much sought-after commodity in hockey—a pure goal scorer, a sniper, a right winger who not only scores in abundance but does it with flair. He's a drawing card on a franchise that is reloading and aiming to recreate the magic that carried the New York Islanders to four straight Stanley Cups from 1980 to 1983.

Palffy attracted plenty of attention at the 1991 World Junior Hockey Championship in Saskatoon, Saskatchewan, while playing with future NHL winger Martin Rucinsky and against such luminaries as Eric Lindros, Pavel Bure and Doug Weight.

Only Bure, with 12 goals and Rucinsky, with nine, scored more than Palffy's six goals at that tournament.

Palffy has lived up to the promise he showed playing on that bronze medal-winning club with the Islanders.

"When Ziggy has the puck, there's a little mystery to the game," says Islanders general manager Mike Milbury. "His greatest asset is his imagination—you just don't know what he's going to do."

### Czech overture

Palffy did not join the Islanders organization full time until the 1993-94 season, preferring to play in the Czech Elite League for two seasons, where he whet the Islanders' appetite by scoring 79 goals in 88 games over those two years.

He then spent the better part of two seasons in the Islanders' farm system before joining the NHL club for good part-way through the 1994-95 season.

In his first full season with the Islanders—1995-96—Palffy led the team in goals (43) and points (87). In 1996-97 he went out and did it again, scoring 48 goals and registering 90 points.

When Palffy scores, he often scores in bunches, too. Over a seven-game span from February 29 to March 12, Palffy scored 11 goals, including back-to-back three-goal hat tricks.

### No pushover

Palffy is no power forward, he's not the big, strong forward like Jaromir Jagr who can dazzle with finesse or simply bull his way past opponents.

At 5-foot-10, Palffy is small by NHL standards, but he's hardly passive. Palffy shows a feisty side if opponents start getting rough.

"He's got an edge to him," says Milbury. "He'll respond to a physical challenge from the other team."

Palffy should take the attention—however distasteful—as something of a compliment. Other teams know they have to stop Palffy when they play the Islanders, even if they have to bend the rules to do it.

It's the price a sniper pays for his brilliance.

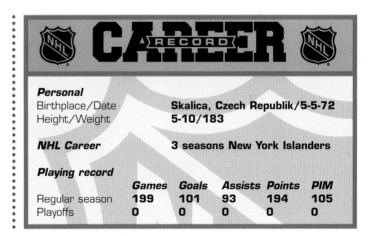

**Zippy Czech:** Ziggy Palffy proved his 43-goal season in 1995-96 was no fluke by scoring 48 more, and 90 points in all, in 1996-97.

## CAREER RECORD

**Personal**

| | |
|---|---|
| Birthplace/Date | Skalica, Czech Republik/5-5-72 |
| Height/Weight | 5-10/183 |

**NHL Career**     3 seasons New York Islanders

**Playing record**

| | Games | Goals | Assists | Points | PIM |
|---|---|---|---|---|---|
| Regular season | 199 | 101 | 93 | 194 | 105 |
| Playoffs | 0 | 0 | 0 | 0 | 0 |

# The Rangers' Good Guy
# MIKE RICHTER

An instrumental force in his team's 1994 Cup win, this goalie's goaltender keeps his cool and always gives his best.

Take it from one of his goaltending brethren: New York Rangers netminder Mike Richter is one of the best around when it comes to winning a big game or series. "There are not many goalers who can win games by themselves, but Mike is capable of doing it," remarked Martin Brodeur, the New Jersey Devils No. 1 backstop. "He did it in the World Cup, and he did it against us."

In the first instance, Brodeur was referring to Richter's stellar play last fall which spearheaded the United States squad to a 2-1 triumph over Canada in the best-of-three series at the first-ever World Cup hockey tournament. The second allusion was to Richter's performance against the Devils in last spring's Eastern Conference semifinal, in which Richter stopped 178 of 182 shots, recorded two shutouts and led the Rangers to a five-game upset of the Devils in the best-of-seven series.

Richter wasn't able to lead an injury-decimated Rangers lineup past the Philadelphia Flyers in the Eastern Conference final, but that didn't detract from the accomplishments of the nimble netminder who grew up a Flyers' fan in Flourtown, Pennsylvania. The Rangers would likely not have got as far as they did without a vintage Richter, who compiled a 2.68 regular-season goals-against average.

## Notorious success

Before the elimination by the Flyers, Richter revived memories of 1994, when he was an instrumental force in the Rangers ending a 54-year Stanley Cup drought. Richter started all 23 of the Rangers playoff games that year, leading the NHL with 16 wins,

posting a 2.07 goals-against average and recording four shutouts, which tied a league record for shutouts in post-season play.

Perhaps Richter's finest moment in that year's playoffs was his 31-save effort in the Rangers' seventh-game double-overtime triumph over New Jersey to win the Eastern Conference finals.

Richter's notoriety earned him guest spots—along with teammates Mark Messier and Brian Leetch—on the David Letterman Show following the Stanley Cup win. Articulate and comfortable as a communicator, Richter, a past winner of the Rangers 'Good Guy Award' for cooperation with the media, was in his element on the popular U.S. late-night television program.

Two years later, Richter was in the spotlight again, when he won the Most Valuable Player Award at the World Cup. With the U.S. team trailing Canada 1-0 in the best-of-three series, Richter made 35 saves in Game 2 as the Americans tied the series and, in Game 3, he kept the U.S. in the game—the team was outshot 22-9 through two periods—enabling it to go on to a 5-2 win in the decisive third game.

## Cool courage

When he's not throwing his body in front of pucks, Richter is deeply involved in social causes. He has won awards for 'Excellence and Humanitarian Concern', and an 'Award of Courage' for his work with hospitals. He has also served as honorary hockey chairman of the Children's Health Fund.

Placid and cool under the constant pressures of trying to stifle some of the game's finest sharpshooters, Richter is equally collected in his approach to his craft. "You have to realize you are probably as good or as bad as the team in front of you," he once explained. "But one of the attractions of being a goaltender is that you are the guy on the spot. There's pressure on everybody, but that's a lot easier to bear than not having the opportunity to deliver under pressure."

**Goalie Winner: Mike Richter's brilliance for Team USA led them to win the first World Cup of Hockey in September. His New York Rangers teammates witness his excellence nearly every game.**

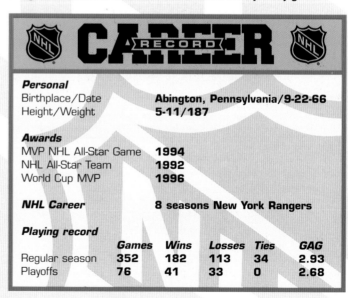

## NHL CAREER RECORD

**Personal**
Birthplace/Date: Abington, Pennsylvania/9-22-66
Height/Weight: 5-11/187

**Awards**
MVP NHL All-Star Game: 1994
NHL All-Star Team: 1992
World Cup MVP: 1996

**NHL Career**: 8 seasons New York Rangers

**Playing record**

|  | Games | Wins | Losses | Ties | GAG |
|---|---|---|---|---|---|
| Regular season | 352 | 182 | 113 | 34 | 2.93 |
| Playoffs | 76 | 41 | 33 | 0 | 2.68 |

<br>

# Mile-High Goaltender
# PATRICK ROY

*Eccentric, miraculous and flawless, Montreal's ex-star has proven his worth in Colorado.*

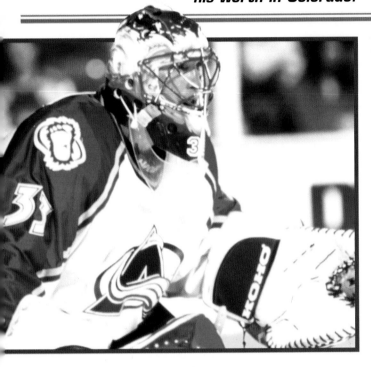

**St. Patrick: Patrick Roy, a demigod in Montreal, was traded to Colorado after delivering an ultimatum to the Canadiens owner last Fall.**

was just this side of miraculous. It's not for nothing the Forum came to be known as St. Patrick's Cathedral during his glory years there.

In 1994, Roy was stricken with appendicitis after two games of the opening-round series against the Boston Bruins and had to be hospitalized. Antibiotics forestalled the need for surgery and Roy rose from his hospital bed to record two straight victories over the Bruins, one a 2-1 overtime thriller at the old Boston Garden in which he made 60 saves.

At his best, Roy is technically flawless, using a butterfly style in which he goes to his knees and splays his leg pads to cover the lower portion of the net, protecting the upper portion with his body and his cat-quick left hand.

### Superstar shock

Roy was Montreal's franchise player, its superstar, so it was stunning on December 2, 1995 when the goaltender, embarrassed by an 11-1 pounding he had absorbed from the Detroit Red Wings, told club president Ronald Corey—on national TV—that he had played his last game with the Montreal Canadiens. Three days later, Roy was traded to Colorado. The Canadiens had ejected St. Patrick from his own Cathedral.

Never mind. Roy would make his new home his shrine. In his first season with the Avalanche, he backstopped Colorado to the Stanley Cup. In 1996-97, he was brilliant again, but the Avalanche were eliminated in the semifinals by the eventual Stanley Cup champion Detroit Red Wings.

The legend of St. Patrick had simply relocated to a new address.

**D**uring games, the rookie goaltender talked to his goalposts, and before each game started, he skated 40 feet in front of his net, turned and stared intently at his workplace, skated hard right at the crease, veered away at the last second, then settled into his work station for another night of brilliance.

Even among goaltenders, who are known for their eccentricity, Patrick Roy was a classic from his first NHL season in 1986.

Roy was magnificent during the playoffs as the Canadiens, with a rookie-laden club, won the Stanley Cup, surprising the hockey world.

Roy won the Conn Smythe Trophy, winning 15 and losing just five playoff games and posting a goals-against average of 1.92. He had staked his claim to the title of the best goalie in the NHL.

The next three seasons, he won the William Jennings Trophy, for the goalie whose team allows the fewest goals against. Three times (1989-90, 1992) Roy also won the Vezina Trophy, awarded to the league's best goalie, as voted on by the general managers.

Roy refined his goaltending technique the hard way. As a junior goalie, playing for the sad sack Granby Bisons of the Quebec Major Junior Hockey League, it was not uncommon for Roy to face 60- or 70-shot barrages.

### Stellar start

When he arrived in the NHL as a regular, Roy was only 20, and had played one single, solitary game in minor pro hockey, but he was seasoned, which he quickly proved.

Roy has been at his best in pressure situations. His stellar play led the Canadiens to three Stanley Cup finals (1986, 1989, 1993), and two Cup championships.

Both those years, he won the Conn Smythe Trophy as the most valuable player in the playoffs. His performance in the 1993 Stanley Cup playoffs, when the Canadiens won ten of 11 overtime games,

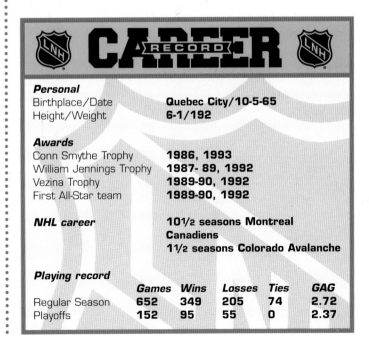

# CAREER RECORD

**Personal**
Birthplace/Date — Quebec City/10-5-65
Height/Weight — 6-1/192

**Awards**
Conn Smythe Trophy — 1986, 1993
William Jennings Trophy — 1987-89, 1992
Vezina Trophy — 1989-90, 1992
First All-Star team — 1989-90, 1992

**NHL career** — 10½ seasons Montreal Canadiens / 1½ seasons Colorado Avalanche

**Playing record**

| | Games | Wins | Losses | Ties | GAG |
|---|---|---|---|---|---|
| Regular Season | 652 | 349 | 205 | 74 | 2.72 |
| Playoffs | 152 | 95 | 55 | 0 | 2.37 |

*This rising star has lived up to his promise, but despite high scores, failed to lift the Avalanche to a second straight Cup victory.*

He's not big, in fact, he's almost small by National Hockey League standards, but Joe Sakic is water-bug elusive, a slick, clever passer, an accurate shooter and perhaps the most unassuming superstar in hockey.

Sakic was a first-round draft pick by the then-Quebec Nordiques in 1987. He was taken 15th overall after a monster season (60 goals, 133 points) with the Swift Current Broncos of the Western Hockey League.

When he joined the once-mighty Nordiques, for the 1988-89 season, they had just finished last in the Adams Division and were about to embark on the darkest period in franchise history. They would finish last overall in the NHL the next three years in a row. Sakic's NHL apprenticeship did not come easy.

## Nordique blues

Sakic was fortunate enough to have Nordiques' star center Peter Stastny around for most of his first two seasons as a role model. Sakic, it turned out, didn't need that much guidance.

He scored 23 goals and added 39 assists for 62 points in his first season, then recorded the first of four 100-plus point seasons the very next year, when he led the Nordiques with 39 goals and 63 assists.

When the Nordiques traded Stastny, their first real superstar, to the New Jersey Devils in 1990, the torch had been passed to the smallish, shifty Sakic. The Nordiques would soon surround Sakic with some of the best young talent in the game.

As the club improved, adding players like Owen Nolan, Mats Sundin, Curtis Leschyshyn, Stephane Fiset, Valeri Kamensky et al, expectations began to soar, also.

In 1992-93, the Nordiques made the playoffs for the first time in five years and drew provincial rival Montreal Canadiens as their first-round opponent. The talent-rich Nordiques won the first two games.

But Montreal goalie Patrick Roy stiffened and the Canadiens stunned the Nordiques, winning the next four games in a row. The critics howled, many of them at Sakic, but the quiet-spoken Sakic took the loss as a learning experience.

The following season, the Nordiques slumped as a team. They missed the playoffs again.

In the lockout-shortened 1994-95 season, Sakic's 19 goals and 43 assists put him fourth in league scoring and the Nordiques finished first overall in the Eastern Conference, then lost to the more experienced Rangers in the opening round of the Stanley Cup playoffs.

## Colorado dawn

In Colorado's first full season in Denver, Sakic collected 120 points, finishing third in the regular-season scoring race. Then he guided the Avalanche to the Stanley Cup, winning the Conn Smythe Trophy as the most valuable player in the playoffs.

In 1997, Sakic was the second-leading scorer in the playoffs (behind Eric Lindros) with 25 points, including eight goals, but it wasn't enough to lift the Avalanche to their second straight Cup victory.

He is a sniper in his prime, but entered the off-season with a shadow of uncertainty over him since he is a restricted free agent, his contract having expired.

**Little Joe:** Sakic suffered through some brutal seasons with a rebuilding team in Quebec, but enjoyed his finest scoring year in 1995-96 in Colorado.

## CAREER RECORD

**Personal**

| | |
|---|---|
| Birthplace/Date | Burnaby, British Columbia/ 7-7-69 |
| Height/Weight | 5-11/185 |

**Awards**

| | |
|---|---|
| All-Star Game Participant | 1990, 1994 |
| Conn Smythe Trophy | 1996 |

**NHL Career**   9 seasons Quebec Nordiques/ Colorado Avalanche

**Playing record**

| | Games | Goals | Assists | Points | PIM |
|---|---|---|---|---|---|
| Regular season | 655 | 307 | 513 | 820 | 261 |
| Playoffs | 50 | 33 | 37 | 70 | 30 |

# TEEMU SELANNE

*After his surprise debut in the NHL as a fully-formed star with the Jets, the Finn is now high-scoring for Anaheim.*

W hen you blend world-class skill and offensive creativity with eye-popping speed, you really discombobulate a defense. That description fits Teemu Selanne perfectly.

Selanne, The Finnish Flash, blazed through the National Hockey League in his first season with the Winnipeg Jets, scoring 76 goals and adding 56 assists to shatter the records for most goals.

### Fully-grown rookie

The 6-foot, 200-pound Finnish speedster zoomed into the NHL in 1994 at 22, two or three years older than the average rookie. To say he made the adjustment from Jokerit in the Finnish Elite League with ease is to understate the magnitude of his achievement.

Selanne recorded his first three-goal hat trick in his fifth NHL game. In late February that season, Selanne scored four goals in a victory over the Minnesota (now Dallas) Stars.

He produced a string of scoring streaks that left Jets fans dizzy: an eight-game scoring streak (nine goals and 11 assists); a five-game goal-scoring streak in which he recorded 11 goals; a nine-game goal-scoring streak in which he scored 14 goals; a 17-game points streak that produced 20 goals and 14 assists. He rocketed through the Jets' final six games, scoring 13 goals and adding two assists.

In his first NHL playoff game, against the Vancouver Canucks, he not only scored a goal, he recorded another three-goal hat trick.

His Calder Memorial Trophy award as the top rookie in the league was expected. Astonishing was his arrival as a fully formed superstar, competing with both rookies *and* the best players.

His 76 goals tied for the league lead with Alexander Mogilny and he was selected as the right winger on the first All-Star team.

### Kid start

Selanne was a mature player upon arrival in North America because he had not hurried his development in his native Finland.

He grew up in the minor hockey system in Helsinki, playing for KalPa-Espoo from the age of five. By nine, he was competing against players two years his senior, and at 16 he joined Jokerit,

## CAREER RECORD

**Personal**

| | |
|---|---|
| Birthplace/date | Helsinki, Finland/7-3-70 |
| Height/Weight | 6-0/200 |

**Awards**

| | |
|---|---|
| Calder Memorial Trophy | 1994 |
| First All-Star Team | 1994 |

**NHL Career**

3½ seasons Winnipeg Jets
1½ seasons Anaheim Mighty Ducks

**Playing record**

| | Games | Goals | Assists | Points | PIM |
|---|---|---|---|---|---|
| Regular Season | 337 | 214 | 237 | 451 | 123 |
| Playoffs | 17 | 11 | 7 | 18 | 7 |

one of the most successful of the teams in the Finnish Elite League for five seasons before he made the jump to the NHL.

"It is good to play there and get better and then come (to the NHL) later, when you are ready," he has said. "I had dreams to play in the World Championship and the Olympic Games before I came here and when I came here, I had done all that. I left with a clear conscience."

It's also clear that the Mighty Ducks plan to construct a championship team around Selanne and Paul Kariya, who give Anaheim one of the swiftest, most highly skilled duos in all of hockey.

The pair combined for 95 goals and 208 points in 1996-97, including 51 goals and 109 points for team leader Selanne.

It seems clear there is plenty more excitement coming from these two marquee players for years to come.

## ICE TALK

"WHEN I WAS YOUNGER, THE NHL WAS JUST A DREAM BECAUSE I DID NOT KNOW HOW MUCH OF A SACRIFICE IT TOOK TO MAKE IT TO THIS LEVEL. BUT WHEN I WAS 18 OR 19, I STARTED HAVING MORE SUCCESS AND THEN MY GOAL WAS TO PLAY IN THE NHL."

*TEEMU SELANNE*

**Finnish Flash:** Selanne left Winnipeg reluctantly, but quickly warmed to life in California, particularly since he was paired with Paul Kariya, another talented speedster.

# BRENDAN SHANAHAN

The Detroit Red Wings were so eager to welcome rugged left winger Brendan Shanahan into the fold that the team delayed a morning practice so that Shanahan, who was on a flight from Hartford following his trade from the Whalers last October 9, could join them.

There were definitely great expectations for Shanahan—and with good reason. While Detroit was the fourth stop for the quintessential power forward, Shanahan had established a reputation as one of the NHL's premier players. Selected No. 2 overall by New Jersey in the 1987 entry draft, Shanahan scored 81 goals in his last three seasons with the Devils prior to being dealt to St. Louis, where he topped 50 goals in two of his three seasons, and then it was on to Hartford, where he had 78 points in 74 games in 1995-96.

Disgruntled in Hartford, Shanahan pressed for a trade because the club wasn't a contender, and the cash-strapped franchise really couldn't afford to keep him. Enter the Red Wings, a team that had both the money and contending status, and needed a productive, strapping forward to put it over the top.

## Fighting start

The October 9 trade saw Shanahan and defenseman Brian Glynn head to Detroit for Keith Primeau, a hulking forward who still hadn't blossomed offensively, veteran defenseman Paul Coffey, and a first-round pick in the 1997 entry draft. "I don't look at this as the end of something," Shanahan said when he learned of the trade. "I look at it as the beginning. The Red Wings' game is to win the Stanley Cup, and that's my game, too."

They were prophetic words indeed. Shanahan fit into the Red Wings lineup like a glove, blending strong physical play—he got into his first fight four minutes into his first game with Detroit—along with a knack around the net to score 46 goals and collect 87 points in 79 regular-season games. He also racked up 131 minutes in penalties.

Shanahan contributed nine goals and eight assists in 20 post-season games, helping the Red Wings end a 52-year Stanley Cup drought. It was mission accomplished, both for Shanahan and the Red Wings, who were still smarting from a four-game sweep by the New Jersey Devils in the Stanley Cup final two years earlier.

## Missing link

Shanahan said watching the Devils, his former team, win the Cup, only increased his yearning to join a contender. "I saw friends and fans I know celebrate that Cup win, and it hit pretty close to home," said Shanahan, who had left New Jersey when St. Louis signed him as a free agent in July, 1991. The Devils were awarded defenseman Scott Stevens as compensation for signing Shanahan. "I really thought I was going to get a Cup win in St. Louis," added Shanahan. But in July, 1995, he was on the move again—to Hartford for defenseman Chris Pronger. To some, the Blues made the trade for economic reasons. Shanahan believes it was because Blues coach Mike Keenan "wanted to bring in his own guys."

In his only full season with the Whalers, Shanahan was named the team captain, a testimony to his leadership abilities. When he arrived in Detroit, he was immediately made an assistant captain to captain Steve Yzerman.

"I know that I am a missing piece of the puzzle," Shanahan said after joining the Red Wings. "But just a piece. I'm not the guy who's going to change things."

His teammates who giddily paraded around the ice at the Joe Louis Arena early last June, as well as the long-suffering Red Wings fans, would undoubtedly dispute Shanahan's claim.

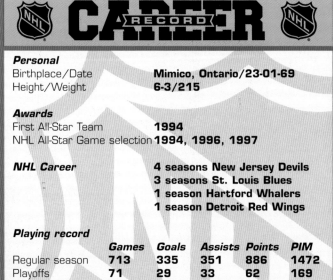

## CAREER RECORD

**Personal**

| | |
|---|---|
| Birthplace/Date | Mimico, Ontario/23-01-69 |
| Height/Weight | 6-3/215 |

**Awards**

| | |
|---|---|
| First All-Star Team | 1994 |
| NHL All-Star Game selection | 1994, 1996, 1997 |

**NHL Career**

4 seasons New Jersey Devils
3 seasons St. Louis Blues
1 season Hartford Whalers
1 season Detroit Red Wings

**Playing record**

| | Games | Goals | Assists | Points | PIM |
|---|---|---|---|---|---|
| Regular season | 713 | 335 | 351 | 886 | 1472 |
| Playoffs | 71 | 29 | 33 | 62 | 169 |

**Puzzle Piece:** Power forward Brendan Shanahan added grit, drive, leadership and offense to the already powerful Detroit Red Wings, who acquired him from the Hartford Whalers.

# MATS SUNDIN

*With his effortless offensive drive, this scorer is set to spearhead Toronto's urgent efforts to rejuvenate its team.*

**M**ats Sundin had franchise player written all over him when he was drafted first overall in the 1989 Entry Draft. As things have unfolded, Sundin has filled that office for not one franchise, but two.

Big, strong, a swift, powerful skater with a hard, accurate shot and an impressive bag of creative offensive tricks, Sundin certainly has the requisite tools to be the key player wherever he earns his pay cheque.

For four years, Sundin was one of the building blocks around whom the Quebec Nordiques were going to surge from the ashes to contend for a Stanley Cup.

But Sundin only had one shot at Stanley Cup playoff action with Quebec (now the Colorado Avalanche). That was in 1992-93, the year Sundin scored 47 goals and totalled 114 points in all, tops on the talent-rich Nordiques, whose lineup boasted Joe Sakic and Valeri Kamensky.

## Tall hustler

The Nordiques won the first two games of their only playoff series that spring against the Montreal Canadiens, but that was it. The Canadiens would ride the goaltending brilliance of Patrick Roy to the Stanley Cup championship that season, while the Nordiques would take a year to recover from the shock. The following season, they missed the playoffs altogether.

For many, a lasting image of that Stanley Cup opening-round failure is that of then-Nordiques head coach Pierre Page yelling in Sundin's ear on national TV as the seconds ticked down on the final loss of the series.

Some fans, too, can be critical of Sundin, whose sublime offensive achievements often appear too effortless.

"Sometimes it doesn't look like bigger guys hustle as much as the little guy who has to take maybe three strides while the bigger guy takes one," Sundin says. "I'm known to have been criticized sometimes, when people say that I'm kind of cruising around or pacing myself. I'm 6-foot-4 1/2, almost 6-foot-5, and I know that when I'm on the ice, I'm always working hard."

**Northern Light: One of the few bright spots for the lowly Toronto Maple Leafs in 1996-97 was the play of Mats Sundin, their offensive leader.**

## Toronto hope

Following the 1993-94 season, Sundin was traded to the Toronto Maple Leafs in a blockbuster trade that sent popular Maple Leafs winger Wendel Clark to Quebec.

If there was pressure in replacing the fan favorite Clark in Toronto, it has not been evident. Sundin has led the Maple Leafs in scoring all three seasons he has played there.

Over that span, Sundin has scored 97 goals, including 41 (and 97 points) in 1996-97, when he was the only bright light in a dismal Toronto season that saw veterans Doug Gilmour, Kirk Muller and Larry Murphy dispatched to other teams as the Maple Leafs desperately attempted to swap aging talent for young prospects.

Only 26, Sundin remains central to the Maple Leafs youth movement—and its future.

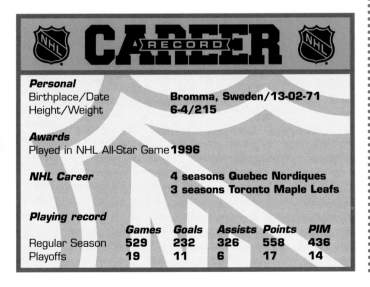

# CAREER RECORD

**Personal**
Birthplace/Date     Bromma, Sweden/13-02-71
Height/Weight     6-4/215

**Awards**
Played in NHL All-Star Game **1996**

**NHL Career**     **4 seasons Quebec Nordiques**
    **3 seasons Toronto Maple Leafs**

**Playing record**

| | Games | Goals | Assists | Points | PIM |
|---|---|---|---|---|---|
| Regular Season | 529 | 232 | 326 | 558 | 436 |
| Playoffs | 19 | 11 | 6 | 17 | 14 |

*The qualities that made this U.S. high-scorer the NHL's youngest captain continue to bolster Phoenix.*

**Captain Courageous: If the Phoenix Coyotes are going to live up to their considerable potential, it will be due to the leadership and talent of players like Keith Tkachuk.**

after Winnipeg matched a five-year, $17-million offer sheet he had signed with the Chicago Blackhawks after he became a restricted free agent. Tkachuk quickly became the fans' target.

Despite the pressure, Tkachuk lived up to the trust shown him when he was named captain by scoring 41 goals and adding 40 assists and staking a solid claim to being one of the best young power forwards in hockey.

But it was in 1995-96 and 1996-97 that Tkachuk really blossomed. He scored 50 goals in 1995-96 and 52 in 1996-97, the franchise's first in its new home in Phoenix as the Coyotes, not the Jets.

The scoring achievement made him just the second U.S.-born player to score 50 or more goals in two different seasons (the other is Pat LaFontaine). Tkachuk, just 24, is poised to set a new standard for scoring excellence for American-born players.

### Smile for the hitman

The 1996-97 preseason was when Tkachuk established himself on the international hockey stage by helping lead Team USA to the gold medal in the inaugural World Cup of Hockey in September.

He scored five goals in seven games and managed to find an outlet for his renowned toughness, too, breaking the nose of Claude Lemieux in a fight.

"There were a lot of toothless smiles around the league," said Phoenix winger Jim McKenzie.

Tkachuk's style always has involved blending physical toughness with offensive skill. He's a brutally effective corner man, and a nearly immovable object when he plants himself in front of the opponents' goal crease to discombobulate the opposition.

His multi-faceted play has provoked many a smile—toothless and otherwise—among the fans in Phoenix.

To long-suffering fans in hockey-crazed Winnipeg, Keith Tkachuk was nothing less than the saviour when he arrived there as a 19-year-old following the 1992 Winter Olympics in Albertville, France.

It did not take him long to demonstrate he belonged in The Show. In his first complete season—1992-93—Tkachuk scored 28 goals and racked up 201 minutes in penalties.

The following season, Tkachuk was named captain of the Jets at the tender age of 21, the youngest captain in franchise history. Being captain of the Jets was no trivial responsibility, and Tkachuk has the grey hair to prove it.

"Try being captain of the Winnipeg Jets at age 21 and see what it does to your hair," Tkachuk once said.

### Making the grade

When he joined the Jets, they were in the middle of one of their periodic rebuilding campaigns but still underachieving, despite the likes of Teemu Selanne and Alexei Zhamnov in the lineup. To make matters worse, the club was in rocky financial shape. Tkachuk, through no fault of his own, put them deeper in a hole

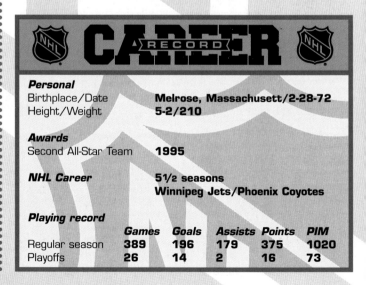

## CAREER RECORD

**Personal**

Birthplace/Date: **Melrose, Massachusett/2-28-72**
Height/Weight: **5-2/210**

**Awards**

Second All-Star Team: **1995**

**NHL Career**: **5½ seasons**
**Winnipeg Jets/Phoenix Coyotes**

**Playing record**

| | Games | Goals | Assists | Points | PIM |
|---|---|---|---|---|---|
| Regular season | 389 | 196 | 179 | 375 | 1020 |
| Playoffs | 26 | 14 | 2 | 16 | 73 |

**This steady, strong offensive power scorer has carved himself a center place in the Senators' strengthening line-up.**

When the Ottawa Senators drafted Alexei Yashin second overall in the NHL Entry Draft in 1992, his name hardly resonated with that city's hockey fans. For starters, the Senators were expected to select Roman Hamrlik, a feisty, skilled defenseman from the Czech Republic.

A lot of Russians were well known to North American hockey fans before they crossed the Atlantic. Not Yashin.

Unlike, for example, Valeri Bure or Alexander Mogilny, Yashin had not made a name for himself as a junior virtuoso. To a lot of Ottawa fans, Yashin was simply the first of a slew of Russians, and other Europeans, claimed in the first round of that draft.

"The greatest thing that ever happened to this franchise was losing a coin flip," John Ferguson, the Senators' director of player personnel at the time, boasted. "Last February I said Yashin would be rookie-of-the-year."

Yashin would not win the Calder Trophy, but he took a run at it, in his own creative, if somewhat methodical fashion.

He certainly isn't the typical Russian player. Compared to speed merchants like Bure, Mogilny and Sergei Fedorov, Yashin's a plodder, strong on his skates, clever with the puck, but no end-to-end flash.

## Interludes in Russia

Yashin, as it happened, was in no hurry to get to Ottawa after he was drafted. Rather than endure the inevitable growing pains of an expansion franchise's first season, Yashin played an extra year with Moscow Dynamo, and joined the Senators for the start of the 1993-94 season, along with another rookie—Alexandre Daigle, the first overall pick in the 1993 Entry Draft.

He obviously was worth the wait. In his first season, Yashin scored 30 goals and totalled 79 points, tops on the Senators that season. He also was a finalist for the Calder Trophy as the NHL's best first-year player.

He managed such a productive season despite the fact that the Senators traded winger Bob Kudelski, Yashin's linemate, who was enjoying a career season, part-way through the year.

The following season, the lockout-shortened 1994-95 campaign, Yashin put together a 44-point season in 47 games, including 21 goals.

Having established himself as Ottawa's top player, Yashin chafed knowing that the under-achieving Daigle was earning far more than he. And so he became a contract holdout in 1995-96. He began that year playing for CSKA in Moscow, and sitting out almost half the season before signing and rejoining the Senators.

It took the big, strong Russian most of the rest of that season to regain the form he had shown as a rookie, yet he still managed 39 points in 46 games for Ottawa.

## Growing strong

In 1996-97, the Senators fortunes improved dramatically. Under general manager Pierre Gauthier and head coach Jacques Martin, both of whom had been hired by the Senators part-way through the 1995-96 season, the club took a run at making the playoffs for the first time in the club's young history.

Not surprisingly, Yashin helped lead the charge, scoring 35 goals and adding 45 assists to lead the Senators in scoring. The Senators set franchise records for victories (31) and points (77), and received strong performances from Daigle (26 goals, 51 points) and sophomore winger Daniel Alfredsson (24 goals, 71 points).

Making their first playoff appearance, the Senators pushed the Buffalo Sabres to seven games before losing

Like the Senators, Yashin, who turns 24 this November, is young and still improving. Slow and steady, but also creative and spectacular, Yashin is the capstone player around whom the Senators are building a legitimate contender.

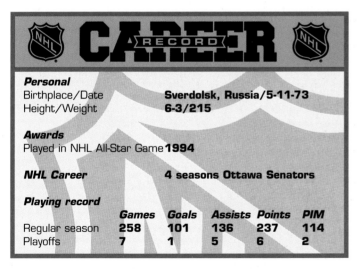

## CAREER RECORD

**Personal**
Birthplace/Date: Sverdolsk, Russia/5-11-73
Height/Weight: 6-3/215

**Awards**
Played in NHL All-Star Game 1994

**NHL Career** — 4 seasons Ottawa Senators

**Playing record**

| | Games | Goals | Assists | Points | PIM |
|---|---|---|---|---|---|
| Regular season | 258 | 101 | 136 | 237 | 114 |
| Playoffs | 7 | 1 | 5 | 6 | 2 |

**Able Alexei:** Yashin's strong offensive contribution was a key reason the Ottawa Senators took a step up toward respectability in 1996-97 by qualifying for the playoffs for the first time ever.

# THE STANLEY CUP
## THE ULTIMATE GOAL

It's known as the National Hockey League's second season and it may well be the most exciting post-season tournament in professional sports. The Stanley Cup playoffs stretch from mid-April to mid-June as 16 of the NHL's 26 teams compete for the Stanley Cup, one of the most cherished pieces of sporting silverware in the world. The champion must win four best-of-seven series—16 games out of a possible 28 in total, all played after the 82-game regular season concludes in mid-April.

This annual North American Rite of Spring has unfolded, in various formats, since 1893, one year after Lord Stanley, the Earl of Preston and Governor-General of Canada, donated the challenge cup to symbolize the hockey championship of Canada.

Lord Stanley returned to England without ever seeing a championship game or personally presenting the trophy that bears his name. He wasn't around when the Montreal Amateur Athletic Association hockey club became the first winner of the trophy. He certainly could not have foreseen that his trophy would become the property of the National Hockey League, which did not exist until 1917 and did not assume control of the Stanley Cup competition until the 1926-27 season.

Still, the rich and colorful history attached to the silver cup that Lord Stanley purchased for 10 guineas ($48.67 Cdn) more than lives up to the spirit of the annual hockey competition he envisoned more than 100 years ago.

The institution of the trophy kicked off a parade of legendary performances. In 1904, One-Eyed Frank McGee scored a record five goals in an 11-2 victory for the Ottawa Silver Seven over the Toronto Marlboros. The following year, McGee scored 14 goals for the Silver Seven, who demolished the Dawson City Nuggets 23-2. The Nuggets had journeyed to Ottawa via dogsled, boat and train to challenge for Lord Stanley's Cup.

Alberta Magic: Few would have guessed that Wayne Gretzky's fourth Stanley Cup in Edmonton would be his last in an Oiler uniform.

### A special time

The quality of competition has tightened considerably since those early days, and transportation is decidedly less rustic, also. But the mystique of the best four-out-of-seven game final series still holds powerful appeal for hockey fans.

The Stanley Cup final can pit speed and finesse against size and toughness, slick offense versus stingy defense, age against youth and, sometimes, brother against brother. The first time that happened was March 16, 1923 when the Denneny brothers, Cy and Corb, and the Boucher siblings, George and Frank, faced off against each other. Cy and George were members of the Ottawa Senators, Corb and Frank played for the Vancouver Maroons. Ottawa won that game 1-0 and went on to capture the Stanley Cup.

In a playoff game between the Montreal Canadiens and the

Cup of Honor: Lanny McDonald (left), the Calgary Flames' bearded veteran, capped off a 16-year NHL career with a Stanley Cup triumph in 1989.

Quebec Nordiques in the 1980s, Montreal's Mark Hunter missed a golden opportunity to pot an overtime winner at one end, then watched, crestfallen as older brother Dale put the game away for the Nordiques (now the Colorado Avalanche) at the other end.

The Stanley Cup tournament is a special event, when there's no time for injuries to heal, so the great ones simply play through the pain, no matter how excruciating. Hall of Fame defenseman Jacques Laperriere once played the finals with a broken wrist, goaltender John Davidson gritted his teeth and played with a wonky knee in the 1979 finals. Montreal left winger Bob Gainey once completed a playoff series against the New York Islanders with not one but two shoulder separations. And in 1964, Toronto Maple Leafs defenseman Bob Baun scored an overtime winner with a broken ankle in Game 6, then played Game 7 without missing a shift. He then spent two months on crutches recuperating. No doubt, the Stanley Cup ring helped soothe his pain.

The Stanley Cup is about unlikely heroes, like Montreal goalie Ken Dryden being called up from the minors to backstop Montreal to a first-round upset over the heavily favored Boston Bruins in 1971, then going on to win the Conn Smythe Trophy, not to mention the Stanley Cup, both before winning the Calder Trophy as rookie-of-the-year the following season.

It's a showcase for the game's greatest stars, like Maurice (Rocket) Richard, who once scored five goals in a playoff game in 1944. Richard's record of six career playoff overtime goals has stood up for 36 years.

### A fitting showcase

In the 1990s, the first round of the playoff tournament has captivated hockey fans, providing some stunning upsets, like the expansion San Jose Sharks knocking out the Detroit Red Wings in seven games in 1994. The Sharks rolled right to the Western Conference semifinal, extending the Toronto Maple Leafs to seven games before losing.

In 1993, the New York Islanders surprised the Washington Capitals in the opening round, then stunned the two-time defending champion Pittsburgh Penguins in the division final, a series victory that helped pave the way for Montreal's surprising Stanley Cup triumph. The Canadiens had fallen behind 2-0 to the talent-rich Quebec Nordiques before winning four straight games to eliminate their provincial rivals from the tournament.

There are those who criticize the Stanley Cup playoffs as far too long, who suggest, not without justification, that hockey is simply not meant to be played in June, taxing the ice-making machinery, the fans' attention span and the players' fitness level.

Few would dare to suggest, however, that the two-month-long tournament is not a fitting showcase for professional hockey. Boring is something the Stanley Cup playoffs most certainly are not.

Lord Stanley never knew what he missed; nor had he any idea how rich a sporting tradition he initiated all those years ago.

# COMING OUT

## Unexpected finalists Minnesota North Stars fell to the Lemieux-led Pittsburgh Penguins offense.

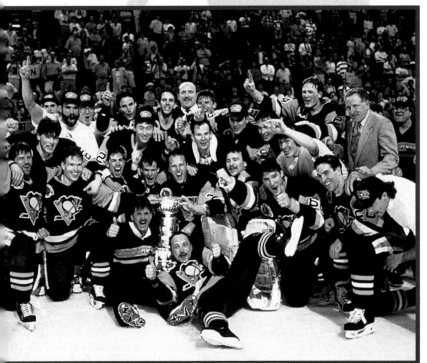

**A New Dynasty?:** When Mario Lemieux led the Pittsburgh Penguins to their first Stanley Cup in 1991 it seemed as if a new era had dawned in the NHL—the Lemieux Era.

This Stanley Cup final matchup was closer than it might have looked. The North Stars were managed by former Philadelphia Flyers great Bobby Clarke and coached by Bob Gainey, the top defensive forward for the great Montreal Canadiens teams of the 1970s. It took a while for the Clarke-Gainey plan to kick in, but it worked almost to perfection in the playoffs.

The Stars had won fewer regular-season games (27) than any of the teams that qualified for the playoffs, but the pieces of the team puzzle fit nicely together in the post-season.

Goaltender Jon Casey was superb, and ably supported by defensemen like Mark Tinordi and Neil Wilkinson. The forwards were veterans like Bobby Smith, Neal Broten, Brian Propp and Brian Bellows, and young stars like Mike Modano, Dave Gagner and Ulf Dahlen. Gainey had the team playing a sound defensive style.

The Stars surprised most just by advancing to the final, having beaten Chicago, St. Louis and Edmonton.

### The Lemieux threat

Most saw this as the North Stars' opportunity to be humiliated by Mario Lemieux and company. Then the North Stars won Game 1.

The Penguins evened the series in Game 2 but they were hardly on a roll. In Game 3, Minnesota grabbed a 2-1 series lead by beating Pittsburgh 3-1.

Lemieux, due to a sore back, didn't play in that game, and just as well—it featured some rough play. Pittsburgh's Stevens received a game misconduct in the third period after he speared an opponent.

Lemieux was back in Game 4, scoring a goal and setting up another as the Penguins evened the series at 2-2 with a 5-3 victory.

The Penguins kicked their potent offense into gear in Game 5, rolling to a 4-0 first-period lead. Lemieux scored the first goal and assisted on both of Mark Recchi's goals as the Penguins outshot the Stars 18-7 in the first 20 minutes.

### First Cup

The Penguins won their first Stanley Cup in Minneapolis, crushing the Stars 8-0 as Lemieux scored once and added three assists. Lemieux led all scorers in the final series with 12 points, including five goals. He also won the Conn Smythe Trophy as the top performer in the playoffs.

1991 is remembered as the coming-out party for Mario Lemieux and his talented teammates. Jaromir Jagr, a brilliantly creative forward, did not score a single goal in his first Stanley Cup final series.

## ★★★★ RESULTS ★★★★

|  | Game | Site | Winner | Score | GWG |
|---|---|---|---|---|---|
| May 15 | Game 1 | Pittsburgh | Minnesota | 5-4 | Bobby Smith |
| May 17 | Game 2 | Pittsburgh | Pittsburgh | 4-1 | Kevin Stevens |
| May 19 | Game 3 | Minnesota | Minnesota | 3-1 | Bobby Smith |
| May 21 | Game 4 | Minnesota | Pittsburgh | 5-3 | Bryan Trottier |
| May 23 | Game 5 | Pittsburgh | Pittsburgh | 6-4 | Ron Francis |
| May 25 | Game 6 | Minnesota | Pittsburgh | 8-0 | Ulf Samuelsson |

# 1992 Stanley Cup Finals
# VICTORY REPLAY

## Mario Lemieux and the Penguins started the playoffs slowly, then rolled to eleven straight victories and their second straight Stanley Cup.

It was the second time around in the finals for Mario Lemieux and the Pittsburgh Penguins, and they were gathering momentum. Down 3-1 to the Washington Capitals in the first round of the playoffs, they reeled off three straight victories to move past their divisional rivals.

Penguins general manager Craig Patrick had tinkered with the lineup. Gone were Paul Coffey and Mark Recchi. In were defenseman Kjell Samuelsson, power forward Rick Tocchet and winger Shawn McEachern, plus veteran Ken Wregget.

Scotty Bowman, who had been the club's director of scouting, had replaced head coach Bob Johnson, who died in November 1991. Bowman had piloted the Montreal Canadiens to five Stanley Cups in the 1970s.

### Tight odds

In Game 1 of the final series, the Blackhawks jumped to a 3-0 first-period lead.

Phil Bourque got one back for the Penguins late in the opening period, but Brent Sutter restored the Blackhawks three-goal lead at 11:36 of the second period. Then the Penguins showed their mettle.

Tocchet and Lemieux sliced the lead to one goal before the end of the second period. And Jaromir Jagr tied the game with his first goal of the finals in the third.

When Blackhawks defenseman Steve Smith was whistled for hooking with 18 seconds left in the game, the Penguins seized the opportunity.

Just 13 seconds before the end of regulation time, Lemieux beat Chicago goaltender Ed Belfour on the power play to win the game for Pittsburgh.

Lemieux was front and center in Game 2, as well, scoring to lift the Penguins to a 3-1 victory and a 2-0 series lead as the final shifted to Chicago Stadium.

### Depth of talent

In Game 3, the Penguins showed that they were fully capable of excelling in a tight-checking playoff game by posting a 1-0 victory.

And in Game 4, they won in a 6-5 shootout as the Blackhawks failed to match goals.

The teams entered the third period tied 4-4, but goals by Larry Murphy and Ron Francis gave the Penguins the cushion they needed.

After their slow playoff start, the Penguins had won 11 straight games, including a semifinal sweep of the Boston Bruins.

Lemieux won the Conn Smythe Trophy for the second straight year, the second player to win the playoff MVP award two straight years.

Emergent Star: Jaromir Jagr arrived as an NHL star in helping Pittsburgh win a second straight Stanley Cup in 1992.

## ★★★★ RESULTS ★★★★

|  | Game | Site | Winner | Score | GWG |
|---|---|---|---|---|---|
| May 26 | Game 1 | Pittsburgh | Pittsburgh | 5-4 | Mario Lemieux |
| May 28 | Game 2 | Pittsburgh | Pittsburgh | 3-1 | Mario Lemieux |
| May 30 | Game 3 | Chicago | Pittsburgh | 1-0 | Kevin Stevens |
| June 1 | Game 4 | Chicago | Pittsburgh | 6-5 | Ron Francis |

# 1993 Stanley Cup Finals
# OVERTIME POWER PLAY

**Goaltender Patrick Roy—St. Patrick to his Montreal fans—backstops the Canadiens to ten straight overtime victories and a surprise Cup.**

## ★★★★★ RESULTS ★★★★★

| | Game | Site | Winner | Score | GWG |
|---|---|---|---|---|---|
| June 1 | Game 1 | Montreal | Los Angeles | 4-1 | Luc Robitaille |
| June 3 | Game 2 | Montreal | Montreal | 3-2 (OT) | Eric Desjardins |
| June 5 | Game 3 | Los Angeles | Montreal | 4-3 (OT) | John LeClair |
| June 7 | Game 4 | Los Angeles | Montreal | 3-2 (OT) | John LeClair |
| June 9 | Game 5 | Montreal | Montreal | 4-1 | Kirk Muller |

**Captain Kirk: Montreal's surprise Stanley Cup in 1993 was due in significant part to the gritty play of Kirk Muller.**

Patrick Roy's legend reached its zenith this year as his goaltending keyed ten straight overtime victories by Montreal en route to their 24th Stanley Cup victory. The Canadiens had upset favored Quebec, swept the Buffalo Sabres and beaten the New York Islanders to reach the final series.

Los Angeles, led by Wayne Gretzky, had advanced past the Calgary Flames, Vancouver Canucks and the Toronto Maple Leafs.

In Game 1 of the Stanley Cup final, Luc Robitaille's two goals powered the Kings to a 4-1 victory. In Los Angeles, this was supposed to be the year Gretzky led the Kings to a championship.

All was going well for them, Roy or no Roy, when catastrophe struck. Canadiens captain Guy Carbonneau had noticed that Kings defenseman Marty McSorley used a stick blade whose curvature exceeded the legal one inch limit.

With just 1:45 remaining in the third period and the Kings leading 2-1, referee Kerry Fraser measured the stick. As 18,000 fans and a vast TV audience watched, the blade was shown to be clearly over the limit. McSorley was banished to the penalty box for two minutes.

During the ensuing power play, Montreal defenseman Eric Desjardins beat Kings goalie Kelly Hrudey to tie the game, sending it into overtime.

Just 51 seconds later, Desjardins scored again, lifting Montreal to a 3-2 victory. The series was tied 1-1.

### Confidence restored

It gave Montreal new life.

When the series moved to LA, the Canadiens twice extended the Kings to overtime.

Twice in a row, power forward John LeClair scored the game-winner.

The Canadiens returned to the Forum leading the series 3-1. The demoralized Kings were frustrated by Roy, whose nearly flawless play infused his teammates with confidence.

In Game 5, McSorley, seeking to make amends for his stick gaffe, scored a rare goal to lift the Kings into a 1-1 tie. It wasn't enough.

Kirk Muller, with the Stanley Cup-winning goal, made it 2-1 before the second period was over and Stephan Lebeau padded Montreal's lead with a power-play goal at 11:31 of the period. Paul DiPietro's third-period goal was merely insurance.

The Canadiens clinched the Cup with an emphatic victory in which the Kings managed just 19 shots—only five in the final period— at Roy.

Roy won the Conn Smythe Trophy as the most valuable player in the playoffs, the second time he won the award.

# 1994 Stanley Cup Finals
# We Won, We Won

## The long-suffering Rangers silenced their many critics by winning their first Stanley Cup championship in fifty four years.

The biggest game in New York's first Stanley Cup triumph in 54 years probably came not in the exciting, final against Vancouver, but in the seven-game semifinal against New Jersey.

It was before Game 6, with the Devils holding a 3-2 series lead, that Rangers captain Mark Messier guaranteed a New York victory to push the series to a seventh game. Then he backed up his prediction with three goals as the Rangers won 4-2 to send the series to a seventh game.

### Team for a win

In the final, Vancouver grabbed a 1-0 lead, winning 3-2, but the Rangers methodically rolled to a 3-1 series lead.

Rangers' general manager Neil Smith had carefully constructed a championship team, blending talented draft selections like goalie Mike Richter, Brian Leetch, Alexei Kovalev and Sergei Nemchinov with veterans acquired through trades.

Messier was the centerpiece acquisition, but the cast of players included ex-Oilers like Glenn Anderson, Jeff Beukeboom, Adam Graves, Kevin Lowe, Craig MacTavish and Esa Tikkanen, and role players such as Stephane Matteau, Brian Noonan and Jay Wells.

The Vancouver Canucks, meanwhile, had built their team around Russian speedster Pavel Bure and Trevor Linden, their on-ice leader, who would have to go head-to-head with Messier.

### An end to waiting

In Game 5, the Canucks spoiled the party at Madison Square Garden by stunning the Rangers 6-3 as Geoff Courtnall and Bure each scored twice. That meant both teams—and the Cup iself—had to make another trip to Vancouver, where the Canucks tied the series, by posting a 4-1 victory.

The final score in Game 7 was 3-2 for the Rangers, but New York was in command of the game, without question.

Leetch and Graves provided a 2-0 first-period lead, and after Linden's short-handed goal sliced the lead to one goal early in the second, Messier responded with a power-play score in the 14th minute that restored the New York lead to two goals.

Linden's power-play goal at 4:50 of the third period gave the Canucks renewed hope, but the Rangers were able to hold them off to bring the Cup back to their fans for the first time since 1940. The victory touched off days of celebrations and tributes to the Rangers.

Defenseman Leetch won the Conn Smythe Trophy, becoming the first American-born player to do so. He led all playoff scorers with 34 points, including 11 goals.

**Broadway Championship: Head coach Mike Keenan piloted the Rangers to the Stanley Cup in 1994, 54 years after their previous championship in 1940.**

## ★★★★ RESULTS ★★★★

|  | Game | Site | Winner | Score | GWG |
|---|---|---|---|---|---|
| May 31 | Game 1 | New York | Vancouver | 3-2 (OT) | Greg Adams |
| June 2 | Game 2 | New York | NY Rangers | 3-1 | Glenn Anderson |
| June 4 | Game 3 | Vancouver | NY Rangers | 5-1 | Glenn Anderson |
| June 7 | Game 4 | Vancouver | NY Rangers | 4-2 | Alexei Kovalev |
| June 9 | Game 5 | New York | Vancouver | 6-3 | David Babych |
| June 11 | Game 6 | Vancouver | Vancouver | 4-1 | Geoff Courtnall |
| June 14 | Game 7 | NY Rangers | NY Rangers | 3-2 | Mark Messier |

# DEVILS' TRAP

## Once described as a "Mickey Mouse" franchise by Wayne Gretzky, the Devils received their due with a stunning upset over Detroit.

| | Game | Site | Winner | Score | GWG |
|---|---|---|---|---|---|
| June 17 | Game 1 | Detroit | New Jersey | 2-1 | Claude Lemieux |
| June 20 | Game 2 | Detroit | New Jersey | 4-2 | Jim Dowd |
| June 22 | Game 3 | New Jersey | New Jersey | 5-2 | Neal Broten |
| June 24 | Game 4 | New Jersey | New Jersey | 5-2 | Neal Broten |

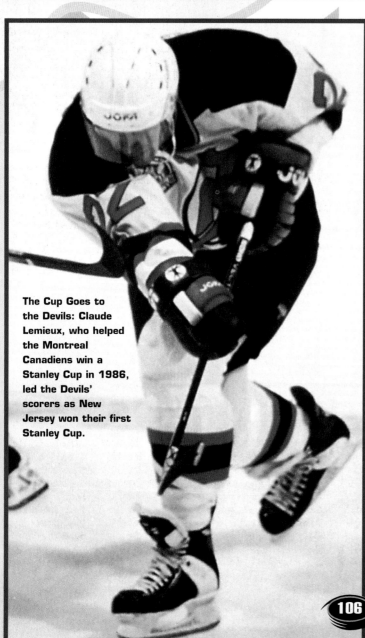

The Cup Goes to the Devils: Claude Lemieux, who helped the Montreal Canadiens win a Stanley Cup in 1986, led the Devils' scorers as New Jersey won their first Stanley Cup.

The New Jersey Devils sprung a speed trap on Detroit in 1995 and stopped the flashy Red Wings dead in their tracks in a too-brief Stanley Cup final series. The trap—known as the neutral-zone trap and designed to choke off an opponent's attack in the neutral zone and create turnovers—couldn't have been a surprise to the Red Wings. New Jersey head coach Jacques Lemaire had the Devils using the delayed forechecking system throughout the lockout-shortened 1994-95 season.

The Devils had no easy route to the final. They had withstood the Philadelphia Flyers, who had dismissed the New York Rangers.

The Red Wings, the top team in the league during the 48-game regular season, had cruised to the final, losing just two games in three series along the way.

But the Devils rode the flawless goaltending of Martin Brodeur, the crashing, banging ensemble work of their forwards and the physical play of defensemen like Scott Stevens and Ken Daneyko to the Stanley Cup. And they made it look easy.

### No chance

In three of the four series games, the Devils held the potent Red Wings—the likes of Fedorov, Yzerman, Kozlov and Sheppard—to fewer than 20 shots. The Wings managed just seven scores in the four games against New Jersey.

In Game 1, Claude Lemieux scored the game-winner in the third period. It was his 12th goal of the playoffs and he would score 13 to lead all playoff snipers before the series was over.

In Game 2, the Devils broke open a 2-1 game with three straight third-period goals for a 2-0 lead.

In Game 3, the Devils raced to a 5-0 lead. Fedorov and Yzerman just managed to score power-play goals within the game's final three minutes.

Game 4 was similarly one-sided, as the Devils held the Red Wings to just 16 shots in winning 5-2 again to capture the first Stanley Cup in franchise history.

Red Wings head coach Scotty Bowman termed the defeat "humiliating."

Lemieux won the Conn Smythe Trophy for his steady playoff scoring, and longtime Devils veterans like John MacLean, Bruce Driver, and Ken Daneyko won their first Stanley Cup after years of struggling in mediocrity.

The Devils gained bragging rights in the all-important New York City media market. Long the forgotten franchise, third in the public imagination behind the Rangers and Islanders, it was the Devils' turn to bask in some Stanley Cup glory.

# 1996 Stanley Cup Finals

# Avalanche on a Roll

**Upstart third-year expansion team Florida Panthers were on a playoff roll to victory until Colorado Avalanche swept their hopes away.**

The Colorado Avalanche and the Florida Panthers were surprise Stanley Cup finalists in the playoff year that will forever be known as the Year of the Rat. Fans at the Miami Arena brought a new ritual to Stanley Cup play—tossing toy plastic rats onto the ice after a Panthers goal. Rats rained down on the Boston Bruins, Philadelphia Flyers, and Pittsburgh Penguins as each was eliminated.

With nightly miracles by John Vanbiesbrouck in goal, a sound, aggressive defensive system, and total commitment to hard work, the Panthers got on an effective playoff roll—first-year head coach Doug MacLean had them believing they could defeat anyone.

But in the final they confronted a team with far more talent, size, speed, and skill than they could contain.

In Game 1, Tom Fitzgerald scored to give the Panthers a 1-0 first-period lead, but the Avalanche's superior firepower showed up in the second period. Scott Young, Mike Ricci and Uwe Krupp scored consecutive goals in a span of two minutes 49 seconds as momentum shifted irrevocably to Colorado.

## Outgunned

The outmanned Panthers were swept aside in Game 2 as Colorado took a 2-0 series lead with a 8-1 win. Swedish forward Peter Forsberg was the scoring star with three goals.

Goaltender Patrick Roy was the key to Colorado's Game 3 victory, a 3-2 squeaker in Miami which saw the toy rats make their first series appearance. Avalanche winger Claude Lemieux, back from a two-game suspension, converted a pass from Valeri Kamensky at 2:44 of the opening period.

Then, at 9:14, Florida's Ray Sheppard prompted the first rat shower, scoring on the power play to tie the game, and Rob Niedermayer scored a 2-1 lead just over two minutes later.

But the Avalanche soon dominated, with Mike Keane scoring at 1:38 and Sakic beating Vanbiesbrouck for the game-winner on a breakaway at 3:00. A brilliant Roy held off the Panthers until game's end.

Game 4 was a festival of saves by both Roy and Vanbiesbrouck—turning away 119 shots between them over 104 minutes and 31 seconds.

Colorado defenseman Uwe Krupp ended the third-longest game in Stanley Cup history when his slap shot from the right point at 4:31 of the third overtime period handed the Avalanche their first Stanley Cup—and the only rain of rats for the opposing team at the Miami Arena.

The rats symbolized a fairy tale Stanley Cup run for the Panthers. Colorado's performance was embodied by their team captain, Joe Sakic, who led all playoff scorers with 18 goals, 16 assists and 34 points, to earn the Conn Smythe Trophy.

Rush for the Cup: Colorado's Valeri Kamensky couldn't solve Panthers' netminder John Vanbiesbrouck on this rush, but in the end it was Patrick Roy of the Avalanche who won the goalies' duel as the Avalanche swept Florida 4-0 to claim their first Stanley Cup.

## ★★★★ RESULTS ★★★★

|  | Game | Site | Winner | Score | GWG |
|---|---|---|---|---|---|
| June 4 | Game 1 | Denver | Colorado | 3-1 | Mike Ricci |
| June 6 | Game 2 | Denver | Colorado | 8-1 | Rene Corbet |
| June 8 | Game 3 | Miami | Colorado | 3-2 | Joe Sakic |
| June 10 | Game 4 | Miami | Colorado | 1-0 (3OT) | Uwe Krupp |

# RED WINGS SOAR

## A dominating total team effort swept Detroit from 42 years of disappointment to a Stanley Cup victory for Hockeytown, USA.

Detroit put 42 years of Stanley Cup disappointment behind it in June 1997 by sweeping away the overmatched Philadelphia Flyers to win their first championship since 1955. In that bygone time, the heroes were the legendary Gordie Howe, Terry Sawchuk, (Terrible) Ted Lindsay and Sid Abel.

The 1997 champions were led by Steve Yzerman, their classy captain, goaltender Mike Vernon, who won the Conn Smythe Trophy as the most valuable player in the playoffs, and Sergei Fedorov.

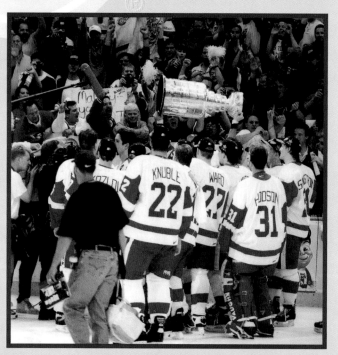

**Worth the Wait: It had been 42 years since the Red Wings and their fans shared a Stanley Cup moment, so the Joe Louis Arena faithful and their heroes savored the thrill of ultimate victory in grand style.**

But, just as the Red Wings had suffered an embarrassing collective collapse in 1995 when the New Jersey Devils swept them in four straight in the Stanley Cup final series, this time their dominance over the Flyers was a total team effort, as well.

As frequently happens in the Stanley Cup playoffs, unlikely heroes emerged and shone brightly for the Red Wings and their Hall of Fame head coach, Scotty Bowman.

### Rising to the occasion

In Game 1, the Red Wings grabbed a 2-0 lead on a pair of Flyers defensive lapses. On the first, checking line center Kris Draper stripped Flyers captain Eric Lindros of the puck and sped away on a two-on-nothing break with Kirk Maltby during a Flyers power play. The pair of speedy Wings exchanged passes before Maltby finished off the rush by lifting a shot over a spread-eagled Ron Hextall to give the Wings an early lead.

On the second goal Philadelphia defenseman Kjell Samuelsson made an ill-conceived pass that Joey Kocur intercepted just inside the Flyers' blue line. He then danced in, with Yzerman along as a decoy. Hextall guessed that the modestly talented Kocur would pass to the future Hall of Famer Yzerman. Instead, Kocur held the puck and flicked a shot high over Hextall, and it was 2-0.

Detroit's fourth goal of the game, scored on a routine shot from just inside the blue line by Steve Yzerman, had the biggest impact on the series, though. That goal apparently convinced Philadelphia head coach Terry Murray to switch to backup goalie Garth Snow for the second game of the series.

Snow didn't last long. He, too, was victimized on a pair of long-range shots as Detroit lost Game 2.

Hextall was back in goal for Game 3, when Detroit's offensive gears meshed smoothly, and the Red Wings whacked the Flyers 6-1. The next day, Flyers coach Murray suggested his players were "choking" in an apparent attempt to motivate his overmatched team.

The Flyers, who held the lead in the series for just two minutes, certainly brought more intensity to Game 4 of the series, but to little avail.

The coup de grace was applied by unlikely scoring hero Darren McCarty, who scored the Cup-winning goal on a sublime rush on which he feinted magically past Flyers defenseman Janne Niinimaa, then swept the puck past a sliding Hextall on the backhand.

This prompted a dance of ecstasy by McCarty, a foreshadowing of a night-long party by the long-suffering Detroit fans.

Finally, the Stanley Cup had come back to stay, for a while at least, in the city that bills itself as Hockeytown, USA.

## ★★★★★ RESULTS ★★★★★

| | Game | Site | Winner | Score | GWG |
|---|---|---|---|---|---|
| May 31 | Game 1 | Philadelphia | Detroit | 4-2 | Sergei Fedorov |
| June 3 | Game 2 | Philadelphia | Detroit | 4-2 | Kirk Maltby |
| June 5 | Game 3 | Detroit | Detroit | 6-1 | Sergei Fedorov |
| June 7 | Game 4 | Detroit | Detroit | 2-1 | Darren McCarty |

# Stanley Cup Results 1927-1997 (NHL assumed control of the Cup in 1927)

| Year | W/L | Winner | Coach | Runner-up | Coach |
|------|-----|--------|-------|-----------|-------|
| 1997 | 4-0 | Detroit | Scott Bowman | Philadelphia | Terry Murray |
| 1996 | 4-0 | Colorado | Marc Crawford | Florida | Doug MacLean |
| 1995 | 4-0 | NJ Devils | Jacques Lemaire | Detroit | Scott Bowman |
| 1994 | 4-3 | NY Rangers | Mike Keenan | Vancouver | Pat Quinn |
| 1993 | 4-1 | Montreal | Jacques Demers | LA Kings | Barry Melrose |
| 1992 | 4-0 | Pittsburgh | Scott Bowman | Chicago | Mike Keenan |
| 1991 | 4-2 | Pittsburgh | Bob Johnson | Minnesota | Bob Gainey |
| 1990 | 4-1 | Edmonton | John Muckler | Boston | Mike Milbury |
| 1989 | 4-2 | Calgary | Terry Crisp | Montreal | Pat Burns |
| 1988 | 4-0 | Edmonton | Glen Sather | Boston | Terry O'Reilly |
| 1987 | 4-3 | Edmonton | Glen Sather | Philadelphia | Mike Keenan |
| 1986 | 4-1 | Montreal | Jean Perron | Calgary | Bob Johnson |
| 1985 | 4-1 | Edmonton | Glen Sather | Philadelphia | Mike Keenan |
| 1984 | 4-1 | Edmonton | Glen Sather | NY Islanders | Al Arbour |
| 1983 | 4-0 | NY Islanders | Al Arbour | Edmonton | Glen Sather |
| 1982 | 4-0 | NY Islanders | Al Arbour | Vancouver | Roger Neilson |
| 1981 | 4-1 | NY Islanders | Al Arbour | Minnesota | Glen Sonmor |
| 1980 | 4-2 | NY Islanders | Al Arbour | Philadelphia | Pat Quinn |
| 1979 | 4-1 | Montreal | Scott Bowman | NY Rangers | Fred Shero |
| 1978 | 4-2 | Montreal | Scott Bowman | Boston | Don Cherry |
| 1977 | 4-0 | Montreal | Scott Bowman | Boston | Don Cherry |
| 1976 | 4-0 | Montreal | Scott Bowman | Philadelphia | Fred Shero |
| 1975 | 4-2 | Philadelphia | Fred Shero | Buffalo | Floyd Smith |
| 1974 | 4-2 | Philadelphia | Fred Shero | Boston | Bep Guidolin |
| 1973 | 4-2 | Montreal | Scott Bowman | Chicago | Billy Reay |
| 1972 | 4-2 | Boston | Tom Johnson | NY Rangers | Emile Francis |
| 1971 | 4-3 | Montreal | Al McNeil | Chicago | Billy Reay |
| 1970 | 4-0 | Boston | Harry Sinden | St. Louis | Scott Bowman |
| 1969 | 4-0 | Montreal | Claude Ruel | St. Louis | Scott Bowman |
| 1968 | 4-0 | Montreal | Toe Blake | St. Louis | Scott Bowman |
| 1967 | 4-2 | Toronto | Punch Imlach | Montreal | Toe Blake |
| 1966 | 4-2 | Montreal | Toe Blake | Detroit | Sid Abel |
| 1965 | 4-3 | Montreal | Toe Blake | Chicago | Billy Reay |
| 1964 | 4-3 | Toronto | Punch Imlach | Detroit | Sid Abel |
| 1963 | 4-1 | Toronto | Punch Imlach | Detroit | Sid Abel |
| 1962 | 4-2 | Toronto | Punch Imlach | Chicago | Rudy Pilous |
| 1961 | 4-1 | Chicago | Rudy Pilous | Detroit | Sid Abel |
| 1960 | 4-3 | Montreal | Toe Blake | Toronto | Punch Imlach |
| 1959 | 4-1 | Montreal | Toe Blake | Toronto | Punch Imlach |
| 1958 | 4-2 | Montreal | Toe Blake | Boston | Milt Schmidt |
| 1957 | 4-1 | Montreal | Toe Blake | Boston | Milt Schmidt |
| 1956 | 4-1 | Montreal | Toe Blake | Detroit | Jimmy Skinner |
| 1955 | 4-3 | Detroit | Jimmy Skinner | Montreal | Dick Irvin |
| 1954 | 4-3 | Detroit | Tommy Ivan | Montreal | Dick Irvin |
| 1953 | 4-1 | Montreal | Dick Irvin | Boston | Lynn Patrick |
| 1952 | 4-0 | Detroit | Tommy Ivan | Montreal | Dick Irvin |
| 1951 | 4-1 | Toronto | Joe Primeau | Montreal | Dick Irvin |
| 1950 | 4-3 | Detroit | Tommy Ivan | NY Rangers | Lynn Patrick |
| 1949 | 4-0 | Toronto | Hap Day | Detroit | Tommy Ivan |
| 1948 | 4-0 | Toronto | Hap Day | Detroit | Tommy Ivan |
| 1947 | 4-2 | Toronto | Hap Day | Montreal | Dick Irvin |
| 1946 | 4-1 | Montreal | Dick Irvin | Boston | Dit Clapper |
| 1945 | 4-3 | Toronto | Hap Day | Detroit | Jack Adams |
| 1944 | 4-0 | Montreal | Dick Irvin | Chicago | Paul Thompson |
| 1943 | 4-0 | Detroit | Jack Adams | Boston | Art Ross |
| 1942 | 4-3 | Toronto | Hap Day | Detroit | Jack Adams |
| 1941 | 4-0 | Boston | Cooney Weiland | Detroit | Ebbie Goodfellow |
| 1940 | 4-2 | NY Rangers | Frank Boucher | Toronto | Dick Irvin |
| 1939 | 4-1 | Boston | Art Ross | Toronto | Dick Irvin |
| 1938 | 3-1 | Chicago | Bill Stewart | Toronto | Dick Irvin |
| 1937 | 3-2 | Detroit | Jack Adams | NY Rangers | Lester Patrick |
| 1936 | 3-1 | Detroit | Jack Adams | Toronto | Dick Irvin |
| 1935 | 3-0 | Mtl. Maroons | Tommy Gorman | Toronto | Dick Irvin |
| 1934 | 3-1 | Chicago | Tommy Gorman | Detroit | Herbie Lewis |
| 1933 | 3-1 | NY Rangers | Lester Patrick | Toronto | Dick Irvin |
| 1932 | 3-0 | Toronto | Dick Irvin | NY Rangers | Lester Patrick |
| 1931 | 3-2 | Montreal | Cecil Hart | Chicago | Dick Irvin |
| 1930 | 2-0 | Montreal | Cecil Hart | Boston | Art Ross |
| 1929 | 2-0 | Boston | Cy Denneny | NY Rangers | Lester Patrick |
| 1928 | 3-2 | NY Rangers | Lester Patrick | Mtl. Maroons | Eddie Gerard |
| 1927 | 2-0-2 | Ottawa | Dave Gill | Boston | Art Ross |

# THE ALL-STAR GAME

It's ironic that the NHL All-Star Game, sometimes labeled a non-contact version of hockey, came into being because of an unfortunate incident that ended a player's career. The first, unofficial All-Star game was a benefit for Ace Bailey, who had been gravely injured in a regular-season game between the Toronto Maple Leafs and the Boston Bruins on December 12, 1933.

Bruins' star Eddie Shore had been knocked down while carrying the puck up the ice. Enraged, he charged Bailey, who had not been the culprit, and upended him viciously. Bailey's head struck the ice, knocking him unconscious. Bailey never played again.

On February 14, 1934, the Maple Leafs played a team of NHL All-Stars at Maple Leaf Gardens in a benefit for Bailey. More than $23,000 Cdn. was raised for Bailey, but the format did not exactly capture the imagination of the league's governors.

Two more unofficial All-Star games were staged, both owing to personal tragedy. In November 1937, a game was organized after the death following complications from a broken leg of Montreal Canadiens star Howie Morenz.

And in 1939, a similar game was held to benefit the widow of Babe Siebert, who had drowned that summer.

## It's official

The first official All-Star Game was held in 1947, with the reigning Stanley Cup champions, the Toronto Maple Leafs, playing an All-Star team. The Stars won 4-3, establishing the format that would remain for most of the next two decades.

The Dream Game notion was that the true test of just how good the Stanley Cup champions were was to pit the best players from around the league against them. There was one obvious flaw with this set-up. The All-Star team selections often were dominated, understandably, by members of the Stanley Cup champions.

In 1958-59, for example, the Montreal Canadiens placed four players on the first All-Star team and two on the second team. Inevitably, the All-Star team that faced the champions took the ice minus several of its best players.

The league experimented with a different format for two years in the early 1950s, pitting the first All-Star team against the Second Team, but otherwise did not deviate from the Stars against the Stanley Cup champions until 1969.

This was the first All-Star Game following the first major expansion in NHL history, a project that doubled the size of the league from six to 12 teams.

From 1969 through 1971, the All-Star Game pitted the stars from the so-called Original Six against the stars from the six expansion clubs. That period featured the first All-Star Game

held in an expansion city when St. Louis played host to the game in 1970.

The established stars of the East won that game 4-1, but the expansion stars surprised the Original Six when they won the 1971 game in Boston 2-1.

In 1972, the first of a series of realignments shifted the established Chicago Blackhawks into the West Division, and further expansion would continue to alter the makeup of the division.

By 1975, the league had grown to 18 teams, organized into two nine-team conferences: the Prince of Wales Conference; and the Clarence Campbell Conference, named after the longtime president of the NHL.

The Wales did All-Star battle with the Campbells until 1994, when the NHL realigned its conferences and divisions geographically, replacing the Campbell with the Western Conference, and the Wales with the Eastern. The Central and Pacific Divisions comprise the Western Conference, while the Atlantic and Northeast Divisions make up the Eastern.

## New trends

The league also had new uniforms designed, in teal and violet colors, and placed new emphasis on the skills competition, a fan friendly feature the NHL had borrowed from a highly successful skills format used in the National Basketball Association, an opportunity for the fans to see what the players do best — shoot, skate, and score.

The game itself remains an exhibition, a non-contact shootout which showcases plenty of offensive flash but involves little or no bodychecking and little commitment to defense. The goaltenders often have to perform at their best, and just as often they are buried in an avalanche of shots.

Injuries are rare in the All-Star Game, since no one is dishing out any bodychecks. Penalties are rare, too. The 1992 and 1994 games were penalty-free, while the 1993 game involved a single infraction, a minor penalty handed out to defenseman Dave Manson.

The NHL front office sees the All-Star Game as a chance to market its stars and win new fans. In 1996 the NHL with Fox Sports, made a splashy entrée into the sport by introducing its FoxTrax puck at the All-Star Game. To TV viewers, the puck appeared with a blue aura highlighting it for greater visibility. Fired at high speed, the blue aura turned into a red rocket and the speed at which the puck was shot was displayed on the screen.

Purists in Canada howled, but the high-tech gimmick certainly drew plenty of publicity for the league in the United States.

The idea seemed harmless enough.

# *1991* All-Star Game
# *Patriots in Chicago*

## CAMPBELL 11 - WALES 5

Those who attended the 1991 All-Star Game at Chicago Stadium may well remember it more for the roar throughout the national anthems than for the game. The Stadium was renowned for the roar, but the mid-season exhibition came just a few days after the onset of the Persian Gulf War. The 18,472 fans who packed the colorful, old arena that afternoon came prepared to express themselves about the war against Saddam Hussein.

There were plenty of ovations, including one for longtime Chicago star Denis Savard, who had been traded to the Montreal Canadiens, but the building vibrated during the National Anthem, when the fans had other things on their minds.

Many of the players thoughts were elsewhere, also.

"I was standing next to Mark Messier during the national anthems," marveled Wayne Gretzky. "I said to him, 'This is really unbelievable.'

''I've heard it as loud in here before, but never as emotional. The flags of both countries, the banners, the vibrations. You could tell the fans, like us, were thinking of other things."

In the days leading up to the game, Gretzky had even suggested it be cancelled.

"I still feel the same," he said after the game. "It doesn't seem right that we're here having a good time while soldiers are getting killed in the Persian Gulf.

"During intermissions between periods, we came down to the locker room and watched news updates. But there was such a mood in that rink, such patriotism. It was good for hockey. It was a good show, period."

### Missed out

The other controversy involved a player not chosen to play in the game, Chicago goaltender Ed Belfour. Campbell coach John Muckler had chosen Bill Ranford, whom he coached with the Edmonton Oilers, and the fans also expressed themselves on that issue.

"Ed-die, Ed-die, Ed-die," they chanted. All game long.

When it was over, an unrepentant Muckler cracked a joke about the heckling.

"I thought Eddie Ranford played a great game," he said.

So did Toronto Maple Leafs' star Vincent Damphousse, who scored four goals for the Campbell Conference to take home the Most Valuable Player award.

Vinny's Day: In 1991, Vincent Damphousse scored four times to earn Most Valuable Player honors.

# Gunning for Goals in Philly

## CAMPBELL 10 - WALES 6

The Golden Brett was the star of the show in 1992 in Philadelphia. He scored twice and assisted on another to lead the Campbells over the Wales. This game was not only the typical All-Star no-hitter, it was a game in which no penalties were called, an All-Star Game first. There was nothing to get in the way of five-on-five gunning for goals.

Six goaltenders faced 83 shots in all in this shootout, with Washington Capitals goalie Don Beaupre having the toughest time. He yielded six goals on 12 shots in the second period, as the Campbell Conference built an 8-3 lead. Both of Hull's goals came against Beaupre.

"I didn't have a chance to look up to see which one of their guns was coming at me," said Beaupre. "For a while it seemed like everything was going by me. There were a lot of tips and rebounds and I'm not ready to go through anything like that anytime soon."

Beaupre and the other goalies had the other players' sympathy, for whatever that might have been worth.

"It's totally unfair for goalies," said Wayne Gretzky. "I think everybody understands this game is going to be like that."

### Fateful pairing

Four first-time all-stars were able to record goals in Philadelphia: Gary Roberts of the Calgary Flames; Owen Nolan of the Quebec Nordiques; Alexander Mogilny of the Buffalo Sabres; and Randy Burridge of the Washington Capitals.

"It was nice getting on the scoreboard," said Burridge. "I've got the puck in my bag and I'll always have it."

The game was notable for the pairing of Gretzky with Hull, a fantasy pairing that would actually come true years later in St. Louis.

**All-Star Theoren: In 1992, Theoren Fleury and the Campbell Conference beat the Wales Conference.**

As All-Star teammates, Gretzky and Hull combined for three goals and three assists.

"I've said this a million times—I've always wanted a chance to play with Wayne," said Hull. "Sitting next to Wayne and Stevie Y (Yzerman of the Detroit Red Wings) in the dressing room was unbelievable. Those guys are my idols in this game."

# 1993 All-Star Game
# Campbell Blues in Montreal

## WALES 16 - CAMPBELL 6

**W**ayne Gretzky is certainly not a stranger to All-Star games, having been selected a first-team all-star eight times and a second-team player five times. But the spotlight was on him at the All-Star Game in Montreal for an entirely different reason.

Rumors were circulating rapidly that the man many consider the best player in the history of the game was going to be traded to the Toronto Maple Leafs. Los Angeles Kings owner Bruce McNall was forced to hold a news conference to deny everything.

### Big deal

Once the controversy subsided and the game began, everybody scored, or so it seemed. Even Brad Marsh, a cautious defenseman for the expansion Ottawa Senators potted one, earning a standing ovation from the Montreal Forum fans.

"Kevin Stevens made a great pass," Marsh said later. "I just put my stick on the ice and it went in off it. I've gone whole seasons without scoring a goal, so any time I do score, it's a big deal."

The goal was all the sweeter for Marsh, who had been embarrassed during the target-shooting portion of the skills competition when he failed to hit a single target in eight tries.

"I knew I was in trouble after I missed the first six," Marsh said. "My excuse is that I'm not supposed to be shooting at targets, anyway."

Mike Gartner took home the MVP award by scoring four goals and adding an assist. The Wales Conference built a 9-0 lead by early in the second period, and a 12-2 lead after 40 minutes of play, as they strafed goalies Ed Belfour and Mike Vernon for six goals each.

Things could have been much worse for the Campbell team when it's considered that Mario Lemieux missed the game.

Lemieux, who had been diagnosed with Hodgkin's Disease four weeks earlier, was undergoing treatment and unable to play. But he was introduced before the game to the fans at the Forum, who gave a five-minute standing ovation to the Montreal-born superstar.

**All-Star Shootout:** The teams combined for a record 22 goals in the 1993 All-Star Game, including six in the first period against goalie Ed Belfour.

# NHL goes United Nations

## EASTERN 9 - WESTERN 8

The NHL had been realigned into Eastern and Western Conferences and hip new uniforms had been designed in time for this game, which was another penalty-free contest. Despite the lopsided result, there was sparkling goaltending, and it was a good thing, considering the teams combined for a record 102 shots.

Mike Richter stopped 19 of the 21 shots the Eastern Conference unleashed at him. Only Paul Coffey and Sandis Ozolinsh beat him.

The acrobatic Richter stopped Vancouver speedster Pavel Bure five times, including twice on breakaways, as the Madison Square Garden fans roared their approval.

"I didn't want to come into this game and not be tested," said Richter. "You're playing against the best in the world. If they pepper you with a bunch of shots and you're feeling good, it's fantastic. You want more."

More was what the winning Eastern Conference team got—more money. The victory was worth $5,000 U.S. for each winning player as the NHL decided to sweeten the pot for All-Star participants in an effort to add some competitive zip to the often tepid game.

"If they're giving you $5,000, you might as well try to win it," reasoned Rangers defenseman Brian Leetch.

Still, the All-Stars do have one unwritten rule, no matter how competitive they or the league might try to intensify things: no hitting.

"We didn't do any checking but at least we got into each other's way," said Chicago defenseman Chris Chelios, with a laugh.

The game also illustrated the growing international make-up of the NHL. Among the participants there were five Russians, two Latvians, a Czechoslovakian, a Finn, eight Americans and 24 Canadians.

One of the Latvians—Sandis Ozolinsh—and one of the Russians—rookie Alexei Yashin—each scored two goals. Yashin's second was the gamewinner for the Eastern Conference.

"It was all luck," said Yashin, the only rookie in the game.

Some of his peers—notably Wayne Gretzky—didn't agree with Yashin.

"He's a tremendous talent," said Gretzky. "I see a lot of Mario (Lemieux) in him.

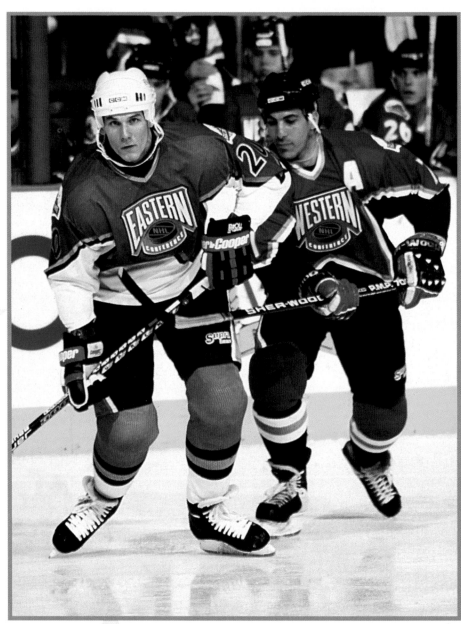

Beginner's Luck: Alexei Yashin, the only rookie in the game, scored two goals including the winner in 1994.

"He's got good puck sense and Mario's size. To be doing what he's doing on an expansion team (Ottawa) is a credit to him, along with his coming over from Russia for his first year."

For his part, Gretzky had two assists, giving him 19 points lifetime in All-Star competition, tying Gordie Howe's record for points in All-Star games. Gretzky, though, collected his 19 points in 14 games, compared to 23 appearances for Howe.

# 1996 All-Star Game
## FoxTraxing in Boston

The 1995 All-Star Game was one of the casualties of the lockout-shortened 1994-95 season. The 1996 All-Star was held in Boston, but not at historic Boston Garden, which had officially closed before the season began.

Literally inches away from the funky, intimate Garden, the Bruins owners had built the FleetCenter, a state-of-the-art, 17,565-seat amphitheater.

The center of attention during the game, at least for fans watching on Fox, was a high-tech puck the network had designed to enhance viewers' ability to follow the disk in the heat of the action.

The FoxTrax puck, fashioned with infrared-emitting diodes, gave off a pale blue haze as it slid about the ice in its debut.

When a player teed up a shot at 120-kilometres-an-hour or faster, the puck became a red rocket as it zoomed netward, with a comet-like tail, describing its flight path for the viewers.

The puck was a public relations smash as the NHL and Fox generated plenty of media attention.

Hockey purists in Canada sniffed at the innovation, but Fox, attempting to boost interest in the sport across the United States, was encouraged by the fancy puck.

### Local hero

The game, meanwhile, provided the perfect ending for Bruins fans, and gave them a chance to salute one of the game's greatest stars, Boston captain and wheelhorse defenseman Ray Bourque, who was playing in his 14th All-Star Game.

The early thunder in the game belonged to goaltender Martin Brodeur, who pitched a shutout in the first period, stopping 12 shots from the best of the West. The Buffalo Sabres goaltender, Dominik Hasek, faced 13 shots for the Eastern team in the third period, giving up just one goal.

It was a relatively low-scoring affair, as these things go, but the final one was a masterpiece.

That one came at 19:23 of the final period, when Bourque beat Toronto Maple Leafs goalie Felix Potvin to hand the victory to the Eastern team, take the MVP award and bask in the heat of an enormous ovation from the Boston fans.

**Hometown Hero: Boston Bruins defenseman Ray Bourque thrilled the Boston fans when he scored the winner in 1996.**

# Knowing the Way in San Jose

## EASTERN 11 – WESTERN 7

This was the All-Star game in which the local hero called his shot before firing in the final goal in his three-goal hat-trick and still couldn't win the All-Star game most valuable player award.

It was the All-Star game in which the guy who did win the MVP also scored a hat-trick but was booed by the understandably partisan crowd at the San Jose Arena, home of the Sharks.

"They booed me and they'll probably boo me next time I come here," said Montreal Canadiens winger Mark Recchi, whose three-goal performance helped the East All-Stars outscore the West. "I thought (the media) would give it to the home-town boy. That would have been Owen Nolan, the Sharks' power forward who also scored three goals, including one at 17:57 of the third period on Buffalo Sabres goaltender Dominik Hasek.

That one was special. Nolan pointed to an opening, then promptly threaded the needle with a shot that cleanly beat The Dominator. The goal didn't win the game for the West, but the spectacle brought the house down. The media members were apparently unmoved.

For openers, Nolan scored his first two goals, which came late in the second period, just eight seconds apart—an All-Star Game record. No big deal, the media ruled, awarding the MVP to Recchi, the latest in a lengthy line of Montreal Canadiens snipers.

"There are a lot of great all-stars who have played for the Canadiens," Recchi said. "I'm told I remind some of (Hall of Famer) Yvan Cournoyer, which is quite an honor."

### Due honors

The 47th All-Star game also was an occasion to pay homage to some of the greatest players ever to play in the NHL, including the Magnificent One, Mario Lemieux.

Out of respect for Lemieux, East coach Doug MacLean sent Lemieux out for the game's final shift along with Wayne Gretzky and Mark Messier, with Raymond Bourque and Paul Coffey on defense.

"That was impressive," West goaltender Andy Moog said, ignoring the fact that he was beaten for six goals in the second period. "As I watched them, I thought, Gretz has 18 years, Mark 17, Bourque 18, Coffey 18 and Mario about 13 or 14. It was a nice tribute to the elder statesmen."

As with most NHL All-Star games, this was another chance for the snipers to shine and goalies to cringe. Even Patrick Roy, who can lay a strong claim to being the best goalie in the business, was beaten for four goals on 15 shots. He handled the blitzkrieg with his customary aplomb.

"You accept the risk when you accept the invitation," Roy said. "I enjoy everything about this weekend—except the game."

But the 17,422 fans who jammed the Arena enjoyed the game just fine, thanks.

**Eastern Blitz:**
**Eric Lindros and the Eastern Conference prevailed over the Western Conference in a goal-scoring spectacular in the 1997 NHL All-Star game.**

# All-Star Game Results 1947-1997

| Year | Venue | Score | Coaches |
|---|---|---|---|
| 1997 | San Jose | Eastern 11, Western 7 | Doug MacLean; Marc Crawford |
| 1996 | Boston | Eastern 5, Western 4 | Doug MacLean; Scott Bowman |
| 1994 | New York | Eastern 9, Western 8 | Jacques Demers; Barry Melrose |
| 1993 | Montreal | Wales 16, Campbell 6 | Scott Bowman; Mike Keenan |
| 1992 | Philadelphia | Campbell 10, Wales 6 | Bob Gainey; Scott Bowman |
| 1991 | Chicago | Campbell 11, Wales 5 | John Muckler; Mike Milbury |
| 1990 | Pittsburgh | Wales 12, Campbell 7 | Pat Burns; Terry Crisp |
| 1989 | Edmonton | Campbell 9, Wales 5 | Glen Sather; Terry O'Reilly |
| 1988 | St. Louis | Wales 6, Campbell 5(OT) | Mike Keenan; Glen Sather |
| 1986 | Hartford | Wales 4, Campbell 3(OT) | Mike Keenan; Glen Sather |
| 1985 | Calgary | Wales 6, Campbell 4 | Al Arbour; Glen Sather |
| 1984 | New Jersey | Wales 7, Campbell 6 | Al Arbour; Glen Sather |
| 1983 | NY Islanders | Campbell 9, Wales 3 | Roger Neilson; Al Arbour |
| 1982 | Wash. | Wales 4, Campbell 2 | Al Arbour; Glen Sonmor |
| 1981 | Los Angeles | Campbell 4, Wales 1 | Pat Quinn; Scott Bowman |
| 1980 | Detroit | Wales 6, Campbell 3 | Scott Bowman; Al Arbour |
| 1978 | Buffalo | Wales 3, Campbell 2 (OT) | Scott Bowman; Fred Shero |
| 1977 | Vancouver | Wales 4, Campbell 3 | Scott Bowman; Fred Shero |
| 1976 | Philadelphia | Wales 7, Campbell 5 | Floyd Smith; Fred Shero |
| 1975 | Montreal | Wales 7, Campbell 1 | Bep Guidolin; Fred Shero |
| 1974 | Chicago | West 6, East 4 | Billy Reay; Scott Bowman |
| 1973 | New York | East 5, West 4 | Tom Johnson; Billy Reay |
| 1972 | Minnesota | East 3, West 2 | Al McNeill; Billy Reay |
| 1971 | Boston | West 2, East 1 | Scott Bowman; Harry Sinden |
| 1970 | St. Louis | East 4, West 1 | Claude Ruel; Scott Bowman |
| 1969 | Montreal | East 3, West 3 | Toe Blake; Scott Bowman |
| 1968 | Toronto | Toronto 4, All-Stars 3 | Punch Imlach; Toe Blake |
| 1967 | Montreal | Montreal 3, All-Stars 0 | Toe Blake; Sid Abel |
| 1965 | Montreal | All-Stars 5, Montreal 2 | Billy Reay; Toe Blake |
| 1964 | Toronto | All-Stars 3, Toronto 2 | Sid Abel; Punch Imlach |
| 1963 | Toronto | All-Stars 3, Toronto3 | Sid Abel; Punch Imlach |
| 1962 | Toronto | Toronto 4, All-Stars1 | Punch Imlach; Rudy Pilous |
| 1961 | Chicago | All-Stars 3, Chicago 1 | Sid Abel; Rudy Pilous |
| 1960 | Montreal | All-Stars 2, Montreal 1 | Punch Imlach; Toe Blake |
| 1959 | Montreal | Montreal 6, All-Stars 1 | Toe Blake; Punch Imlach |
| 1958 | Montreal | Montreal 6, All-Stars 3 | Toe Blake; Milt Schmidt |
| 1957 | Montreal | All-Stars 5, Montreal 3 | Milt Schmidt; Toe Blake |
| 1956 | Montreal | All-Stars 1, Montreal 1 | Jim Skinner; Toe Blake |
| 1955 | Detroit | Detroit 3, All-Stars 1 | Jim Skinner; Dick Irvin |
| 1954 | Detroit | All-Stars 2, Detroit 2 | King Clancy; Jim Skinner |
| 1953 | Montreal | All-Stars 3, Montreal 1 | Lynn Patrick; Dick Irvin |
| 1952 | Detroit | 1st Team 1, 2nd Team 1 | Tommy Ivan; Dick Irvin |
| 1951 | Toronto | 1st Team 2, 2nd Team 2 | Joe Primeau; Hap Day |
| 1950 | Detroit | Detroit 7, All-Stars 1 | Tommy Ivan; Lynn Patrick |
| 1949 | Toronto | All-Stars 3, Toronto 1 | Tommy Ivan; Hap Day |
| 1948 | Chicago | All-Stars 3, Toronto 1 | Tommy Ivan; Hap Day |
| 1947 | Toronto | All-Stars 4, Toronto 3 | Dick Irvin; Hap Day |

# All-Star Hockey Mosts

**Most Games Played**
23    Gordie Howe, from 1948 through 1980.

**Most Goals**
12    Wayne Gretzky, in 15 appearances.

**Most Points, One Game**
6    Mario Lemieux, Wales, 1988 (3 goals, 3 assists)

**Most Goals In One Game**
4    Wayne Gretzky, Campbell, 1983
     Mario Lemieux, Wales, 1990
     Vincent Damphousse, Campbell, 1991
     Mike Gartner, Wales, 1993

**Most Goals, Both Teams, One Game**
22    Wales 16, Campbell 6, 1993 at Montreal

# THE HOCKEY HALL OF FAME

The building that houses the state-of-the-art Hockey Hall of Fame in Toronto is a former Bank of Montreal that was built in the previous century. It's appropriate that the National Hockey League showcases its rich history in a vintage 1885 building. After all, the first recorded advertisement for a hockey game comes from the same era, having been placed in the *Montreal Gazette* in 1875.

The game that came to be known as hockey had been played for decades across Canada by that time, in a variety of forms, with a variety of names. Its 'invention' was a product of rural isolation and the need for some activity to enliven the months-long winter.

Unlike baseball, though, hockey has no Abner Doubleday, no personage who can be said, however inaccurately, to have invented the game, no bucolic equivalent of Cooperstown to cherish as the cradle of the game.

Numerous hockey historians make cases for the game originating in, variously, Kingston, Ontario, or Montreal or a certain rural pond in Nova Scotia. Which claim is the most legitimate? Flip a coin.

But if there is no one mythology surrounding the location of the Hockey Hall of Fame it doesn't seem to matter. The ultra-modern facility is fraught with lore, rich in tradition, bursting with memories.

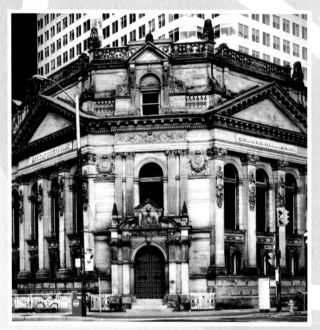

Hall of Honor: The great rotunda in the imposing Hockey Hall of Fame in Toronto is a fitting setting for the array of plaques honoring all the greats of the NHL game.

## Golden memories

The Hall fills 51,000 square feet of space at BCE Place in downtown Toronto, a modern skyscraper that incorporates the century-old former bank building into its sprawling complex.

The displays include a surprisingly life-like re-creation of the fabled Montreal Canadiens dressing room in the old Forum, a large collection of the many strikingly artistic protective masks worn by the league's goaltenders over the years, and interactive displays that enable visitors, for example, to try their hand at play-by-play description of some of the game's golden moments.

The centerpiece of the building, which opened on 18 June 1993, is the Great Hall, a magnificent dome-ceilinged room that proudly showcases the plaques honoring the members as well as the NHL's glittering family of trophies.

The most famous trophy in the collection, of course, is the Stanley Cup, donated by Lord Stanley in 1893, the oldest trophy continuously competed for by professional athletes in North America.

The plaques honor the Hall of Fame's 304 members: 207 players; 84 builders (coaches, general managers, owners) and 13 referees and linesmen.

There also are 55 members from the media—broadcasters and print reporters—whose work helped raise awareness about, and helped foster the mythology of the game.

The broadcast members are awarded the Foster Hewitt Memorial Award, named after the legendary play-by-play man whose "He shoots, he scores" became a recreational rink mantra for all Canadian hockey fans. The print members are awarded the Elmer Ferguson Memorial Award. Ferguson, who worked for the *Montreal Herald*, covered the 1917 meeting at which the NHL was formed, and followed the game for years afterward.

## Honor for a league

The Hall of Fame was first established in 1943, its early members first honored in 1945. But a permanent location to house the legacy of the game wasn't found until 26 August 1961, when the collection was set up in a building on the grounds of the Canadian National Exhibition on Toronto's lakeshore.

The current location updates the museum for the 1990s and the coming century. Which is not surprising for the Hall of Fame of a league that has more than quadrupled in size in the past 30 years.

Inductees are honored at a special ceremony held each fall. In the Fall of 1996, four new members entered the Hall: former Toronto Maple Leafs defenseman Borje Salming; ex- New York Islanders head coach Al Arbour; Bobby Bauer, a star with the Boston Bruins in the 1930s, 1940s and early 1950s; and broadcaster Bob Cole.

Arbour entered the Hall one year following Bill Torrey, the architect of the great Islanders teams that Arbour coached to four straight Stanley Cup victories in the early 1980s.

Bauer was a member of the legendary Bruins Kraut Line, along with Woody Dumart, who was inducted into the Hall in 1992, and Milt Schmidt, a member since 1961.

# Mario Lemieux—A Player for the Ages

**H**is name means, literally, 'The Best' and Mario Lemieux may well have been the best who ever played in the National Hockey League. His extraordinary skills earned him the nickname, The Magnificent One, a moniker he lived up to time and time again during his 13-year career with the Pittsburgh Penguins. Little wonder, then, that the custodians of the Hockey Hall of Fame chose to waive the normal three-year waiting period and usher Lemieux directly into the Hall in the fall of 1997.

He entered the Hall loaded down with scoring records, NHL awards, a brilliant player whose achievements were all the more remarkable given the adversity he overcame.

In the lockout-shortened 1994-95 season, Lemieux did not play at all. He took time off to give his chronically aching back time to heal, and to recover from the effects of radiation therapy to overcome Hodgkin's Disease, the treatable form of cancer that sidelined him in 1992-93.

## Battered triumphs

In the 1990s alone, Lemieux missed more than 200 regular-season games owing to illness or injury. Brilliant as he was, he might have carved an even more special place in the NHL record book had his health not tripped him up.

Not once during his career did Lemieux play every game during the regular season.

Despite a staggering string of injuries, Lemieux left the NHL having won the Calder Trophy as the NHL's top rookie in 1985, as its Most Valuable Player in 1986, 1988 and 1992, as its scoring champion in 1988, 1989, 1992, 1993, 1996, and 1997, and as the Most Valuable Player in the Stanley Cup playoffs in 1991 and 1992.

Four times Lemieux was a first-team All-Star, and twice he led the Penguins to the Stanley Cup. In 1993, the year he sat out 20 games during treatment for Hodgkin's Disease, Lemieux won the Bill Masterton Trophy as the NHL player best embodying the qualities of perseverance and dedication to his sport.

Lemieux, a jealous guardian of his privacy and off-season time, earned a reputation as a reluctant international competitor. Yet, when he did compete for Canada, he performed brilliantly.

In 1985, Lemieux helped Canada win a silver medal at the

**Hero of Honor:** Preternaturally gifted, and possessing a flair for the dramatic, Mario Lemieux didn't disappoint his home fans, scoring a picture-perfect goal in his final game at the Civic Arena.

World Hockey Championship. In 1987, he scored 11 goals in nine games, including the final two game-winning goals to lift Canada to victory in the Canada Cup tournament, forerunner to the World Cup of Hockey.

A commanding 6-foot-3 and 220 pounds, Lemieux possessed a deceptively swift, undeniably graceful stride, magical puckhandling skills, and creative resources like none before him.

"Guys had no idea how to defend him," said longtime New York Islanders general manager Bill Torrey. "I don't know of anyone who has frozen players like Mario.

"He could beat you with his stickhandling, his shot, or just by holding on to the puck. Defensemen would drop down thinking he was going to shoot. Goalies would commit before he did. On breakaways, he was the best I've ever seen."

## Unselfish scorer

And Lemieux had a remarkable flair for the dramatic. When the NHL All-Star game was held in Pittsburgh in 1990, he made the mid-season exhibition his personal showcase, scoring four goals in front of his adoring fans.

In his early years with the Penguins, Lemieux's playmaking brilliance made scoring stars out of a succession of players—like Warren Young and Rob Brown—who quickly receded into obscurity, their run-of-the-mill skills exposed, after they were traded away from Pittsburgh, away from Mario.

"Lemieux was such a great playmaker that people sometimes overlook what a great goal scorer he was," said Detroit Red Wings head coach Scott Bowman, who coached him in Pittsburgh. "He was the best of all time.

"He could put a puck exactly where he wanted. If he wasn't so unselfish, he'd have scored more goals."

Still, he managed 613 regular-season goals in just 745 games, the highest goals-per-game average (.823) in NHL history.

He left the NHL holding or sharing 15 NHL scoring records. Yet what most will remember is the magic that was Mario.

"Almost every night he showed you something new, something you had never seen before," said Craig Patrick, the Penguins' general manager.

He was—and is—a player for the ages.

Inspirational Leader: Bobby Clarke overcame limited natural ability and diabetes through sheer hard work and dedication to become the key player on the Philadelhia Flyers in the 1970s.

**JEAN BELIVEAU:** center. A native of Victoriaville, Quebec, Beliveau became a star center with the Quebec Aces of the Quebec Senior League. Le Colisée in Quebec, where the Aces played their games, was nicknamed the House that Beliveau Built, but it wasn't his hockey home for long. In 1952, Beliveau joined the Montreal Canadiens, who held his pro rights. He remained with them for his entire 18-year NHL career, and led the Canadiens to ten Stanley Cup victories. He was the first winner of the Conn Smythe Trophy as the most valuable player in the playoffs and twice won the Hart Trophy. He retired after leading the Canadiens to the Stanley Cup in 1970-71, having played 1125 NHL games and scored 507 goals.

**HECTOR (TOE) BLAKE:** left winger, coach. Blake played 578 NHL games, scoring 235 goals and adding 292 assists. The left wing beside center Elmer Lach and right winger Maurice Richard on the legendary Punch Line, Blake was nicknamed the Old Lamplighter for his scoring prowess. Many regard him as the best coach in the history of the NHL. For 13 seasons he coached the Canadiens, who won eight Stanley Cups under his regime, including five straight from 1956-60. He retired after coaching his eighth Cup victory in 1968.

**MIKE BOSSY:** right winger. As a junior star, Bossy was considered a soft player, a one-dimensional scorer whose offensive skills would be muted in the NHL, whose defensive skills would be a liability. The Montreal Canadiens, among other teams,

passed on Bossy in the Entry Draft and lived to regret it. Bossy became the best right winger in the NHL in the 1980s, scoring 573 goals in just 752 regular-season games. For nine straight years, he scored 50 or more goals. He was the sniper on the Trio Grande—a line with Bryan Trottier at center and Clark Gillies at left wing. Bossy added 85 goals in 129 playoff games as he helped the New York Islanders win four straight Stanley Cup championships from 1980-83. Chronic back trouble forced him into retirement in 1987.

**JOHNNY BOWER:** goaltender. Scar-faced Bower didn't make it to the NHL for good until he was 34. He played 11 seasons for the Toronto Maple Leafs, helping them win four Stanley Cups, including the fabled upset in 1967 when an aging Toronto team beat the favored Montreal Canadiens. Bower and Terry Sawchuck shared the goaltending duties that season, as well as the Vezina Trophy as the best netminding duo in the league. He retired after the 1969-70 season, the only one in which he wore a protective mask.

**SCOTTY BOWMAN:** coach, general manager. He apprenticed in the Montreal Canadiens system under Sam Pollock before becoming the coach of the expansion St. Louis Blues, whom he led to three straight Stanley Cup finals. Repatriated to the Canadiens as head coach in 1971, he led them to five Stanley Cup victories. He worked for the Sabres from 1979 to 1987 but didn't return to the Stanley Cup final until 1992, with the Penguins, replacing the late Bob Johnson as head coach. As head coach of the

Detroit Red Wings, Bowman added the 1997 Stanley Cup to his résumé as the most successful coach in NHL history with well over 800 victories.

**CLARENCE CAMPBELL:** NHL president, 1947-78. Campbell was a Rhodes Scholar and won the Order of the British Empire after working as a prosecutor with the Canadian War Crimes Commission in Germany. He is remembered mostly as the man who suspended Maurice (Rocket) Richard after he slugged linesman Cliff Thompson in March 1955. Campbell's presence at the Forum on March 16, 1955 touched off a riot by outraged Montreal fans. But Campbell withstood that storm. His most notable achievement came in 1968, when he oversaw the expansion of the NHL from six to 12 teams. Before he retired in 1978, the league had grown to 18 teams.

Straight On: Al Arbour coached one of the best teams in the history of the NHL during the New York Islanders' run of four straight Stanley Cups in the 1980s.

**GERRY CHEEVERS:** goaltender. Starting goalie for the Boston Bruins in the Bobby Orr-Phil Esposito era. Known as a great money goaltender, Cheevers was at his best in the playoffs. He helped Boston win the Stanley Cup in 1970 and 1972.

**BOBBY CLARKE:** center, coach, general manager. In 1968-69, Clarke piled up 137 points with the Flin Flon Bombers of the Western Hockey League, but many teams were leery of his diabetic condition and he was taken 17th overall in the NHL entry draft. He proved the skeptics wrong, playing 15 NHL seasons for the Philadelphia Flyers, winning the Hart Trophy three times and leading the Flyers to two straight Stanley Cups in the early 1970s. He was the first player on a post-1967 expansion team to score 100 or more points in a season. His grit, determination and leadership were central to the Flyers becoming the first expansion club ever to win the Stanley Cup.

**YVAN COURNOYER:** right winger. Cournoyer's speed earned him the nickname 'The Roadrunner,' but he was anything but birdlike. His speed came from thickly muscled legs that teammate Ken Dryden once compared to "two enormous roasts spilling over his knees." When he joined the Montreal Canadiens in 1963-64, Cournoyer was used as a power-play specialist. He developed into one of the most explosive forwards in the game, scoring 428 goals in 16 seasons, and helping Montreal win ten Stanley Cups. He was the Canadiens captain for their four-straight Stanley Cup run in the 1970s.

**MARCEL DIONNE:** center. Dionne was chosen second overall behind Guy Lafleur in the 1970 entry draft and played most of his career in brilliant obscurity. After racking up 366 points in four seasons with Detroit, Dionne was traded to the Los Angeles Kings, where he quietly piled up points for years, centering the Triple Crown Line with wingers Charlie Simmer and Dave Taylor. He won a scoring championship with the Kings and ended his 18-year career with 731 goals and 1,040 assists, but no Stanley Cup victories.

**KEN DRYDEN:** goaltender. Dryden, 23-year-old law student and a 6-foot-4, 210-pound giant, backstopped the Montreal Canadiens to a surprise Stanley Cup victory in 1970-71 after playing just six regular-season games with the club. He was awarded the Conn Smythe Trophy as the most valuable player in the playoffs, and followed that up by winning the Calder Trophy (rookie-of-the-year) the next season. Dryden played eight seasons for the Canadiens, helping them win six Stanley Cups, while winning the Vezina Trophy five times. He retired after the 1978-79 season, after helping the Canadiens win a fourth straight Cup. On March 2, 1971, he made hockey history when he faced brother Dave Dryden of the Buffalo Sabres. The pair were the first goaltending brothers ever to face each other in goal. In 1997, Ken Dryden returned to the NHL for the first time since 1979 when he was named president of the Toronto Maple Leafs.

**The Roadrunner: Montreal Canadiens sniper Yvan Cournoyer used blazing speed to zoom past opponents and score big goals.**

**PHIL ESPOSITO:** center, coach, general manager. Esposito was a competent, but unremarkable center for the Chicago Blackhawks when he was traded, with Ken Hodge and Fred Stanfield, to the Boston Bruins in 1967 for Hubert (Pit) Martin, Jack Norris and Gilles Marotte. Esposito blossomed as a Bruin, becoming the first player to score more than 100 points in a season. He won five scoring titles in eight-and-a-half seasons in Boston, where he and Bobby Orr led the Bruins to two Stanley Cups. He won two Hart Trophies and scored 55 goals or more in five straight seasons. He played 18 seasons in all, scoring 717 goals and adding 873 assists. He retired in 1981, finishing his career as a New York Ranger.

**BILL GADSBY:** defenseman. Gadsby played standout defense for Chicago, New York Rangers and the Detroit Red Wings for 20 seasons over three decades, stretching from 1946-47 to 1965-66.

Gadsby was fortunate to have a career at all. When he was 12, he and his mother were returning from England when the ship they were traveling on was torpedoed and sunk. He was rescued after spending five hours in the frigid Atlantic. In 1952, he overcame a bout of polio so severe doctors told him he would never play again. He played—well enough to be named an All-Star seven times. Strangely, he never won a Stanley Cup.

**BERNARD (BOOM-BOOM) GEOFFRION:** left wing. Geoffrion earned his nickname by becoming the first to consistently use the slap shot as an offensive weapon in the 1950s. He won the Calder Trophy in 1952 and led the NHL in scoring in 1955. He was the second player, after teammate Maurice Richard, to score 50 goals in a season and helped Montreal win five Stanley Cups. He frequently played the point (defense) on the power play to take advantage of his booming shot. He also coached, briefly, for the New York Rangers, Atlanta Flames and Montreal Canadiens.

**ED GIACOMIN:** goaltender. "Ed-die, Ed-die" was the chant at Madison Square Gardens during Giacomin's decade as the No. 1 goaltender for the Rangers in the late 1960s and early 1970s. Giacomin shared the Vezina Trophy and won 226 games for the Rangers, while endearing himself to the tough Garden fans with his acrobatic style.

**DOUG HARVEY:** defenseman. Many consider Harvey, who played 20 NHL seasons from 1947-48 to 1968-69, the best defenseman in the history of the game. He won the Norris Trophy as the league's best defenseman seven times and helped the Montreal Canadiens win six Stanley Cups. He was the point man on the great Montreal power-play unit that included Jean Beliveau, Maurice (Rocket) Richard, Dickie Moore and Bernard (Boom-Boom) Geoffrion. The power-play unit was so effective that the NHL altered its rules so that a penalized player could leave the penalty box before his two minutes was up if the opposing team scored a goal. It was said of Harvey that he was so skilled he could control the tempo of a game, speeding its pace or slowing it down to suit the situation.

**GORDIE HOWE:** right winger. Howe, a physically powerful, awesomely talented but shy and humble farm boy from Floral, Saskatchewan, fully earned the nickname Mr. Hockey. Howe played 26 seasons, 34 pro seasons in all, covering five decades from 1946-47 to 1979-80. He played 1767 NHL games, scored 801 goals, added 1049 assists. At one time, he held NHL records for most games played, most goals, assists, and points in both regular season and playoffs. He became the first NHLer over the age of 50 to score a goal and the first to play on a line with his sons, Mark and Marty.

**GLENN HALL:** goaltender. The man who became known as Mr. Goalie didn't earn the title for nothing. Hall played 18 seasons—ten with Chicago—and was named an All-Star 11 times. He led the NHL in shutouts for six seasons, played in 115 Stanley Cup playoff games and set a league record for most consecutive games by a goalie—502, stretching from 1955 to November 7, 1962. He finished his remarkable career sharing goaltending duties with fellow Hall of Famer Jacques Plante in St. Louis, where he backstopped the Blues to three straight Stanley Cup final appearances.

**BOBBY HULL:** left winger. Blond-haired and dimple-cheeked handsome and built like an Adonis, Hull also had blazing speed (29.7 mph top speed) and a frighteningly hard slap shot that once was clocked at 118.3 mph. Hull quickly became known as The Golden Jet in the NHL. He scored 610 goals in a 16-year NHL career during which he became the first player ever to record more than one 50-goal season (he had five). He won the Art Ross Trophy as the league's top scorer three times, the Lady Byng Trophy once, the Hart twice. He led the Blackhawks to the Stanley Cup in 1961, the first of his 50-goal seasons. He was the first big-name superstar to jump to the World Hockey Association when he signed a $1 million Cdn. contract with the Winnipeg Jets.

**GEORGE (PUNCH) IMLACH:** coach, general manager, Toronto Maple Leafs, Buffalo Sabres. Imlach was a bundle of superstitions and hockey acumen who piloted the Maple Leafs to four Stanley Cups in the 1960s. In 1970-71 he gave the expansion Buffalo Sabres instant credibility when he became their first coach and general manager. Imlach was instantly recognized by his trademark lucky fedoras. His superstition prevented him from changing suits when his team was on a winning streak.

**GUY LAFLEUR:** right winger. Lafleur, lightning-fast, creative and possessed of a

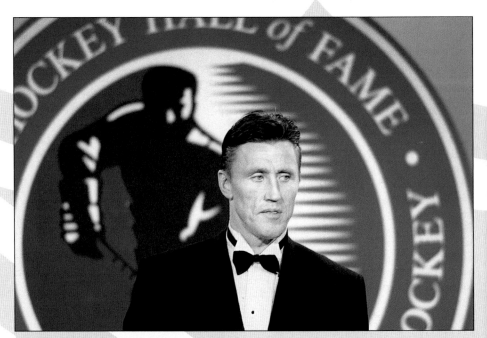

Old World Flash: Swedish defenseman Borje Salming brought an elegant skating stride and a large basket of skills to the Toronto Maple Leafs in the early 1970s. He was the first true European superstar in the NHL.

wicked slap shot was the NHL's dominant scorer of the 1970s. He was the first to score 50 goals or more in six consecutive seasons and six straight 100-point seasons. He also was the youngest player in history to score 400 goals and attain 1,000 points. He helped the Canadiens win five Stanley Cups, including four straight during his heyday from 1976-79.

**TED LINDSAY:** left winger. Terrible Ted Lindsay, one of the toughest players the NHL has ever seen, played on the famous Production Line with Gordie Howe and center Sid Abel. He helped the Red Wings win four Stanley Cups from 1948 to 1955. Lindsay channelled his combativeness into setting up the NHL Players' Association, which many believe led to his being traded to the Chicago Blackhawks in 1957.

**FRANK MAHOVLICH:** left winger. The man better known to hockey fans as The Big M possessed a booming slap shot and perhaps the smoothest, most powerful skating stride the game has ever seen. He scored 48 goals as a 23-year-old with Toronto in 1961 and helped the Maple Leafs win four Stanley Cups in the 1960s. Traded to Detroit in 1968, Mahovlich played on a line with Gordie Howe and Alex Delvecchio. Detroit traded him to Montreal in 1971 and The Big M set a playoff scoring record with 27 points and 14 goals to lead the Canadiens to the Stanley Cup. He also helped the

Canadiens win the Cup in 1973.

**LANNY MCDONALD:** right winger. McDonald scored 500 goals and added 506 assists in his 16-year career with Toronto, Colorado and Calgary. McDonald teamed up with Sittler as a potent one-two punch with the Maple Leafs until club owner Harold Ballard traded him to Colorado, largely out of spite. McDonald concluded a distinguished career in style, scoring a goal in Calgary's Cup-winning game against the Montreal Canadiens in 1989, the only Cup victory of his career.

**STAN MIKITA:** center. Born in Czechoslovakia, Mikita entered the NHL as a feisty, clever centerman, but he underwent a transformation into a gentlemanly player winning the Art Ross, Hart and Lady Byng trophies in 1967 and 1968, the first player ever to win all three in a single season. He is credited with introducing the curved stick blade to the NHL, by accident, it turns out. An angry Mikita tried to snap his stick blade by closing the door to the team bench on it. The stick bent, but did not break, and Mikita discovered it enhanced his shooting immensely.

**FRANK NIGHBOR:** center, defenseman. They called Nighbor the Pembroke Peach and he is credited with perfecting the poke check. He played 13 seasons in the NHL, from 1917-18 to 1929-30. He won five Stanley Cups, one with the Vancouver Millionaires in 1915, four more with the Ottawa Senators. In 1923, he became the first winner of the Hart Trophy as the NHL's most valuable player. In 1925, he was the first recipient of the Lady Byng Trophy, awarded to the league's most sportsmanlike player.

**BOBBY ORR:** defenseman. Played junior hockey for the Oshawa Generals and joined the Boston Bruins, at age 18, in 1966-67. Orr, one of the fastest skaters in the NHL in his time, revolutionized the defense position. With his quick acceleration, excellent straightahead speed and lateral mobility, Orr played defense like a point guard in basketball. More often than not, it was Orr who led the Bruins' offensive attacks, dishing a pass off to a teammate, or going end to end to take a shot on goal. He scored 296 goals in his 13 NHL seasons and was the first defenseman to score more than 40 goals and record more than 100 points in a season. He was the first defenseman to win the Conn Smythe Trophy. He also won the Norris Trophy eight times, the Hart three times and twice won the league scoring championship. He led the Bruins to two Stanley Cups. His career was foreshortened by a series of knee injuries.

**BRAD PARK:** defenseman. Contemporary of Orr and Potvin. Park played 17 years in the NHL, never for a team that missed the playoffs; but never for a team that won the Stanley Cup. He was named a first-team All-Star five times and became the second defenseman in NHL history to record 500 assists—after Orr. He scored 213 goals and added 683 assists in his career, which, like Orr's, was plagued by knee injuries. Early in his career, Park revived the seemingly lost art of the open-ice body check. Often cast in the shadow of first Orr, then Denis Potvin, Park was a superb two-way defenseman.

**GILBERT PERREAULT:** center. Won two Memorial Cups while a member of the Montreal Junior Canadiens. Perreault was the first draft pick of the Buffalo Sabres, for whom he played his entire 17-year career. Perreault centered the dangerous French Connection line with wingers Rene Robert and Richard Martin, amassing 1,336 points (512 goals) in his brilliant career. A virtuoso performer, Perreault was a strong, fast, slightly bow-legged skater, whose head

and shoulder fakes and quicksilver stickhandling mystified opponents. The Sabres built a credible NHL franchise in Buffalo around Perreault, who retired after the 1987-88 season.

**JACQUES PLANTE:** goaltender. Plante redefined his position. He was the first to roam away from the goal crease to handle loose pucks in the corners and along the end boards. After he suffered a nasty facial cut in a game in 1959, Plante donned a protective mask of his own design and, over the protests of his coach, Toe Blake, wore one from then on. Plante played 19 years in the NHL, with Montreal, New York, Toronto, St. Louis and Boston, but his years in Montreal were his finest. He won seven Vezina Trophies, six Stanley Cups and one Hart Trophy during his career.

**DENIS POTVIN:** defenseman. After a brilliant five-year junior career with the Ottawa 67s that Potvin began as a 14-year-old, the defenseman joined the New York Islanders as their indisputable franchise player. He led the Islanders to four straight Stanley Cups in the early 1980s. Potvin, a rugged, highly skilled player, chafed at comparisons with Orr. When his 15-year career was over, Potvin had recorded more goals (310), assists (742) and points (1,052) than any defenseman in NHL history.

**Big Bird: Larry Robinson was one of the famous Big Three defenseman in Montreal, with Guy Lapointe and Serge Savard in the 1970s.**

**MAURICE RICHARD:** right winger. The Rocket, as he was known, was a passionate presence on the ice who often saved his most brilliant performances for the most dramatic of circumstances. Among the 82 playoff goals he scored, 18 were gamewinners, six of those in sudden-death overtime. He was the first player to score 50 goals in 50 games in a single season and the first to score 500 in his career. He scored 544 goals during his career, won eight Stanley Cups and won the Hart Trophy. Ironically, the man many consider the league's best-ever pure scorer, never won the Art Ross Trophy as the leading NHL's leading scorer.

**TERRY SAWCHUK:** goaltender. Many consider Sawchuck to be the best goalie who ever played in the NHL. He posted an NHL-record 103 shutouts during his 21-year career, which saw him play for Detroit, Toronto, Boston, Los Angeles and New York Rangers. In 1952, Sawchuck carried the Red Wings to a Stanley Cup, posting four shutouts in Detroit's eight straight victories, and allowing just five goals overall. Sawchuck won the Vezina Trophy three times, including one award he shared with Johnny Bower for Toronto in 1967.

**DARRYL SITTLER:** center. Sittler was the heart and soul of some exciting Toronto Maple Leafs teams in the 1970s. He is remembered, as much as anything, for one brilliant night when he scored six goals and added four assists in an 11-4 Maple Leafs victory over the Boston Bruins in 1976. The same year, he scored five goals in a playoff game against the Flyers. He was the first member of the Maple Leafs to score 100 points in a season. He finished his career with 484 goals.

**VLADISLAV TRETIAK:** goaltender. In a perfect world, Tretiak, the brilliant goaltender for the Soviet Red Army and Soviet national teams, might have played for the Montreal Canadiens, who held his NHL rights. As a 20-year-old, Tretiak established himself as an excellent goaltender in the eight-game Canada-Soviet Summit Series in 1972. Viktor Tikhonov, the legendary Soviet coach, pulled Tretiak after the first period in the famous Miracle on Ice loss to the U.S. team at the Winter Olympics in 1980 in Lake Placid. Tikhonov would admit later this was his biggest regret as a coach.

# HOCKEY HALL OF FAME MEMBERSHIP ROSTER
## (PLAYERS ONLY)

**SID ABEL:** center, Detroit Red Wings (1938-43 and 1945-52), Chicago Blackhawks (1952-54). Inducted 1969.

**JACK ADAMS:** forward, Toronto Arenas (1917-19), Toronto St. Pats (1922-26), Ottawa Senators (1926-27). Inducted 1959.

**SYL APPS:** center, Toronto Maple Leafs (1936-43 and 1945-48). Inducted 1961.

**GEORGE ARMSTRONG:** center, Toronto Maple Leafs (1949-71). Inducted 1975.

**IRVINE (ACE) BAILEY:** forward, Toronto St. Pats (1926-27), Toronto Maple Leafs (1927-34). Inducted 1975.

**DAN BAIN:** forward, Winnipeg Victorias (1895-1902). Inducted 1945.

**HOBEY BAKER:** forward, Princeton University (1910-1914). Inducted 1945.

**BILL BARBER:** right winger, Philadelphia Flyers (1972-84). Inducted 1990.

**MARTY BARRY:** forward, NY Americans (1927-28), Boston Bruins (1929-35), Detroit Red Wings (1935-39), Montreal Canadiens (1939-40). Inducted 1965.

**ANDY BATHGATE:** right winger, NY Rangers (1952-63), Toronto Maple Leafs (1963-65), Detroit Red Wings (1965-67), Pittsburgh Penguins (1967-68 and1970-71). Inducted 1978.

**JEAN BELIVEAU:** center, Montreal Canadiens (1950-51 and 1952-71). Inducted 1972.

**CLINT BENEDICT:** goaltender, Ottawa Senators (1912-24), Montreal Maroons (1924-30). Inducted 1965.

**DOUG BENTLEY:** forward, Chicago Blackhawks (1939-44 and 1945-52), NY Rangers (1953-54). Inducted 1964.

**MAX BENTLEY:** forward, Chicago Blackhawks (1940-43 and 1945-48), Toronto Maple Leafs (1947-53), NY Rangers (1953-54). Inducted 1966.

**HECTOR (TOE) BLAKE:** left winger, Montreal Maroons (1934-35), Montreal Canadiens (1935-48). Inducted 1966.

**LEO BOIVIN:** defenseman, Boston Bruins (1954-66), Detroit Red Wings (1965-67), Pittsburgh Penguins (1967-69), Minnesota North Stars (1968-70). Inducted 1986.

**DICKIE BOON:** forward, Montreal AAAs (1899-03), Montreal Wanderers (1904-06). Inducted 1952.

**MIKE BOSSY:** right winger, New York Islanders (1977-87). Inducted 1991.

**EMILE (BUTCH) BOUCHARD:** defenseman, Montreal Canadiens (1941-1956). Inducted 1966.

**FRANK BOUCHER:** forward, Ottawa Senators (1921-22), NY Rangers (1926-38 and 1943-44). Inducted 1958.

**GEORGE BOUCHER:** forward, Ottawa Senators (1915-1929), Montreal Maroons (1928-31), Chicago Blackhawks (1931-32). Inducted 1960.

**JOHNNY BOWER:** goaltender, NY Rangers (1953-55 and 1956-57), Toronto Maple Leafs (1958-70), Vancouver Canucks (1954-55). Inducted 1976.

**RUSSELL (DUBBIE) BOWIE:** forward, Montreal Victorias (1898-1908). Inducted 1945.

**FRANK BRIMSEK:** goaltender, Boston Bruins (1938-43 and 1945-49), Chicago Blackhawks (1949-50). Inducted 1966.

**HARRY (PUNCH) BROADBENT:** forward, Ottawa Senators (1912-15 and 1918-24 and 1927-28), Montreal Maroons (1924-27), NY Americans (1928-29). Inducted1962.

**WALTER (TURK) BRODA:** goaltender, Toronto Maple Leafs (1936-43 and 1945-52). Inducted 1967.

**JOHN BUCYK:** left winger, Detroit Red Wings (1955-57), Boston Bruins (1957-78). Inducted 1981.

**BILLY BURCH:** forward, Hamilton Tigers (1922-25), NY Americans (1925-32), Boston/Chicago (1932-33). Inducted 1974.

**HARRY CAMERON:** forward, Toronto Blue Shirts (1912-16), Montreal Wanderers (1916-17), Toronto Arenas (1917-19), Ottawa Senators (1918-19), Montreal Canadiens (1919-20), Toronto St. Pats (1919-23). Inducted 1962.

**GERRY CHEEVERS:** goaltender, Toronto Maple Leafs (1961-62), Boston Bruins (1965-72 and 1975-80). Inducted 1985.

**FRANCIS (KING) CLANCY:** defenseman, Ottawa Senators (1921-30), Toronto Maple Leafs (1930-37). Inducted 1958.

**AUBRY (DIT) CLAPPER:** defenseman, Boston Bruins (1927-47). Inducted 1947.

**BOBBY CLARKE:** center, Philadelphia Flyers (1969-84). Inducted 1987.

**SPRAGUE CLEGHORN:** forward, Montreal Wanderers (1911-17), Ottawa Senators (1918-21), Toronto St. Pats (1920-21), Montreal Canadiens (1921-25), Boston Bruins (1925-28). Inducted 1958.

**NEIL COLVILLE:** forward, NY Rangers (1935-42 and 1944-49). Inducted 1961.

**CHARLIE CONACHER:** forward, Toronto Maple Leafs (1929-38), Detroit Red Wings (1938-39), NY Americans (1939-41).

**ALEX CONNELL:** goaltender, Ottawa Senators (1924-31 and 1932-33), Detroit Falcons (1931-32), NY Americans (1933-34), Montreal Maroons (1934-35 and 1936-37). Inducted 1958.

**BILL COOK:** forward, Saskatoon Crescents (1921-26), NY Rangers (1926-37). Inducted 1952.

**FRED JOSEPH (BUN) COOK:** forward, Boston Bruins/New York Rangers (1926-37). Inducted 1995.

**ART COULTER:** defenseman, Chicago Blackhawks (1931-36), NY Rangers (1935-42). Inducted 1974.

**YVAN COURNOYER:** right winger, Montreal Canadiens (1963-79). Inducted 1982.

**BILL COWLEY:** forward, St. Louis Eagles (1934-35), Boston Bruins (1935-47). Inducted 1968.

**RUSTY CRAWFORD:** forward, Quebec Bulldogs (1912-17), Toronto Arenas (1917-19), Ottawa Senators (1917-18), Vancouver Maroons (1925-26). Inducted 1962.

**JACK DARRAGH:** forward, Ottawa Senators (1910-1924). Inducted 1962.

**ALLAN (SCOTTY) DAVIDSON:** forward, Toronto Blueshirts (1912-14). Inducted 1950.

**CLARENCE (HAP) DAY:** defenseman, Toronto St. Pats (1924-26), Toronto Maple Leafs (1926-37), NY Americans (1937-38). Inducted 1961.

**ALEX DELVECCHIO:** center, Detroit Red Wings (1950-74). Inducted 1977.

**CY DENNENY:** forward, Toronto Shamrocks (1914-15), Toronto Arenas (1915-16), Ottawa Senators (1916-28), Boston Bruins (1928-29). Inducted 1959.

**MARCEL DIONNE:** center, Detroit Red Wings (1971-75), LA Kings (1975-87), NY Rangers (1987-89). Inducted 1992.

**GORDIE DRILLON:** forward, Toronto Maple Leafs (1936-42), Montreal Canadiens (1942-43). Inducted 1975.

**GRAHAM DRINKWATER:** forward, Montreal AAAs (1892-93), Montreal Victorias (1893, 1895-98), McGill University (1894-95), Montreal Victorias (1899).

**KEN DRYDEN:** goaltender, Montreal Canadiens (1970-73 and 1974-79). Inducted 1983.

**WOODY DUMART:** forward, Boston Bruins (1935-42 and 1945-54). Inducted 1992.

**TOMMY DUNDERDALE:** forward, Winnipeg Victorias (1906-08), Toronto Shamrocks (1909-10), Quebec Bulldogs (1910-11), Victoria Aristocrats 1911-15 and 1918-23), Portland Rosebuds (1915-18), Saskatoon/Edmonton (1923-24). Inducted 1974.

**BILL DURNAN:** goaltender, Montreal Canadiens (1943-50). Inducted 1964.

**MERVYN (RED) DUTTON:** defenseman, Montreal Maroons (1926-30), NY Americans (1930-36). Inducted 1958.

**CECIL (BABE) DYE:** forward, Toronto St. Pats (1919-26), Hamilton Tigers (1920-21), Chicago Blackhawks (1926-28), NY Americans (1928-29), Toronto Maple Leafs (1930-31) Inducted 1970.

**PHIL ESPOSITO:** center, Chicago Blackhawks (1963-67), Boston Bruins (1967-76), NY Rangers (1975-81). Inducted 1984.

**TONY ESPOSITO:** goaltender, Montreal Canadiens (1968-69), Chicago Blackhawks (1969-84). Inducted 1988.

**ARTHUR FARRELL:** forward, Montreal Shamrocks (1896-1901). Inducted 1965.

**FERNIE FLAMAN:** defenseman, Boston Bruins (1944-51 and 1954-61), Toronto Maple Leafs (1950-54). Inducted 1965.

**FRANK FOYSTON:** forward, Toronto Blueshirts (1912-16), Seattle Metros (1915-24), Victoria Aristocrats (1924-26), Detroit Cougars (1926-28). Inducted 1958.

**FRANK FREDERICKSON:** forward, Victoria Aristocrats (1920-26), Boston Bruins (1926-29), Detroit Falcons (1926-27 and 1930-31), Pittsburgh Pirates (1928-30). Inducted 1958.

**BILL GADSBY:** defenseman, Chicago Blackhawks (1946-54), NY Rangers (1954-61), Detroit Red Wings (1961-66). Inducted 1970.

**BOB GAINEY:** left winger, Montreal Canadiens (1973-89). Inducted 1992.

**CHUCK GARDINER:** goaltender, Chicago Blackhawks (1927-34). Inducted 1945.

**HERB GARDINER:** defenseman, Montreal Canadiens (1926-29), Chicago Blackhawks (1928-29). Inducted 1958.

**JIMMY GARDNER:** forward, Montreal AAAs (1900-03), Montreal Wanderers (1903-11), New Westminster Royals (1911-13), Montreal Canadiens (1913-15). Inducted 1962.

**BERNARD (BOOM BOOM) GEOFFRION:** left winger, Montreal Canadiens (1951-64), NY Rangers (1966-68). Inducted 1972.

**EDDIE GERARD:** forward, Ottawa Victorias (1907-08), Ottawa Senators (1913-23). Inducted 1945.

**EDDIE GIACOMIN:** goaltender, NY Rangers (1965-76), Detroit Red Wings (1975-78). Inducted 1987.

**ROD GILBERT:** forward, NY Rangers (1960-78). Inducted 1982.

**BILLY GILMOUR:** forward, Ottawa Senators (1902-06 and 1908-09 and 1915-16), Montreal Victorias (1907-08). Inducted 1962.

**FRANK (MOOSE) GOHEEN:** defenseman, St. Paul Athletic Club (1914-28). Inducted 1952.

**EBBIE GOODFELLOW:** forward, Detroit Cougars (1928-30), Detroit Falcons (1930-33), Detroit Red Wings (1933-43). Inducted 1963.

**MIKE GRANT:** defenseman, Montreal Victorias (1893-1902). Inducted 1950.

**WILF (SHORTY) GREEN:** forward, Hamilton Tigers (1923-25), NY Americans (1925-27). Inducted 1962.

**SI GRIFFIS:** forward, Rat Portage Thistles (1902-06), Kenora Thistles (1906-07), Vancouver Millionaires (1911-19). Inducted 1950.

**GEORGE HAINSWORTH:** goaltender, Montreal Canadiens (1926-33 and 1936-37), Toronto Maple Leafs (1933-37). Inducted 1961.

**GLENN HALL:** goaltender, Detroit Red Wings (1952-53 and 1954-57), Chicago Blackhawks (1957-67), St. Louis Blues (1967-71). Inducted 1975.

**JOE HALL:** forward, Winnipeg Victorias (1903-05), Quebec Bulldogs (1905-06 and 1910-17), Brandon (1906-07), Montreal AAAs (1907-08), Montreal Shamrocks (1907-08 and 1909-10), Montreal Wanderers (1908-09), Montreal Canadiens (1917-19). Inducted 1961.

**DOUG HARVEY:** defenseman, Montreal Canadiens (1947-61), NY Rangers (1961-64), Detroit Red Wings (1966-67), St. Louis Blues (1967-69). Inducted 1973.

**GEORGE HAY:** forward, Chicago Blackhawks (1926-27), Detroit Cougars (1927-30), Detroit Falcons (1930-31), Detroit Red Wings (1932-34). Inducted 1958.

**RILEY HERN:** goaltender, Montreal Wanderers (1906-11). Inducted 1962.

**BRYAN HEXTALL:** forward, NY Rangers (1936-44 and 1945-48). Inducted 1969.

**HARRY (HAP) HOLMES:** goaltender, Toronto Blueshirts (1912-16), Seattle Metros (1915-17 and 1918-24), Toronto Arenas (1917-19), Victoria Aristocrats (1924-26), Detroit Cougars (1926-28).

**TOM HOOPER:** forward, Rat Portage Thistles (1901-05), Kenora Thistles (1906-07), Montreal Wanderers (1907-08), Montreal AAAs (1907-08). Inducted 1962.

**REGINALD G. (RED) HORNER:** defenseman, Toronto Maple Leafs (1928-40). Inducted 1965.

**TIM HORTON:** defenseman, Toronto Maple Leafs, 1949-70), NY Rangers (1969-71), Pittsburgh Penguins (1971-72), Buffalo Sabres (1972-74). Inducted 1977.

**GORDIE HOWE:** right winger, Detroit Red Wings (1946-71), Houston Aeros (1973-77), New England Whalers (1977-79), Hartford Whalers (1979-80). Inducted 1972.

**SYD HOWE:** forward, Ottawa Senators (1929-30 and 1932-34), Philadelphia Quakers (1930-31), Toronto Maple Leafs (1931-32), St. Louis Eagles (1934-35), Detroit Red Wings (1934-46). Inducted 1965.

**HARRY HOWELL:** defenseman, NY Rangers (1952-69), Oakland Seals (1969-70), LA Kings (1970-73). Inducted 1979.

**ROBERT MARVIN (BOBBY) HULL:** left winger, Chicago Blackhawks (1957-72), Winnipeg Jets (1972-80), Hartford Whalers (1979-80). Inducted 1983.

**BOUSE HUTTON:** goaltender, Ottawa Senators (1898-1904). Inducted 1962.

**HARRY HYLAND:** forward, Montreal Shamrocks (1908-09), Montreal Wanderers (1909-11 and 1912-17), New Westminster Royals (1911-12), Montreal/Ottawa (1917-18). Inducted 1962.

**DICK IRVIN:** forward, Portland Rosebuds (1916-17), Regina Capitals (1921-25), Portland Capitals (1925-26), Chicago Blackhawks (1926-29). Inducted 1958.

**HARVEY (BUSHER) JACKSON:** forward, Toronto Maple Leafs (1929-39), NY Americans (1939-41), Boston Bruins (1941-44). Inducted 1971.

**IVAN WILFRED (CHING) JOHNSON:** defenseman, NY Rangers (1926-37), NY Americans (1937-38). Inducted 1958.

**ERNIE JOHNSON:** forward, Montreal Victorias (1903-05), Montreal Wanderers (1905-11), New Westminster Royals (1911-14), Portland Rosebuds (1914-18), Victoria Aristocrats (1918-22). Inducted 1952.

**TOM JOHNSON:** defenseman, Montreal Canadiens (1947-48 and 1949-63), Boston Bruins (1963-65). Inducted 1970.

**AUREL JOLIAT:** forward, Montreal Canadiens (1922-38). Inducted 1947.

**GORDON (DUKE) KEATS:** forward, Toronto Blue Shirts (1915-17), Edmonton Eskimos (1921-26), Boston & Detroit (1926-27), Detroit & Chicago (1927-28) Chicago Blackhawks (1928-29). Inducted 1958.

**LEONARD (RED) KELLY:** defenseman, center, Detroit Red Wings (1947-60), Toronto Maple Leafs (1960-67). Inducted 1969.

**TED (TEEDER) KENNEDY:** forward, Toronto Maple Leafs (1942-55 and 1956-57). Inducted 1966.

**DAVE KEON:** center, Toronto Maple Leafs (1960-75), Hartford Whalers (1979-82). Inducted 1986.

**ELMER LACH:** center, Montreal Canadiens (1940-54). Inducted 1966.

**GUY LAFLEUR:** right winger, Montreal Canadiens (1971-85), NY Rangers (1988-89), Quebec Nordiques (1989-91). Inducted 1988.

**EDOUARD (NEWSY) LALONDE:** forward, Montreal Canadiens (1910-11 and 1912-22), NY Americans (1926-27). Inducted 1950.

**JACQUES LAPERRIERE:** defenseman, Montreal Canadiens (1962-74). Inducted 1987.

**JACK LAVIOLETTE:** defenseman, Montreal Nationals (1903-07), Montreal Shamrocks (1907-09), Montreal Canadiens (1909-18). Inducted 1962.

**HUGH LEHMAN:** goaltender, New Westminster Royals (1911-14), Vancouver Millionaires (1914-26), Chicago Blackhawks (1926-28). Inducted 1958.

**JACQUES LEMAIRE:** left winger, center, Montreal Canadiens (1967-79). Inducted 1984.

**PERCY LESUEUR:** goaltender, Ottawa Senators (1905-14), Toronto Shamrocks (1914-15), Toronto Blueshirts (1915-16). Inducted 1961.

**HERBIE LEWIS:** forward, Detroit Cougars (1928-30), Detroit Falcons (1930-33), Detroit Red Wings (1933-39). Inducted 1989.

**TED LINDSAY:** left winger, Detroit Red Wings (1944-58 and 1964-65), Chicago Blackhawks (1957-60). Inducted 1966.

**HARRY LUMLEY:** goaltender, Detroit Red Wings (1943-50), Chicago Blackhawks (1950-52), Toronto Maple Leafs (1952-56), Boston Bruins (1957-60).

**MICKEY MACKAY:** forward, Vancouver Millionaires (1914-19 and 1920-24), Vancouver Maroons (1924-26), Chicago Blackhawks (1926-28), Boston & Pittsburgh (1928-29), Boston Bruins (1929-30). Inducted 1952.

**FRANK MAHOVLICH:** left winger, Toronto Maple Leafs (1956-68), Detroit Red Wings (1968-71), Montreal Canadiens (1971-74). Inducted 1981.

**JOE (PHANTOM) MALONE:** forward, Quebec Bulldogs (1908-09 and 1910-17), Waterloo (1909-10), Montreal Canadiens (1917-24), Hamilton Tigers (1921-22). Inducted 1950.

**SYLVIO MANTHA:** defenseman, Montreal Canadiens (1923-36), Boston Bruins (1936-37). Inducted 1960.

**JACK MARSHALL:** forward, Winnipeg Victorias (1900-01), Montreal Victorias (1901-03), Montreal Wanderers (1903-05 and 1906-07 and 1909-12 and 1915-17), Montreal Shamrocks (1907-09), Toronto Tecumsehs (1912-13), Toronto Ontarios (1913-14), Toronto Shamrocks (1914-15). Inducted 1965.

**FRED MAXWELL:** forward, Winnipeg Monarchs (1914-16), Winnipeg Falcons (1918-25). Inducted 1962.

**LANNY MCDONALD:** right winger, Toronto Maple Leafs (1973-80), Colorado Rockies (1980-82), Calgary Flames (1982-89). Inducted 1992.

**Frank McGee:** forward, Ottawa Senators (1902-06). Inducted 1945.

**BILLY MCGIMSIE:** forward, Rat Portage Thistles (1902-03 and 1904-06), Kenora Thistles (1906-07). Inducted 1962.

**GEORGE MCNAMARA:** defenseman, Montreal Shamrocks (1907-09), Halifax Crescents (1909-12), Waterloo (1911), Toronto Tecumsehs (1912-13), Ottawa (1913-14), Toronto Shamrocks (1914-15), Toronto Blueshirts (1915-16), 228th Battalion (1916-17). Inducted 1958.

**STAN MIKITA:** center, Chicago Blackhawks (1958-80). Inducted 1983.

**RICHARD (DICKIE) MOORE:** left winger, Montreal Canadiens (1951-63), Toronto Maple Leafs (1964-65), St. Louis Blues (1967-68). Inducted 1974.

**PADDY MORAN:** goaltender, Quebec Bulldogs (1901-09 and 1910-17), Halleybury Comets (1909-10). Inducted 1958.

**HOWIE MORENZ:** forward, Montreal Canadiens (1923-34 and 1936-37), Chicago Blackhawks (1934-36), NY Rangers (1935-36). Inducted 1945.

**BILL MOSIENKO:** forward, Chicago Blackhawks (1941-55). Inducted 1965.

**FRANK NIGHBOR:** center, Ottawa Senators (1915-29), Toronto Maple Leafs (1929-30). Inducted 1947.

**REGINALD NOBLE:** forward, Toronto Arenas (1917-19), Toronto St. Patricks (1919-25), Montreal Maroons (1924-27), Detroit Cougars (1927-32), Detroit & Montreal (1932-33). Inducted 1962.

**BUDDY O'CONNOR:** forward, Montreal Canadiens (1941-47), NY Rangers (1947-51). Inducted 1988.

**HARRY OLIVER:** forward, Boston Bruins (1926-34), NY Americans (1934-37). Inducted 1967.

**BERT OLMSTEAD:** left winger, Chicago Blackhawks (1948-51), Montreal Canadiens (1950-58), Toronto Maple Leafs (1958-62). Inducted 1985.

**ROBERT (BOBBY) ORR:** defenseman, Boston Bruins (1966-76), Chicago Blackhawks (1976-79). Inducted 1979.

**BERNARD PARENT:** goaltender, Boston Bruins (1965-67), Philadelphia Flyers (1967-71 and 1973-79), Toronto Maple Leafs (1970-72). Inducted 1984.

**BRAD PARK:** defenseman, NY Rangers (1968-76), Boston Bruins (1976-83), Detroit Red Wings (1983-85). Inducted 1988.

**LESTER PATRICK:** forward, Brandon (1903-04), Westmount (1904-05), Montreal Wanderers (1905-07), Edmonton (1907-08), Renfrew Cream Kings (1909-10), Victoria Aristocrats (1911-16 and 1918-22), Spokane (1916-17), Seattle Metros (1917-18), Victoria Cougars (1925-26), NY Rangers (1927-28). Inducted 1947.

**JOSEPH LYNN PATRICK:** forward, NY Rangers (1934-43 and 1945-46). Inducted 1980.

**GILBERT PERREAULT:** center, Buffalo Sabres (1970-87). Inducted 1990.

**TOM PHILLIPS:** forward, Montreal AAAs (1902-03), Toronto Marlboroughs (1903-04), Rat Portage Thistles (1904-06), Kenora Thistles (1906-07), Ottawa Senators (1907-08), Vancouver Millionaires (1911-12). Inducted 1945.

**PIERRE PILOTE:** defenseman, Chicago Blackhawks (1955-68), Toronto Maple Leafs (1968-69). Inducted 1975.

**DIDIER PITRE:** forward, Montreal Nationals (1903-05), Montreal Shamrocks (1907-08), Renfrew Millionaires (1908-09), Montreal Canadiens (1909-23). Inducted 1962.

**JACQUES PLANTE:** goaltender, Montreal Canadiens (1952-63), NY Rangers (1963-65), St. Louis Blues (1968-70), Toronto Maple Leafs (1970-73), Boston Bruins (1972-73). Inducted 1978.

**DENIS POTVIN:** defenseman, NY Islanders (1973-88). Inducted 1991.

**WALTER (BABE) PRATT:** defenseman, NY Rangers (1935-43), Toronto Maple Leafs (1942-46), Boston Bruins (1946-47). Inducted 1966.

**JOE PRIMEAU:** defenseman, Toronto Maple Leafs (1927-36). Inducted 1963.

**MARCEL PRONOVOST:** defenseman, Detroit Red Wings (1949-65), Toronto Maple Leafs (1965-70). Inducted 1978.

**BOB PULFORD:** center, Toronto Maple Leafs (1956-70), LA Kings (1970-72). Inducted 1991.

**HARVEY PULFORD:** defenseman, Ottawa Senators (1893-1908). Inducted 1945.

**BILL QUACKENBUSH:** defenseman, Detroit Red Wings (1942-49), Boston Bruins (1949-56). Inducted 1976.

**FRANK RANKIN:** forward, Stratford (1906-09), Eaton's Athletic Association (1910-12), St. Michaels' (1912-14). Inducted 1961.

**JEAN RATELLE:** center, NY Rangers (1962-76), Boston Bruins (1975-81). Inducted 1985.

**CHUCK RAYNER:** goaltender, NY Americans (1940-41), Brooklyn Americans (1941-42), NY Rangers (1945-53). Inducted 1973.

**KENNETH JOSEPH REARDON:** defenseman, Montreal Canadiens (1940-42 and 1945-50). Inducted 1966.

**HENRI RICHARD:** center, Montreal Canadiens (1955-75). Inducted 1979.

**MAURICE (ROCKET) RICHARD:** right winger, Montreal Canadiens (1942-60). Inducted 1961.

**GEORGE RICHARDSON:** forward, 14th Regiment (1906-13), Queens University (1908-09). Inducted 1950.

**GORDON ROBERTS:** forward, Ottawa Senators (1909-10), Montreal Wanderers (1910-16), Vancouver Millionaires (1916-17 and 1919-20), Seattle Metropolitans (1917-18). Inducted 1971.

**LARRY ROBINSON:** defenseman, Montreal Canadiens (1972-90), Los Angeles Kings (1990-92). Inducted 1995.

**ART ROSS:** forward, Westmount (1904-05), Brandon (1906-07), Kenora Thistles (1906-07), Montreal Wanderers (1907-09 and 1910-14 and 1917-18), Halleybury Comets (1909-10), Ottawa Senators (1914-16). Inducted 1945.

**BLAIR RUSSEL:** forward, Montreal Victorias (1899-1908). Inducted 1965.

**ERNIE RUSSELL:** forward, Montreal AAAs (1904-05), Montreal Wanderers (1905-08 and 1909-14). Inducted 1965.

**JACK RUTTAN:** forward, Armstrong's Point (1905-06), Rustler (1906-07), St. Johns College (1907-08), Manitoba Varsity (1909-12), Winnipeg (1912-13). Inducted 1962.

**BORJE SALMING:** defenseman, Toronto Maple Leafs 1973-1989, Detroit Red Wings, 1990. Inducted 1996.

**SERGE SAVARD:** defenseman, Montreal Canadiens (1966-81), Winnipeg Jets (1981-83). Inducted 1986.

**TERRY SAWCHUCK:** goaltender, Detroit Red Wings (1949-55 and 1957-64 and 1968-69), Boston Bruins (1955-57), Toronto Maple Leafs (1964-67), LA Kings (1967-68), NY Rangers (1969-70). Inducted 1971.

**FRED SCANLAN:** forward, Montreal Shamrocks (1897-1901), Winnipeg Victorias (1901-03). Inducted 1965.

**MILT SCHMIDT:** center, Boston Bruins, 1936-42 and 1945-55). Inducted 1961.

**SWEENEY SCHRINER:** forward, NY Americans (1934-39), Toronto Maple Leafs (1939-43 and 1944-46). Inducted 1962.

**EARL SEIBERT:** defenseman, NY Rangers (1931-36), Chicago Blackhawks (1935-45), Detroit Red Wings (1944-46). Inducted 1963.

**OLIVER SEIBERT:** forward, Berlin Dutchmen (1900-06). Inducted 1961.

**EDDIE SHORE:** defenseman, Boston Bruins (1926-40). Inducted 1947.

**STEVE SHUTT:** left winger, Montreal Canadiens (1973-1984), LA Kings (1985). Inducted 1993.

**ALBERT CHARLES (BABE) SIEBERT:** defenseman, Montreal Maroons (1925-32), NY Rangers (1932-34), Boston Bruins (1933-36), Montreal Canadiens (1936-39). Inducted 1964.

**JOE SIMPSON:** defenseman, Edmonton Eskimos (1921-25), NY Americans (1925-31). Inducted 1962.

**DARRYL SITTLER:** center, Toronto Maple Leafs (1970-82), Philadelphia Flyers (1982-84), Detroit Red Wings (1984-85). Inducted 1989.

**ALF SMITH:** forward, Ottawa Senators, 1894-1908), Kenora Thistles (1906-07). Inducted 1962.

**BILLY SMITH:** goaltender: LA Kings (1971-72), NY Islanders (1972-89). Inducted 1993.

**CLINT SMITH:** forward, NY Rangers (1936-43), Chicago Blackhawks (1943-47). Inducted 1991.

**REGINALD JOSEPH (HOOLEY) SMITH:** forward, Ottawa Senators (1924-27), Montreal Maroons (1927-36), Boston Bruins (1936-37), NY Americans (1937-41). Inducted 1972.

**TOMMY SMITH:** forward, Ottawa Victorias (1905-06), Brantford Indians (1908-10), Cobalt Silver Kings (1909-10), Galt (1910-11), Moncton (1911-12), Quebec Bulldogs (1912-16 and 1919-20), Ontarios (1914-15), Montreal Canadiens (1916-17). Inducted 1973.

**ALLAN STANLEY:** defenseman, NY Rangers (1948-55), Chicago Blackhawks (1954-56), Toronto Maple Leafs (1958-68), Philadelphia Flyers (1968-69). Inducted 1981.

**BARNEY STANLEY:** forward, Vancouver Millionaires (1914-19), Calgary Tigers (1921-22), Regina Capitals (1922-24), Edmonton Eskimos (1924-26). Inducted 1962.

**JACK STEWART:** defenseman, Detroit Red Wings (1938-43 and 1945-50), Chicago Blackhawks (1950-52).

**NELSON STEWART:** forward, Montreal Maroons (1925-32), Boston Bruins (1932-35 and 1936-37), NY Americans (1935-40). Inducted 1962.

**BRUCE STUART:** forward, Ottawa Senators (1898-1902 and 1908-11), Quebec Bulldogs (1900-01), Montreal Wanderers (1907-08). Inducted 1961.

**WILLIAM HODGSON (HOD) STUART:** forward, Ottawa Senators (1898-1900), Quebec Bulldogs (1900-06), Montreal Wanderers (1906-08). Inducted 1945.

**FREDERICK (CYCLONE) TAYLOR:** forward, Ottawa Senators (1907-09), Renfrew Cream Kings (1909-11), Vancouver Millionaires (1912-21 and 1922-23). Inducted 1947.

**CECIL R. (TINY) THOMPSON:** goaltender, Boston Bruins (1928-39), Detroit Red Wings (1939-40). Inducted 1959.

**VLADISLAV TRETIAK:** goaltender, Central Red Army (1969-84), Soviet National Team (1969-84). Inducted 1989.

**HARRY TRIHEY:** forward, Montreal Shamrocks (1896-1901). Inducted 1950.

**NORM ULLMAN:** center, Detroit Red Wings (1955-67), Toronto Maple Leafs (1967-75), Edmonton Oilers (1975-77). Inducted 1982.

**GEORGES VEZINA:** goaltender, Montreal Canadiens (1910-26). Inducted 1945.

**JACK WALKER:** forward, Toronto Blueshirts (1912-15), Seattle Metros (1915-24), Victoria Cougars (1924-26), Detroit Cougars (1926-28). Inducted 1960.

**MARTY WALSH:** forward, Ottawa Senators (1907-12). Inducted 1962.

**HARRY (MOOSE) WATSON:** left winger, St. Andrews (1915), Aura Lee Juniors (1918), Toronto Dentals (1919), Toronto Granites (1920-25), Toronto Sea Fleas (1931). Inducted 1962.

**RALPH C. (COONEY) WEILAND:** forward, Boston Bruins (1928-32 and 1935-39), Ottawa Senators (1932-34), Detroit Red Wings (1933-35). Inducted 1971.

**HARRY WESTWICK:** forward, Ottawa Senators (1894-98 and 1900-08), Kenora Thistles (1906-07). Inducted 1962.

**FRET WHITCROFT:** forward, Kenora Thistles (1906-08), Edmonton (1908-10), Renfrew Cream Kings (1909-10). Inducted 1962.

**GORDON ALLAN (PHAT) WILSON:** forward, Port Arthur War Veterans (1918-20), Iroquois Falls Eskimos (1921), Port Arthur Bearcats (1923-33). Inducted 1962.

**LORNE (GUMP) WORSLEY:** goaltender, NY Rangers (1952-63), Montreal Canadiens (1963-70), Minnesota North Stars (1969-74). Inducted 1980.

**ROY WORTERS:** goaltender, Pittsburgh Pirates (1925-28), NY Americans (1928-37), Montreal Maroons (1929-30). Inducted 1969.

# GLOSSARY OF HOCKEY TERMS

**Art Ross Trophy:** Awarded to the player who wins the scoring championship during the regular season.

**Assist:** A pass that leads to a goal being scored. One or two, or none, may be awarded on any goal.

**Backchecking:** Skating with an opponent through the neutral and defensive zones to try to break up an attack.

**Backhand:** A pass or shot, in which the player cradles the puck on the off- or backside of the stick blade and propels it with a shoveling motion..

**Back pass:** A pass left or slid backwards for a trailing teammate to recover.

**Blocker:** A protective glove worn on the hand a goaltender uses to hold his stick so that the goalie can deflect pucks away from the net.

**Blue lines:** The lines, located 29 feet from each side of the center red line, which demarcate the beginning of the offensive zone.

**Boarding:** Riding or driving an opponent into the boards. A two- or five-minute penalty may be assessed, at the referee's discretion.

**Boards:** Wooden structures, 48 inches high, topped by plexiglass fencing, that enclose the 200 feet by 85 feet ice surface.

**Bodycheck:** Using the hips or shoulders to stop the progress of the puck carrier.

**Breakaway:** The puck carrier skating toward the opposition's net ahead of all the other players.

**Butt-Ending:** Striking an opponent with the top end of the hockey stick, a dangerously illegal act that brings a five-minute penalty.

**Calder Memorial Trophy:** Awarded to the goaltender, defenseman or forward judged to be the best first-year, or rookie, player.

**Central Scouting Bureau:** An NHL agency that compiles statistical and evaluative information on all players eligible for the Entry Draft. The information, which includes a rating system of all players, is distributed to all NHL teams.

**Charging:** Skating three strides or more and crashing into an opponent. Calls for a two-minute or five-minute penalty at the referee's discretion.

**Conn Smythe Trophy:** Awarded to the top performer throughout the Stanley Cup playoffs.

**Crease:** A six-foot semicircular area at the mouth of the goal that opponents may not enter. Only the goaltender may freeze the puck in this space.

**Crossbar:** A red, horizontal pipe, four feet above the ice and six feet long across the top of the goal cage.

**Crosschecking:** Hitting an opponent with both hands on the stick and no part of the stick on the ice. Warrants a two-minute penalty.

**Defensemen:** The two players who form the second line of defense, after the goalie. Defensemen try to strip opponents of the puck in their own zone and either pass to teammates or skate the puck up-ice themselves to start an attack. When retreating from the opponent's zone, defensemen move back toward their zone by skating backwards, facing the oncoming opponents.

**Deflection:** Placing the blade of the stick in the path of a shot on goal, causing the puck to change direction and deceive the goaltender. A puck may also deflect off a player's skate or pads.

**Delay of game:** Causing the play to stop by either propelling the puck outside the playing surface or covering it with the hand. Warrants a two-minute penalty.

**Delayed penalty:** An infraction, signaled by the referee's upraised right hand, but not whistled until the offending team regains possession of the puck. During the delay, the other team can launch a scoring attack, sometimes by replacing their goaltender with a skater. If the team scores during the delay, the penalized player does not sit out his penalty.

**Elbowing:** Striking an opponent with the elbow. Calls for a two-minute penalty.

**Entry Draft:** An annual event, at which all 26 NHL teams submit claims on young players who have not signed professional contracts. The talent pool consists of players from the Canadian junior leagues, U.S. high schools and universities and European elite and junior leagues.

**Faceoff:** A play that initiates all action in a hockey game, in which the referee or a linesman drops the puck onto a spot between the poised stick blades of two opponents. Marks the start of every period, also occurs after every goal and every play stoppage.

**Fighting:** Players dropping their gloves and striking each other with their fists. Calls for a five-minute penalty and ejection for the player who instigated the fisticuffs.

**Forechecking:** Harassing opponents in their own zone to try to gain possession of the puck.

**Forwards:** Three players—the center and the left and right wingers—comprise a hockey team's forward line. The forwards are primarily attackers whose aim is to score goals.

**Frank J. Selke Trophy:** Awarded to the player judged the best defensive forward in the NHL.

**Goal:** A goal is scored when the puck completely crosses the red goal line and enters the net.

**Goals-Against-Average (GAG):** Average number of goals a goaltender surrenders per game. Determined by multiplying the total number of goals allowed by 60 and dividing that figure by the total number of minutes played.

**Goaltender:** A heavily padded player who protects his team's goal.

**Hart Memorial Trophy:** Awarded to the player judged the most valuable to his team during the NHL regular season.

**Hat Trick:** One player scoring three goals in one game. A player who scores three consecutive goals in one period is said to have scored a 'natural' hat trick.

**High sticking:** Carrying the stick above the shoulder level. Calls for a faceoff if a player strikes the puck in this fashion. Calls for a two- or five-minute penalty if a player strikes an opponent with his stick.

**Holding:** Using the hands to impede the progress of an opponent. Two-minute penalty.

**Hooking:** Using the blade of the stick to impede an opponent. Two-minute penalty.

**Icing the puck:** Shooting the puck from one side of the center red line so that it crosses the opponent's red goal line. Calls for a play stoppage and a faceoff in the offending team's zone.

**Interference:** Using the body or stick to impede an opponent who is not in possession of the puck or was the last one to touch it. Two-minute penalty.

**James Norris Memorial Trophy:** Awarded annually to the player who is judged to be the best defenseman in the NHL.

**Kneeing:** Using the knee to check an opponent. Two-minute penalty.

**Lady Byng Trophy:** Awarded to the player who best combines playing excellence with sportsmanship.

**Linesmen:** Two on-ice officials responsible for calling offside, icing and some infractions, such as too many men on the ice. Linesmen drop the puck for faceoffs excluding those after a goal has been scored.

**Neutral zone:** The area of the ice surface between the two blue lines and bisected by the center red line.

**Neutral-zone trap:** Also called the delayed forecheck. A checking system designed to choke off offensive attacks in the neutral zone and enable the defensive team to regain possession of the puck.

**Offside:** A player who crosses the opposition blue line before the puck does is offside. Play is stopped when this occurs and a faceoff is held outside the blue line. A player also is offside if he accepts a pass that has crossed two lines (e.g. his team's blue line and the center red line). When this occurs, play is stopped and a faceoff is held at the point where the pass was made.

**Original Six:** In common usage, it refers to the six NHL teams in the pre-1968 expansion era: Toronto Maple Leafs; Montreal Canadiens; Boston Bruins; New York Rangers; Chicago Blackhawks; Detroit Red Wings.

**Overtime:** During regular-season play, teams play a five-minute, sudden-death overtime period if the score is tied at the end of regulation time. Teams play as many 20-minute sudden-death overtime periods as is necessary to reach a final result during the entire playoff schedule. Sudden-death means the game is over as soon as a goal is scored.

**Penalty:** A rules infraction which results in a player serving a two- or five-minute penalty in the penalty box, or in expulsion from the game. The penalized player's team must play one man short while he serves a minor or major penalty, but is not so handicapped if the player is assessed a ten-minute misconduct. The player cannot play until his time is up, but the team continues at full on-ice strength. A player assessed a game misconduct penalty cannot play for the rest of the game.

**Penalty kill:** A four- or three-man unit of players assigned to prevent the opposition from scoring while a teammate serves a two- or five-minute penalty.

**Penalty Shot:** Called when an attacking player, on a breakaway, is illegally prevented from getting a shot on goal. The puck is placed at center ice and the fouled player skates in alone on the goaltender.

**Period:** A 20-minute segment, during which time the clock stops at every play stoppage. A hockey game consists of three stop-time periods.

**Playing Roster:** A team may only dress 18 skaters and two goaltenders for each NHL game.

**Plus-Minus:** A 'plus' is credited to a player who is on the ice when his team scores an even-strength or shorthanded goal. A 'minus' is given to a player who is on the ice when an opponent scores an even-strength or shorthanded goal. A player's plus-minus total is the aggregate score of pluses and minuses. It is a barometer of a player's value to his team.

**Point man:** A player, usually a defenseman, who positions himself along the blue line near the boards and orchestrates an attacking team's offensive zone strategy. Often teams try to isolate the point man for a shot on goal.

**Pokecheck:** A sweeping or poking motion with the stick used to take the puck away from an opponent. Perfected by Frank Nighbor of the Ottawa Senators teams in the 1920s.

**Power play:** A situation in which one team has one or two more players on the ice than the other team, owing to penalties assessed. It provides the attacking team with an excellent opportunity to create quality scoring chances.

**Puck:** A vulcanized rubber disk, three inches wide and one inch thick. Game pucks are kept on ice before and during a game, which hardens them even more and helps them slide more quickly.

**Rebound:** A puck bouncing off the boards, the goaltender or the goalposts. A rebound gives an attacker a second chance for a dangerous shot on goal.

**Red line:** The red, center line dividing the ice surface in half. In junior and professional hockey, the red line is used to determine icing calls and offside passes. It is not used in U.S. college hockey.

**Referee:** The chief on-ice official at a hockey game. The referee calls all penalties except too many men on the ice and controls the flow of the game.

**Roughing:** Excessive pushing and shoving that has not escalated to the level of fisticuffs. Two-minute penalty.

**Rink:** A surface 200 feet by 85 feet on which a game of hockey is played.

**Save:** Occurs when a goalie uses his blocker, goalie stick, catching glove or pads to prevent a puck from entering the goal.

**Scout:** A man or woman who travels to junior, college and high school games, evaluating players who will be available in the Entry Draft. NHL teams also have pro scouts, who evaluate the play of opposing teams.

**Shift:** The period of time—usually 35-45 seconds—that a player spends on the ice playing the game. Normally a player will play several shifts each period. Some players log as much as 30 minutes in ice time in any given game.

**Shot On Goal:** Any deliberate attempt by a player to shoot the puck into an opponent's net that, without the intervention of the goaltender, would have scored a goal. Therefore, a shot that hits a goalpost or the crossbar and bounces away, is not a shot on goal.

**Shutout:** A game result in which the opponent does not score a goal, usually owing to excellent work by the goaltender.

**Slap shot:** Shooting the puck by swinging the hockey stick through the disk, in a manner similar to a golf swing, except with the hands several inches apart on the stick.

**Slashing:** Swinging a stick at an opponent. Two-minute penalty.

**Slot, The:** The area in the offensive zone directly in front of the crease, extending back between the two faceoff circles, about halfway toward the blue line. Teams work hard to create scoring opportunities inside this area.

**Spearing:** Using a stick as a weapon, jabbing it, like a spear, into an opponent. Five-minute penalty, with expulsion at the discretion of the referee.

**Stanley Cup:** A silver trophy, originally donated by Lord Stanley, Earl of Preston in 1893 to be emblematic of Canadian hockey supremacy. Since 1926 only NHL teams have competed for the trophy.

**Stickhandle:** Manipulating the puck back and forth, or any direction, with the blade of the stick in order to deceive an opponent and carry the puck up the ice.

**Tip-In:** A goal that results when one player shoots on net and a teammate, positioned near the crease, uses his stick to redirect the puck past the goaltender.

**Vezina Trophy:** Awarded annually to the player judged to be the best goaltender in the NHL.

**Wrist shot:** Shooting the puck by sweeping the stick along the ice, snapping the wrists on the follow-through.

**Zamboni:** The box-like, motor-powered vehicle used to resurface the ice in all NHL arenas. The machine collects the snow that builds up during a period of play and lays down a fresh coat of water, providing a smooth ice sheet to begin each period.

# INDEX